MW00469326

Whistleblowers, Leakers, and Their Networks

DISCARDED
Worthington Libraries

Security and Professional Intelligence Education Series (SPIES)

Series Editor: Jan Goldman

In this post–September 11, 2001, era there has been rapid growth in the number of professional intelligence training and educational programs across the United States and abroad. Colleges and universities, as well as high schools, are developing programs and courses in homeland security, intelligence analysis, and law enforcement, in support of national security.

The Security and Professional Intelligence Education Series (SPIES) was first designed for individuals studying for careers in intelligence and to help improve the skills of those already in the profession; however, it was also developed to educate the public on how intelligence work is conducted and should be conducted in this important and vital profession.

1. *Communicating with Intelligence: Writing and Briefing in the Intelligence and National Security Communities*, by James S. Major. 2008.
2. *A Spy's Résumé: Confessions of a Maverick Intelligence Professional and Misadventure Capitalist*, by Marc Anthony Viola. 2008.
3. *An Introduction to Intelligence Research and Analysis*, by Jerome Clauser, revised and edited by Jan Goldman. 2008.
4. *Writing Classified and Unclassified Papers for National Security*, by James S. Major. 2009.
5. *Strategic Intelligence: A Handbook for Practitioners, Managers, and Users*, revised edition by Don McDowell. 2009.
6. *Partly Cloudy: Ethics in War, Espionage, Covert Action, and Interrogation*, by David L. Perry. 2009.
7. *Tokyo Rose / An American Patriot: A Dual Biography*, by Frederick P. Close. 2010.
8. *Ethics of Spying: A Reader for the Intelligence Professional*, edited by Jan Goldman. 2006.
9. *Ethics of Spying: A Reader for the Intelligence Professional*, Volume 2, edited by Jan Goldman. 2010.
10. *A Woman's War: The Professional and Personal Journey of the Navy's First African American Female Intelligence Officer*, by Gail Harris. 2010.
11. *Handbook of Scientific Methods of Inquiry for Intelligence Analysis*, by Hank Prunckun. 2010.
12. *Handbook of Warning Intelligence: Assessing the Threat to National Security*, by Cynthia Grabo. 2010.
13. *Keeping U.S. Intelligence Effective: The Need for a Revolution in Intelligence Affairs*, by William J. Lahneman. 2011.
14. *Words of Intelligence: An Intelligence Professional's Lexicon for Domestic and Foreign Threats, Second Edition*, by Jan Goldman. 2011.
15. *Counterintelligence Theory and Practice*, by Hank Prunckun. 2012.
16. *Balancing Liberty and Security: An Ethical Study of U.S. Foreign Intelligence Surveillance, 2001–2009*, by Michelle Louise Atkin. 2013.
17. *The Art of Intelligence: Simulations, Exercises, and Games*, edited by William J. Lahneman and Rubén Arcos. 2014.
18. *Communicating with Intelligence: Writing and Briefing in National Security*, by James S. Major. 2014.
19. *Scientific Methods of Inquiry for Intelligence Analysis, Second Edition*, by Hank Prunckun. 2014.
20. *Quantitative Intelligence Analysis: Applied Analytic Models, Simulations and Games*, by Edward Waltz. 2014.
21. *The Handbook of Warning Intelligence: Assessing the Threat to National Security–The Complete Declassified Edition*, by Cynthia Grabo, 2015.
22. *Intelligence and Information Policy for National Security: Key Terms and Concepts*, by Jan Goldman and Susan Maret
23. *Handbook of European Intelligence Cultures*, edited by Bob de Graaff and James M. Nyce—With Chelsea Locke
24. *Partly Cloudy: Ethics in War, Espionage, Covert Action, and Interrogation, Second Edition*, by David L. Perry
25. *Humanitarian Intelligence: A Practitioner's Guide to Crisis Analysis and Project Design*, by Andrej Zwitter
26. *Shattered Illusions: KGB Cold War Espionage in Canada*, by Donald G. Mahar
27. *Intelligence Engineering: Operating Beyond the Conventional*, by Adam D. M. Svendsen
28. *Reasoning for Intelligence Analysts: A Multidimensional Approach of Traits, Techniques, and Targets*, by Noel Hendrickson
29. *Counterintelligence Theory and Practice, Second edition*, by Hank Prunckun
30. *Methods of Inquiry for Intelligence Analysis, Third Edition*, by Hank Prunckun
31. *The Art of Intelligence: More Simulations, Exercises, and Games* edited by William J. Lahneman and Rubén Arcos
32. *Whistleblowers, Leakers, and Their Networks: From Snowden to Samizdat* by Jason Ross Arnold

To view the books on our website, please visit https://rowman.com/Action/SERIES/RL/SPIES or scan the QR code below.

Whistleblowers, Leakers, and Their Networks

From Snowden to Samizdat

Jason Ross Arnold
Virginia Commonwealth University

ROWMAN &
LITTLEFIELD
Lanham • Boulder • New York • London

Executive Editor: Traci Crowell
Editorial Assistant: Deni Remsberg
Executive Marketing Manager: Amy Whitaker

Credits and acknowledgments for material borrowed from other sources, and reproduced with permission, appear on the appropriate page within the text.

Published by Rowman & Littlefield
An imprint of The Rowman & Littlefield Publishing Group, Inc.
4501 Forbes Boulevard, Suite 200, Lanham, Maryland 20706
www.rowman.com

6 Tinworth Street, London SE11 5AL, United Kingdom

Copyright © 2020 by The Rowman & Littlefield Publishing Group, Inc.

All rights reserved. No part of this book may be reproduced in any form or by any electronic or mechanical means, including information storage and retrieval systems, without written permission from the publisher, except by a reviewer who may quote passages in a review.

British Library Cataloguing in Publication Information Available

Library of Congress Cataloging-in-Publication Data Available
ISBN 9781538130551 (cloth : alk. paper)
ISBN 9781538130568 (pbk. : alk. paper)
ISBN 9781538130575 (electronic)

♾™ The paper used in this publication meets the minimum requirements of American National Standard for Information Sciences—Permanence of Paper for Printed Library Materials, ANSI/NISO Z39.48-1992.

Contents

Figures and Tables

Figures

Tables

Chapter 1

Introduction

"If you had unprecedented access to classified networks 14 hours a day 7 days a week for 8+ months, what would you do?"[1] Most people in that position would do nothing but follow the law and leave the documents alone. Besides not wanting to endanger national security, they would know that stealing and sharing state secrets could lead to a felony conviction. But a consequential minority, driven by a mix of motives, have exploited opportunities like that, including the person who posed the rhetorical question—a troubled young U.S. Army private and intelligence analyst then named Bradley Manning. Writing as bradass87 in a May 2010 web chat in which he posed the question, Manning dropped hints that he was the leaker responsible for the previous month's global media spectacle orchestrated by WikiLeaks, the website that specializes in publishing state and corporate secrets.[2]

In April, WikiLeaks had published a classified U.S. Army video shot from a helicopter in Baghdad, Iraq, which showed an American attack on suspected anti-government insurgents. The Apache pilots, hovering over a dusty courtyard, chuckled and hooted while firing machine guns at scurrying men and a van filled with people, all of whom WikiLeaks portrayed as innocent civilians. Among the dead were two Reuters journalists who were following the insurgents, and whose cameras and tripods looked like weapons to the pilots, as the audio recording shows. "At first glance," Manning wrote to a WikiLeaks-connected stranger named Adrian Lamo, "It was just a bunch of guys getting shot up by a helicopter . . . no big deal . . . about two dozen more where that came from right . . . but something struck me as odd with the van thing . . . so I looked into it." Elsewhere in the chat session that helped U.S. authorities identify and arrest him, bradass87 confessed his personal troubles (e.g., "I've been isolated so long"; "I'm a total fucking wreck right now") and made it clear that the video was not all that he leaked. Much more would come out: "It's open diplomacy . . . world-wide anarchy in CSV format . . . it's Climategate with a global scope, and breathtaking depth . . . it's beautiful, and horrifying."[3]

April's release of the army video that WikiLeaks dubbed "Collateral Murder" was the beginning of an eight-month campaign of unauthorized disclosures from Manning's massive trove. In July, WikiLeaks teamed with *The New York Times*, *The Guardian*, and *Der Spiegel* to release tens of thousands of classified military records from the war in Afghanistan, which included information about targets sought, detained, or killed; the locations of those actions; and the number of civilians killed and injured. In October, the organization released nearly 400,000 more military records from the Iraq War. In December, the grand finale: more than 250,000 secret U.S. State Department cables from diplomatic posts all over the world, a release that became known as Cablegate. Furious about its inability to stop WikiLeaks, the U.S. government under President Barack Obama finally managed to contain its founder and leader, Julian Assange, soon after Cablegate broke, although the best they could do was to convince the British government to put him under house arrest while the Swedes investigated sexual assault allegations against him, which had recently emerged with peculiar timing. Despite Assange's troubles, which continued to intensify, WikiLeaks survived, thanks to a growing network of collaborators and supporters.

Weeks before U.S. military prosecutors secured court-martial convictions against Manning in 2013, a second, even larger, megaleak burst, although this one did not directly involve WikiLeaks.[4] Edward Snowden, a government contractor with years of experience working with U.S. intelligence agencies, stole up to 1.77 million top secret National Security Agency (NSA) files, plus 900,000 more from the Defense Department.[5] Instead of WikiLeaks, Snowden handpicked a journalist and a documentary filmmaker to reveal some of the NSA's deepest secrets about its global signals intelligence (SIGINT) and cyberwarfare programs. His partners, Glenn Greenwald and Laura Poitras, published sensational stories using the cache, which immediately captured the world's attention. They soon shared the classified files with other journalists, and then others, who published from the Snowden archive for years.

In the early 2010s, nearly everyone seemed to have a strong opinion about Snowden, Manning, WikiLeaks, the NSA, and the other implicated government agencies. Many celebrated the megaleaks, believing that they documented a wide range of American wrongdoings, from war crimes and the NSA's industrial strength privacy violations to the use of routine, excessive secrecy to cover it all up. They condemned the U.S. government, including President Barack Obama's administration, because of its use of the Espionage Act against leakers, its seemingly unusual pretrial punishment of Manning, and its hard line against

Snowden, who had self-exiled in Russia. Americans were particularly concerned about the NSA leaks, because they appeared to show widespread domestic surveillance and clear civil liberties violations. For those applauding the leaks, Manning and Snowden were righteous "whistleblowers," and their partners in the media were public-spirited publishers who had carried out their democratic duties to hold the U.S. government accountable.

Others found the praise unwarranted. While the leaks may have revealed some wrongdoings, they argued, the harms from the massive unauthorized disclosures far outweighed the benefits. Some NSA defenders conceded that one or more of the NSA's many programs appeared to have crossed the line by involving U.S. citizens' communications, or exceeding standard behavior by major global powers' SIGINT agencies. But they noted that the vast majority of the disclosures provided details about the sources and methods of the NSA's foreign-focused surveillance programs; that is, most had nothing to do with domestic surveillance and Americans' civil liberties. Besides, these critics argued, everything that the NSA did appeared to be authorized by Congressional statutes, compliant with Supreme Court precedents, and overseen by the relevant courts and congressional committees.

A similar complaint was leveled against Manning and WikiLeaks: Perhaps, a few disclosures revealed U.S. wrongdoings, but the vast majority unnecessarily gave competitors and adversaries valuable diplomatic and military secrets. Some who backed the Obama administration's position may have reflexively condemned Manning and Snowden as traitors, but many reasonably believed that the leakers' actions, along with their collaborators, were by and large unjustified.

The gulf between the two views will unlikely be bridged anytime soon. However, many who followed the megaleak stories found themselves somewhere in between hard pro- and anti-leak positions. It is often difficult enough to evaluate the ethics of a single document leak, let alone hundreds of thousands at once. Perhaps Snowden deserved credit for revealing the NSA's domestic metadata collection program, which the U.S. Congress reformed after a thorough public debate.[6] But supporting one leak does not justify all of the others, such as the one that exposed details about a program that tracked Al Qaeda operatives in South Asia.[7] Even if Snowden and his collaborators believed that Americans needed a more robust debate about the U.S. government's global campaign against Al Qaeda, there were other means to elevate the issue on the political agenda that did not potentially damage national security through the unauthorized disclosure of top secret documents.

The debate about which secrets and leaks are justified, of course, started long before the Snowden and Manning sagas. Even a political naïf, educated only on Hollywood movies, would recognize dozens of other high-profile cases, including Daniel Ellsberg (Pentagon Papers; *The Post*), Mark Felt/Deep Throat (Watergate; *All the President's Men*), Erin Brockovich (Pacific Gas and Electric;

Erin Brockovich), Karen Silkwood (Kerr-McGee Corporation; *Silkwood*), and Kathryn Bolkovac (DynCorp/NATO; *The Whistleblower*). The megaleak cases already have films of their own, including Oliver Stone's hagiographic *Snowden*, Poitras's equally one-sided *Citizenfour* (also about Snowden) and Bill Condon's *The Fifth Estate*, a thriller about WikiLeaks.

Outside of the movies, there are hundreds, probably thousands, of other cases in the United States and around the world. No one has ever tallied them all. I tried to do that, probably breaking a Lexis-Nexis server or two in the process. The ever-growing database of secret-spillers can be found at https://sites.google.com/view/secretspillers/home. Readers who notice missing cases are invited to offer suggestions.

What becomes clear when examining each case is that focusing only on the individuals who acquired and passed on secrets leads to an incomplete understanding. In nearly every case, numerous people contribute to the process of extracting and publishing secrets. The story of Snowden's disclosures centers, naturally, on Snowden. But the entire enterprise now encompasses hundreds. At first the network was small: Snowden, Greenwald, Poitras, and a few others at *The Guardian* and *The Washington Post*. But it soon mushroomed to

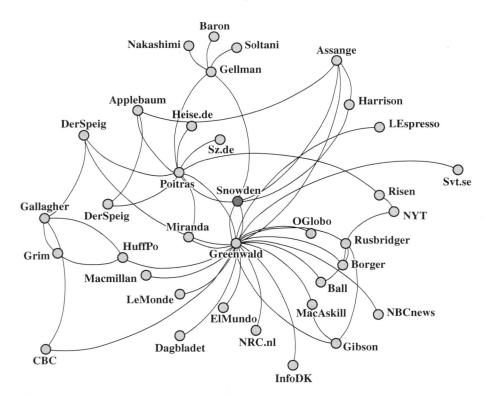

FIGURE 1.1   Network Map Centered on Edward Snowden.

include dozens of journalists and editors in publications around the world. Figure 1.1 provides a snippet of Snowden's network map (all distances, etc., are approximate). Likewise, Daniel Ellsberg, probably the most famous case before Snowden and Manning, worked with many others to release the Pentagon Papers in 1971, including his wife, Patricia Marx Ellsberg; RAND Corporation colleague Anthony Russo; Neil Sheehan and other reporters, editors, and publishers at *The New York Times*, *The Washington Post*, and other papers; U.S. Senator Mike Gravel and his staff; Ellsberg's activist friends Noam Chomsky and Howard Zinn; and many others.[8]

Indeed, nearly every case involves a network of actors coordinating and cooperating to extract and then publish secrets. Far from being about individuals—the lone heroes/anti-heroes who get all of the credit or condemnation—secret-spilling stories almost always involve multiple actors. Two of the recent films make this point clear. *The Post*, about Ellsberg and the Pentagon Papers, focuses more of its attention on the publisher than on Ellsberg. *The Fifth Estate*, with its focus on WikiLeaks and Assange, pushes Manning to the periphery.

Some networks come and go with a single disclosure. But many endure as organized whistleblowing networks, even if they never self-identify that way. Amnesty International and other human rights organizations have developed networks around the world to extract and publish secrets about human rights violations. While it is not all they do, it is central to their mission. Many other organizations do the same. The *Chronicle of Current Events* was an underground newspaper in the Soviet Union which acquired and published government secrets about human rights violations. Powering the *Chronicle* was a clandestine network that withstood fourteen years of sustained KGB hostility. Through its work, and its network, the *Chronicle* became a central player of the dissident pro-democracy movement in the Soviet Union. Another example is WikiLeaks, which has endured since 2006 despite formidable obstacles. Its virtual and social network spans the globe.

Many other species of continuing secret-spilling networks increasingly shape national and international politics: animal welfare organizations whose members sneak into slaughterhouses to document abuses; corruption-reporting websites that invite frustrated citizens to anonymously describe their experiences with bullying, sticky-fingered bureaucrats; and crisis-mapping apps that let citizens, who are caught in riots, armed conflicts, natural disasters, and other calamities, mark their GPS locations and circumstances so that assistance can be targeted and that allow the geographic distribution of the crisis to be studied in real time. New technologies have made the process easier, but the practice and the whistleblowing impulse predates the modern era.

This book covers all of the above: the episodic and the continuous networks that span the globe; the concept and ethics of whistleblowing and the role of technological developments in the evolution and practice of secret-spilling. Chapter 2 grapples with the elusive concept of "whistleblowing" and poses key ethical questions that would-be whistleblowers and their collaborators should ask themselves before proceeding. Chapter 3 examines multiple types of leaking and whistleblowing and makes clear why scholars should focus on networks.

Chapters 4 and 5 focus on continuous whistleblowing networks that have been uniquely effective in exposing human rights violations. Chapter 4 traces the origins, development, network structure, secret-spilling mechanisms, and historical influence of the *Chronicle of Current Events,* the underground Soviet publication. The chapter concludes with a brief comparison of the *Chronicle* with other *samizdat* in Communist countries during the Cold War. Chapter 5 examines the information extraction methods employed by Amnesty International's vast global network of human rights defenders.

Chapters 6 and 7 turn to the ways technological developments, starting with the advent of the Internet, have shaped the history and practice of leaking and whistleblowing. Key cases include WikiLeaks and WITNESS. Chapter 8 focuses on online and offline networks whose members break into organizations to steal and publish their secrets. The chapter's case studies include the political burglary by the Citizens' Commission to Investigate the FBI, the undercover investigations of People for the Ethical Treatment of Animals (PETA), and the endeavors of Anonymous and other hacking groups.

The concluding chapter zooms out, finding would-be whistleblowers in the pre-modern era, long before the term was coined. Eventually, a pivotal technological development, Gutenberg's printing press, provided the means with which would-be whistleblowers could make impactful disclosures. Bartolomé de Las Casas, the Spanish colonial settler turned Dominican friar in the New World, was an early pioneer. With the expansion of publication into the modern era came the increasing prevalence of whistleblowing, a concept that remains among the most poorly developed in the social sciences. The next chapter attempts to correct for that failing.

Notes

1   Evan Hansen, "Manning-Lamo Chat Logs Revealed," *Wired,* July 13, 2011, https://www.wired.com/2011/07/manning-lamo-logs.
2   Manning dropped Bradley for Chelsea in 2013. Bradley, and the male pronoun, are used here because they were the terms that Manning used then, and during the subsequent legal process. Most references to Manning in the book use her chosen name and the female pronouns "she" and "her."
3   Hansen, "Manning-Lamo Chat Logs."
4   Andy Greenberg coined "megaleaks" in an interview with Assange. (Assange: "There should be a cute name for them. [Greenberg:] Megaleaks? [Assange:] Megaleaks. That's good. These megaleaks. . . . They're an important phenomenon, and they're only going to increase.") Andy Greenberg, "An Interview With WikiLeaks' Julian Assange," *Forbes,* November 29, 2010,

https://www.forbes.com/sites/andygreenberg/2010/11/29/an-interview-with-wikileaks-julian-assange/.

[5] See chapter 2 for a discussion of the scale and scope of the document theft.

[6] Glenn Greenwald, "NSA Collecting Phone Records of Millions of Verizon Customers Daily," *The Guardian*, June 6, 2013, https://www.theguardian.com/world/2013/jun/06/nsa-phone-records-verizon-court-order; USA Freedom Act (Uniting and Strengthening America by Fulfilling Rights and Ending Eavesdropping, Dragnet-collection and Online Monitoring Act), Public Law 114–23.

[7] Greg Miller, Julie Tate, and Barton Gellman, "Documents Reveal NSA's Extensive Involvement in Targeted Killing Program," *Washington Post*, October 16, 2013, https://www.washingtonpost.com/world/national-security/documents-reveal-nsas-extensive-involvement-in-targeted-killing-program/2013/10/16/29775278-3674-11e3-8a0e-4e2cf80831fc_story.html.

[8] Daniel Ellsberg, *Secrets: A Memoir of Vietnam and the Pentagon Papers* (New York: Penguin, 2003).

Chapter 2

The Concept of Whistleblowing

Three days after *The Guardian* published the first document from the largest leak of National Security Agency (NSA) secrets in U.S. history a young man named Edward Snowden broke his anonymity and proudly claimed credit (Figure 2.1). "I have no intention of hiding who I am because I know I have done nothing wrong," he said. Although he must have known that coming forward would make him a focal point, he insisted that he did not want the limelight: "I don't want public attention because I don't want the story to be about me. I want it to be about what the U.S. government is doing."[1]

Against Snowden's professed wishes, millions of people turned their focus to him and his riveting leak story.[2] The political debate in the United States quickly divided along lines common to classified leak cases, with one group hailing him as a hero, and the other attacking him as a traitor. It was a revealing but unproductive debate, as both labels are usually no more than rhetorical weapons. Heroism is in the eye of the beholder, while treason's meaning is rooted in law. In the United States, treason convictions require clear evidence of intentional betrayal, which has not materialized in the Snowden case and probably never will.[3]

That so many chose to discuss Snowden in the hero versus traitor frame nevertheless indicated a widespread interest in conceptualizing and ultimately judging his choices in ethical terms. It was a roundabout way of debating whether his unauthorized disclosures were justified and whether he made the correct decision to spill the NSA's secrets. The ensuing stalemate had many causes, not least individuals' divergent perceptions about what righteous whistleblowing entails. Those differences have resulted in part from confusion about what whistleblowing is.

FIGURE 2.1 Edward Snowden via Video Link from Moscow, 2015. *Source*: Andrew Kelly/ Reuters/Newscom.

One thing is clear: there never will be a consensus about Snowden's actions. Even Philip Agee, the Cold War CIA defector who published the names of hundreds of undercover CIA officers and front companies in the 1970s, with help from Cuban and probably Soviet intelligence, still had strong support in left-wing circles in the 2000s. They lauded him in his obituaries, describing him as a "whistleblower."[4] It remains an open question whether Snowden deserves that label or whether he was a mere "leaker" of secrets.

Does Snowden Deserve the Label *Whistleblower*?

When *The Guardian*, *The Washington Post*, and other publications began publishing the Snowden disclosures in June 2013, those who argued that Snowden deserved the desirable label whistleblower had some built-in advantages in the initial public debate. Their claims that the leaked NSA documents showed systematic government abuses resonated with many who had learned to distrust American intelligence agencies by default. Part of that distrust came from broader political and cultural developments that began in the 1960s and 1970s. A flood of disclosures about the intelligence services in particular—for example, about CIA assassinations and regime change operations—provided shocking source material for Hollywood films, *New York Times* bestsellers, and college professors' lectures, all of which painted a sharply negative image of the agencies, which was reinforced by revelations about their post-9/11 work in Iraq and the larger "war on terror."[5] As a result, before the first Snowden-sourced story appeared in June 2013, many were primed to believe a narrative about NSA abuses, which made the unauthorized disclosures seem obviously whistleblowing worthy.

The first disclosures struck many as even worse than the ones from the 1970s. They detailed the NSA's domestic metadata program, which collected AT&T, Sprint, and Verizon's U.S. customers' dialed numbers, call times and durations, and SIM card and serial numbers. They described the PRISM program, which gave the NSA "easy access" (*Guardian*) to servers hosted by Google, Yahoo, and other tech giants. Later stories revealed intercontinental undersea cable taps, undetectable webcam spying, and dozens of other mechanisms the NSA and partner agencies used to allegedly surveil anyone and everyone, regardless of citizenship or suspected wrongdoing. Journalists described a rapacious NSA that spied at will on Americans' phone calls, emails, and Internet browsing, never mind their civil rights and liberties. For understandable reasons—the predispositions plus the new reporting—many distrustful Americans just did not believe President Obama when he said "What I can say unequivocally is that if you are a U.S. person, the NSA cannot listen to your telephone calls, and the NSA cannot target your emails . . . and have not." They dismissed his reassurance that all programs had "very strict supervision by all three branches of government." Skeptics on the left and right accused the U.S. government of engaging in mass, "suspicionless," unconstitutional surveillance.[6]

Snowden's supporters also had an advantage because of his character. His coming out video, broadcast on *The Guardian* webpage, showed an obviously bright, articulate, low-key, clean-cut, twenty-nine-year-old computer whiz, who seemed deeply sincere about his commitment to America's constitutional values. He insisted he had "done nothing wrong." "My sole motive," he claimed, "is to inform the public as to that which is done in their name and that which is done against them."[7]

The intense drama during June 2013 also helped the pro-Snowden cause. Major media networks rushed to Hong Kong to find Snowden and his collaborators, telling the story of his frenzied attempts to dodge American agents who were closing in. Here was this young man, an ostensible lover of liberty, a self-sacrificing truth-teller, holed up in a Hong Kong hotel room, hiding from the feds.[8] Intelligence agency skeptics already knew their answer to the unfolding question at the heart of this real-life spy thriller: Who were the bad guys: the feds, or Snowden and his collaborators? Images from the anti-NSA movie *Enemy of the State*—scowling, secrecy-obsessed, congressman-killing U.S. officials chasing the earnest Will Smith character—probably crossed minds.

It was a compelling narrative, but not one without detractors with cogent questions of their own: Who gave this guy the right to deceive his coworkers, steal possibly millions of top secret documents, and give all of it to handpicked journalists, some of whom seemed indifferent at best to America's national security interests? Why should we allow a twenty-nine-year-old systems administrator—a man without higher education, much life experience, and the long view—to independently determine the difference between necessary or unnecessary secrets? Didn't he understand that the revelations would give everyone from Al Qaeda leaders to the Zimbabwean president U.S. signals intelligence (SIGINT) sources and methods on a silver platter? And then the guy winds up in Vladimir Putin's Russia, whose asylum offer *obviously* came with strings attached! As the story developed—with puzzling discrepancies and murky details about Snowden's time in Hong Kong as well as his interactions with the Russian government[9]—and as the published revelations increasingly described foreign-focused operations against a sharpening backdrop of the programs' sound (albeit contestable) legal underpinnings, his critics' case continued to grow in strength.

Strong pro- and anti-Snowden partisans had their answer to the question of whether he deserved to be called a whistleblower long before the story played out and key details emerged. Fair-minded nonpartisans waited for more information and probably recognized the concept's vagueness, likely even more so after consulting a dictionary. Scholars and dictionary writers have certainly tried to define it. While they have provided some clarity, the definitions range from being inadequate to deeply flawed.

Toward a Better Definition: A Fool's Errand?

Popular Definitions

Our gold standard dictionaries offer definitions of whistleblowing that seem viable at first glance but become unusable upon closer inspection. In the *Oxford English Dictionary* (OED), "to blow the whistle on (a person or thing)" is "to bring an activity to a sharp conclusion, as if by the blast of a whistle; now [usually] by informing on (a person) or exposing (an irregularity or crime)." *Merriam-Webster* defines a whistleblower as "a person who provides information about another's wrongdoing" (MW_1), as well as "a person who tells police, reporters, etc., about something (such as a crime) that has been kept secret" (MW_2).

MW_1's depiction of whistleblowing as the act of providing "information about another's wrongdoing" is so imprecise as to make it useless. If I were to include in this sentence some grisly detail about one of serial killer Jeffrey Dahmer's murders, I would qualify as a whistleblower, according to MW_1, because I provided information about another's wrongdoing. (Set aside the problematic "wrongdoing" for now.) Whistleblowing at a minimum involves unauthorized disclosures of secrets—hidden, exclusive knowledge—not simply "information." The other definitions make this necessary distinction. MW_2 does so explicitly, OED does it implicitly ("exposing").

MW_2's whistleblowers "tell police, reporters, etc., about something (such as a crime) that has been kept secret." That kind of secret-spilling could include just about anything, including truly important revelations in the public interest about, for example, the false imprisonment and torture of a political enemy that only the torturer and his victim know about. But MW_2's secrets could also include some previously unreported piece of evidence from, for example, Dahmer's Milwaukee Police Department file. The definition encompasses a huge array of crime communications down to the absurd, such as a New Yorker telling a police officer that she once saw her neighbor urinating in the alley.[10]

OED's "exposing . . . [a] crime" is similarly vague. "Irregularity" is worse, since it sets the hazy "regular" against the millions of things that are "irregular," including physiological problems, unconventional thoughts, radical artistic innovations, and so forth. We require a better set of boundary conditions.

OED also stipulates that whistleblowing should have a consequence, specifically demanding that it "bring an activity [i.e., crimes or irregularities] to a sharp conclusion." It has an intuitive appeal, in part because of what whistleblowing evokes: Person (X) sees another (Y) doing something wrong; he or she loudly exposes the wrongdoing to make it stop, like a whistle-blowing referee calling a foul that halts gameplay. (The referee simile is ultimately misleading, since an action that prompted a foul call is not a secret to sports fans watching the game.)

OED's "bring . . . to a sharp conclusion" condition, however, sets too high a bar by requiring that whistleblowing have the power to stop bad actions. What if X reveals Y's bad actions but forces outside X's control allows Y to continue doing what he does? Let X be a government official who exposes Y's political corruption. The revelation appears on *The New York Times* front page and leads to a criminal trial. But the trial ends in Y's surprising acquittal, which allows him to resume his shady business. Because X's action did not cause Y to stop, X is not a whistleblower, according to the OED. Overall, the threshold should be lowered to allow X's whistleblowing to *potentially* force Y to stop or to potentially hold Y accountable.

Another problem with OED's sharp conclusion condition involves timing. It absurdly suggests that a whistleblowing opportunity is foreclosed if Y's wrongdoing stops before X can report it. Let's say former U.S. representative William J. Jefferson (Y) died or retired from Congress before anyone, including his former legislative assistant (X), had discovered the $90,000 in bribe money he had stashed in his freezer.[11] In either case (death or retirement), Y could no longer solicit bribes for congressional work, but X could still expose his prior corruption. According to the OED, X's unauthorized disclosures could not be whistleblowing.[12] In general, whistleblowing can involve revelations that happen before (i.e., at the planning stage), during, or after wrongdoings occur.

Other problems plague the OED and MW definitions. First, they are vague about the whistleblowing process. The OED has its whistleblowers "informing on (a person)" or "exposing" their irregularities or crimes. If so, an X could "inform on" a Y just by telling X's roommate, who does nothing with the information. The same vagueness bedevils MW_1 and its whistleblower who "provides information." What a recipient does with a disclosure matters, as we will see.

MW_2 offers an improved version with its whistleblower as "a person who tells police, reporters, etc. about . . . a secret." At least there is some recognition that the secret should wind up in someone's hands who can do something about it, such as publication or criminal investigation. Yet if giving the police evidence of "something (such as a crime)" constitutes whistleblowing, then it appears indistinguishable from mundane forms of citizen–police communications. If X invites Y over for dinner and Y shows off a stolen watch, is it whistleblowing if X calls the police about Y's deeds? Probably not.

The definitions are also vague about the secrets themselves. Which "activities," "irregularities," "wrongdoings," and "crimes" count? How do we distinguish "rightdoings" from wrongdoings? With rare exceptions, human communities disagree about rights and wrongs. An admittedly crude and salacious hypothetical, centered on an overblown caricature of a person, illustrates the problem.

Imagine a nosy, prudish, bigoted, orthodox religious American man, with nineteenth-century sensibilities, who had the personal misfortune of having a gay couple move into the house next door. It didn't take long for him to grow furious about *what they're doing next door, behind those bedroom curtains!* After a bit of pacing and grumbling and a lot of stalking, he caught a glimpse of them doing those *ungodly deviant things*, clearly against the teachings of *The Book*. (They forgot to close the curtains.) He interpreted what he saw as a "wrongdoing," whether or not his neighbors' sexual acts comported with secular law.

A confusing mix of motives prompted the nosy neighbor to take photographs to capture the—in his view—sins. He believed that he had no other choice but to alert the community about the wrongdoers. He published the evidence—all fleshy pictures of groping limbs—on a neighborhood blog, under the heading "The Heathens among Us."

Here we have a protagonist who "provides information about another's wrongdoing" (MW_1), as he and others who share his worldview see it. We could use irregularities or the other common terms instead of wrongdoing and reach the same conclusion about the inadequacy of these words in the whistleblowing context. Overall, universally shared understandings of wrongdoings do exist, such as the proscription of murder and rape, which are human universals, found in every society. But what is right and wrong greatly varies across countries and communities, let alone individuals across the span of their lifetimes of intellectual and ethical development.[13]

Compared with wrongdoings and irregularities, *crimes* might seem to be a superior choice, due to its greater specificity. But there is a clear level of infraction problem, as earlier examples suggested. U.S. crimes include everything from murder and rape to trivialities like writing a check for less than a dollar and transporting dentures across state lines without a dental license.[14] There is also a potential cross-jurisdictional variation problem, in that a crimes-based concept might lead us to accept whatever policymakers proscribe in foreign jurisdictions, such as insulting the king (Thailand, among other places), driving while female (Saudi Arabia, until 2018), or selling gum (Singapore, still).

At the same time, if torture is not banned in country Z, then revealing it there—or possibly elsewhere—would not count as whistleblowing under a strict crimes-based definition. We could add a condition such that a crime in country Z is whistleblowing-worthy for citizens of Q if it is a crime in Q, but that leads right back to the level of infraction problem (e.g., exposing illegal dentures shipping in Z because it is a crime in Q). And we have not even considered the enormous interpretive problem due to many laws' ambiguous and vague language.[15] Debates about Snowden's revelations, for example, have often turned on different interpretations of words in statutes.[16]

Overall, as a standard for evaluating potential cases of whistleblowing, *crime* doesn't pay. It suffers from some of the same semantic problems as *wrongdoings* and *irregularities* (not to mention *activities*, the worst of the bunch). The next section considers the costs and benefits of alternative conceptualizations with even greater specificity.

This section found numerous faults in popular dictionaries' definitions of whistleblowing. It also highlighted several considerations that a better conceptualization must address, including the fact that whistleblowers spill secrets (i.e., not simply "information"); a recognition that not all secrets are whistleblowing-worthy (e.g., the level of infraction issue); the problem of cross-jurisdictional variation in laws and norms; the possibility that whistleblowing can involve revelations that happen before, during, or after the alleged infraction; the identification of the (typically) social nature of whistleblowing, namely the transfer of a secret (or secrets) from one individual to at least one more, specifically a person with some degree of power to use against the accused; and the possibility of holding perpetrators (individuals and/or their organizations) accountable in a way that inflicts real costs on them. The next section evaluates scholarly and legal definitions.

Scholarly and Legal Definitions: The Dilemma of Greater Specificity

Scholarly and legal definitions offer some advantages over popular ones, including greater specificity about whistleblowing-worthy actions. But the efforts at greater precision do not always succeed. For example, Peter Jubb's definition tries to narrow the range of whistleblowing-worthy secrets to "non-trivial illegalit[ies] or other wrongdoing[s]." While *non-trivial* begins to solve the level of infraction problem, what is trivial is debatable and unavoidably subjective. Marcia Miceli and Janet Near focus on "illegal, immoral, or illegitimate practices." However, as the nosy neighbor example illustrated, *immoral* and *illegitimate* are unreliable concepts because people have dissimilar, even contradictory, ideas about what they mean. *Illegal* fails because of the level of infraction and cross-jurisdictional variation problems, among other issues (addressed below).[17]

Some definitions offer more explicit guidance about which infractions are whistleblowing-worthy. Jesselyn Radack, for instance, focuses on evidence of "waste, fraud, abuse, mismanagement, illegality or a danger to health and public safety." Many U.S. government departments and agencies, following the Office of Special Counsel (OSC), use similar language: "a violation of any law, rule, or regulation; gross mismanagement; a gross waste of funds; an abuse of authority; a substantial and specific danger to public health; a substantial and specific danger to public safety." Stuart Dawson's definition identifies corruption, scandal, danger, and malpractice as key whistleblowing-worthy infractions. He then specifies what malpractice means: "negligence, resource wastage, misrepresentation, and safety violations." Corruption and scandal involve actions like "bribery, theft . . . fraud . . . and more recently created legal offences like discrimination in employment."[18]

Despite the more detailed lists of bad actions, the definitions still suffer from serious boundary problems: *Every* perceived instance of waste and mismanagement? *All* rule violations? Which *dangers*? And so forth. The lists require limiting principles.

Even the more specific terms, such as resource wastage, fall short. On the one hand, it seems appealingly specific, with its focus on the misuse of the public's or shareholders' assets. It brings to mind examples like the Department of Defense's (DOD) 1980s procurement scandal, in which the government appeared to vastly overpay for off-the-shelf products, such as coffee pots (purchased for $7,000 each), hammers ($435 to $600), and toilet seats ($600). (In reality, the Department did no such thing; the reported numbers were misleading, "an accounting artifact.")[19] On the other hand, terms like resource wastage, or waste, are unbounded. Let's say Senate dining hall workers routinely throw away mostly empty ketchup bottles instead of consolidating and repurposing the few centimeters of red glop that remain in each. Every day they throw out perfectly good ketchup, and thus every day they waste resources. Legal definitions often offer some guidance by specifying that waste or mismanagement must be "gross" to be whistleblowing-worthy but that just raises the question of how to define *gross*.

Trying to do so runs up to a dilemma; some specificity seems to help, but too much makes for arbitrary cutoff points. Let's say we wanted to make as explicit as possible what constitutes "gross resource wastage." Would we choose a nice, even number,—say, $1,000? If the Senate's ketchup wastage accumulates to a level above $1,000 after ten years, does that wastage count? Or should we arbitrarily bound it in time—$1,000 in one year? What if a case falls below the threshold, but only slightly, say, $994? That seems close enough. But what about $985? Or $950?[20] Any dollar amounts would be arbitrary. The underlying point here is that being explicit about what gross resource wastage constitutes creates its own problems, including the arbitrary quantities problem. A classic case of undesirable specificity in the law involves the Seventh Amendment to the Constitution, which sets a monetary threshold for jury trials using eighteenth-century standards: "In Suits at common law, where the value in controversy shall exceed twenty dollars, the right of trial by jury shall be preserved."

In the interest of greater specificity, we might instead make qualitative distinctions about what counts as a gross waste of funds, gross mismanagement, fraud, and so on. Ketchup wastage at virtually any dollar amount seems beside the point in discussions of resource wastage whistleblowing (except, say, embezzling from the condiment trade in a food service account). Accordingly, we could create a comprehensive, explicitly detailed list of whistleblowing-worthy actions, perhaps ranked according to their level of harm, from whatever sits above ketchup wastage to, say, capital crimes. But who decides? Who gets to create the list, let alone the ranking and cutoff points?

One solution would ask those with the most "local knowledge" to make the determinations. Not only would they best understand the nature of the relevant secrets and resources, but they would be key stakeholders. Of course, many would also be organizational insiders, who might have self-interested reasons to conceal more than is necessary and to prevent people from disclosing those unnecessary secrets. For example, a corporation's insiders might determine that a little corruption gets the job done—the benefits exceed the costs, for the firm, its shareholders, and the public—and therefore conclude that anyone who reveals it should not be considered whistleblowers.

An alternative solution would entail embracing something like the OSC's "reasonable belief" standard in which "a 'whistleblower' discloses information he or she reasonably believes evidences: a violation of any law, rule, or regulation [etc.]" The standard leaves judgments about a violation's significance and harms up to the individual who observes it or encounters evidence of it. It therefore fully concedes the inherent subjectivity of the enterprise and provides a common legal standard with which to evaluate a self-proclaimed whistleblower's actions. But this approach has irremediable flaws.

First, it leads us back to the morass where we started: Snowden claimed that he proceeded prudently and that he reasonably believed the NSA had abused its authority and Americans' civil liberties. Snowden's detractors cast doubt on his claims. Reasonable people disagreed, including about whether Snowden was truthful about his claims.[21] The debate stalled.

Second, a reasonable belief standard likely encourages more secret-spilling than might be justified. However appealing it might be to decentralize the process, to assume the reasonableness and good intentions of secret-spillers, and to leave damage assessment to the post-revelation period, leaning too far in that direction risks too many bad judgments by would-be whistleblowers. In some domains, the harmful consequences of unnecessary disclosures are minor, making relatively excessive secret-spilling a tolerable outcome. But in other domains, such as military engagements and national security intelligence, excessive secret-spilling due to the reasonable belief standard can produce too high a risk. Perhaps *reasonable belief* is appropriate in contexts where the risks of harmful consequences are relatively low. This idea of a consequentialist framework for individuals' whistleblowing decisions is developed below. The next section considers the possibility that a strong philosophical basis for the concept might be superior to a conceptual one expressed in a definition.

Should We Anchor Whistleblowing to Liberalism, or Some Other -Ism?

Philosophers have spent millennia contemplating how to differentiate rights from wrongs, how to balance competing values, how to make ethical tradeoffs. None of the whistleblowing definitions considered so far address those problems sufficiently. One possible solution would involve anchoring the whistleblowing concept to a coherent, widely accepted philosophy or worldview, one that specifies value priorities a priori. For example, we might explicitly link whistleblowing to the liberal tradition, which places its values of individual liberties and rights front and center. From that value-laden base, we could evaluate cases with more resolve and less uncertainty. If an unauthorized disclosure clearly reveals an infringement of someone's civil or human rights, then we can point at the liberal foundation and proclaim the episode a case of whistleblowing. Case closed. It would not matter, for instance, whether a country's laws permit the action, as with the cross-jurisdiction variation problem. People will still disagree about cases, but those conflicts could be moved to the relatively sturdy ground of philosophical debates, from the swamp of extant whistleblowing definitions.

Tethering the whistleblowing concept to liberalism (or another -ism) immediately accomplishes much of the difficult interpretive work for us. It solves vagueness and ambiguity problems. Take, for example, the problematic concept *wrongdoings*. Liberalism provides a framework with which to evaluate alleged wrongdoings. If some perceived wrongdoing clearly violates an individual's rights or liberties, then its revelation would be justified.

Recall the nosy neighbor example, in which the protagonist wants to expose what he considers a wrongdoing: (perceived) immoral sexual deviance in his neighbors' house. In the liberal framework, the man's unauthorized disclosure would not be justified, because his adult neighbors' consensual actions do not violate individual liberties or rights. Indeed, the couple would have a strong case that publication violated their privacy rights. If the nosy neighbor respected the liberal framework, he would still be free to be repulsed, and to follow his religious faith, but not to publish evidence of the perceived wrongdoing (or at least not to expect to be called a whistleblower for doing so). The man's respect for the liberal framework is, of course, a big "if," which illustrates the limits of a framework based on a single philosophy.

Would multiple philosophies work? In such a scenario, the nosy neighbor and like-minded citizens could cite their own philosophical traditions when discussing whistleblowing cases. For example, the nosy neighbor might stand behind St. Augustine, the Christian theologian and philosopher who called homosexuality an "offense against nature" that should always "be held in detestation and should be punished."[22]

By going the multiple philosophies route, we would have competing frameworks with distinctive, coherent value commitments.[23] People would still disagree about whether unauthorized disclosures were justified. But at least they would have more clarity about where their opponents are coming from. Debates about cases would develop into intellectually grounded philosophical debates.

However appealing it is, there are numerous problems with the multiple philosophies solution. First, it brings us back to a problem that surfaced with the reasonable belief standard: the lack of a decision process that selects the best of competing views. This solution has the advantage of established philosophical anchors, compared with the reasonable belief standard's realm of individuals claiming their own reasonableness. But if the aim is to find something closer to a universal set of guidelines for evaluating secret-spilling instances, and for providing guidance to would-be whistleblowers, the multiple philosophies is not the answer. Perhaps a universal framework is a lost cause, but accepting fragmentation at the outset precludes the possibility of getting closer.

Second, a multiple philosophies framework in practice might yield excessive secret-spilling. Depending on the distribution of moral philosophies (and the widespread acceptance of the multiple philosophies standard), we might wind up with secret-spilling run amok, individual rights and liberties be damned. The nosy neighbor, for example, could legitimately claim religious justification in publishing the sex pictures.

Making this fracturing problem worse, followers of the same philosophy do not necessarily share the same interpretation of its main precepts. While liberals agree about the importance of rights and liberties, they have over time developed wildly different understandings about what those concepts entail, and what they do not.[24] Viewpoint diversity can be found in most belief systems, except perhaps the most rigidly defined and enforced ones.

Finally, the multiple traditions solution fails to provide adequate guidance to many would-be whistleblowers. Liberalism, for instance, has little to say about resource wastage (recall the ketchup example). We might invoke economic liberalism's teachings about allocative efficiency to a discussion about resource wastage, but the idea would not go much further than saying, in effect, that waste should be avoided—not whether something counts as excessive waste. It thus does not instruct us about how much waste is acceptable, and consequently, at what point a prospective whistleblower should jump into action. As ridiculous as it sounds, we would still have no way of adjudicating cases of Senate dining hall ketchup wastage.

Leading liberal philosophers, including John Rawls, have recognized and defended liberalism's lack of comprehensiveness.[25] Theological traditions tend to be more comprehensive, but even these lack unity. In the Jewish tradition, rabbinic scholars have argued over proper Torah interpretations for millennia. Same book, many different readings. (Or, as the old joke goes: Ask two Jews, get three opinions.) Christians long ago divided into sects and subsects, as did Muslims. And so forth. Overall, while the multiple philosophies route might offer stronger foundations with which to argue about whistleblower cases, the approach cannot be utilized for the project of developing a better general conceptualization.

The Costs and Benefits of a Consequentialist Approach: Evaluating Snowden's Disclosures

Rahul Sagar's *Secrets and Leaks: The Dilemma of State Secrecy* is an exceptionally well-developed treatise on whistleblowing and leaking. Sagar's focus on classified national security leaks is narrower than mine. (This book often steps out of that realm.) Still, Sagar's normative, consequentialist approach is useful for the present purpose of concept development. It is also useful for would-be whistleblowers, in part by insisting that they focus on the costs and benefits of disclosure. Furthermore, it is a touchstone with which third-party observers can rationally evaluate unauthorized disclosures on procedural and substantive grounds.[26]

For Sagar, an unauthorized disclosure of classified national security information is justified when it meets five conditions. It "(a) reveals an abuse of public authority; (b) is based on clear and convincing evidence; (c) does not pose a disproportionate threat to public safety; (d) is limited in scope and scale as far as is possible; and (e) is made publicly."[27] One of the framework's distinctive features is that it emphasizes the potential negative consequences of a leak, due to its content and size. Would-be whistleblowers with Sagar's framework in their heads would be forced to grapple with a revelation's possible threats to society. No doubt many would-be whistleblowers do that already. Indeed, as a class they probably suffer from weight-of-the-world syndrome more than most. Yet, as evident from the analysis of the definitions above, existing conceptualizations tend not to directly address the downsides of disclosure or include any kind of limiting principle.[28] Sagar's framework incorporates both costs and benefits as well as other factors we have not yet seen in the analysis, such as the quality of the disclosed evidence. It also uses "abuse of public authority" instead of the many alternatives (e.g., wrongdoing or crime), which offers advantages and disadvantages.

Abuses of Public Authority

The phrase *abuses of public authority* has a clarity and specificity that other terms, such as *wrongdoings, illegalities,* and *immoralities,* do not. Gone are the questions about private sexual liaisons (e.g., the nosy neighbor), ketchup wastage, small-ball office supply pilfering, and the like. It homes in on people in authority who abuse their legally allotted power and connotes the willfulness of the perpetrator as well as the bad action's nontriviality.[29] Sagar was not the first to use the phrase in this realm, but his framework is unique for emphasizing it while avoiding the other problematic words.[30] To be sure, whether something counts as an abuse of public authority can be contested. Still, if adopted as a whistleblowing standard, the term would allow for a more focused debate than one about wrongdoings, and so on.

Certainly Snowden's supporters and detractors have disagreed about whether the disclosures revealed abuses of public authority. Snowden described himself as a whistleblower who revealed the NSA's "abuses of power," and his collaborator Glenn Greenwald has used the same phrase. By contrast, the Obama administration's Review Group on Intelligence and Communications Technologies (RGICT)—which included independent academic experts in privacy and First Amendment law (Geoffrey Stone, Cass Sunstein, and Peter Swire), along with former senior intelligence and national security officials

(Richard A. Clarke and Michael Morell)—insisted that no "illegality or other abuse of authority" occurred in the NSA's domestic-based work, even if one could identify "persistent instances of noncompliance" within an otherwise well-functioning, privacy rule-based oversight system.[31]

One positive outcome of the Snowden disclosures was this overdue public debate about how NSA and partner agencies collect, process, and analyze data linked to U.S. persons (citizens and legal residents). Elite and mass concerns about the metadata program, as well as the NSA and FBI's handling of "incidentally" collected U.S. persons data, prompted executive branch initiatives (e.g., RGICT), numerous public congressional hearings, two robust congressional debates before two reauthorizations of Section 702 of the Foreign Intelligence Surveillance Act of 1978 Amendments Act of 2008, and another vigorous debate before Congress passed the USA Freedom Act of 2015 with large bipartisan coalitions in the House (338–88) and Senate (67–32).[32] Many who supported reform viewed the NSA/FBI collection and analysis procedures for U.S. persons as actual or potential systematic abuses of public authority.

Note the important distinction between sporadic versus systematic abuses, which Sagar's standard does not capture as written. Take, for instance, Barton Gellman's *Washington Post* analysis of a leaked NSA internal audit from the Snowden archive, which found that the "NSA broke privacy rules thousands of times per year." Snowden supporters trumpeted the audit as evidence of widespread abuse. After all, the report's statistics do seem incriminating—for instance, 2,776 violations for the twelve-month period ending May 2012. The number becomes less shocking, less indicative of systematic abuse, when it is placed over the denominator, the total number of possible privacy infringements for the audit's time period, which appears to be at least sixty-one million, and possibly four times that. If that estimate is correct, we can infer that infractions happened approximately 0.0011 percent to 0.0046 percent of the time, which hardly reflects widespread or systematic abuse of public authority. Moreover, the audit found that "failure to follow standard operating procedures [SOPs]" constituted only 20 percent (39/195) of the violations that Gellman examined closely, while typographical, training, computer errors, and so on, explained the largest portion of that sample.[33] While it is possible that the "failure to follow SOPs" violations resulted from analysts' intentional efforts to violate privacy rules, the audit does not support that interpretation. And, of course, the very existence of the internal NSA audit shows the agency had at least one self-policing mechanism. There are others.[34] Overall, the NSA audit documents sporadic, not systematic, abuses. Would-be whistleblowers should consider this difference when weighing the costs and benefits of making unauthorized disclosures.

The stark truth about Snowden's megaleak is that the vast majority of the documents published by his journalistic partners revealed foreign-focused programs that had nothing to do with Americans' data and privacy interests. They did not reveal abuses of public authority, as that concept is commonly understood. Consider, for example, the top secret documents Snowden gave to the *South China Morning Post* (SCMP) about the NSA's targeted hacking programs in China. According to the SCMP (a paper overseen by, but not controlled by, the Chinese government), "the documents [that Snowden provided] listed operational details of specific attacks on computers, including internet protocol (IP) addresses, dates of attacks and whether a computer was still being monitored remotely."[35] Clearly, that leak had nothing to do with the privacy rights of Americans or the NSA's abuse of public authority (except, perhaps, in a general critique of intelligence operations, although that was not the critique Snowden and his backers lodged). Greenwald conceded the point when he said "what motivated that leak . . . was a need [for Snowden] to ingratiate himself to the people of Hong Kong and China."[36] Greenwald acknowledges the payoff in that statement, but frames the exchange as one between Snowden and "the people" in the authoritarian country—a place where the government can confiscate materials from a newspaper. Snowden, an experienced intelligence community employee, must have known where the top secret NSA cyberwarfare documents might wind up.

A comprehensive analysis of Snowden leaks to determine the proportion of domestic versus foreign operations—to determine how many potentially meet the abuse of public authority standard—would require access to the complete set of documents that he transferred to Greenwald et al. In lieu of that, the best we can do is evaluate those that have been published. Of the 550-plus news reports based on Snowden's leaks, the vast majority—more than 99 percent—reveal foreign SIGINT operations on non-U.S. person targets, which do not meet the standard.[37] In addition to the one about cyber operations in China, other leaks revealed programs that targeted Taliban email and cell phone communications in Afghanistan; intercepted emails about Iran's secret nuclear weapons program; tracked Al Qaeda operatives in South Asia; and validated CIA assets in Pakistan.[38]

Overall, as is evident from the way it can focus the Snowden disclosures debate, the abuse of public authority standard can be a useful post hoc analytic tool. It also provides conscientious would-be whistleblowers with a clear concept to help frame their thinking when contemplating unauthorized disclosures. But the formulation is not without problems, beyond the systematic versus sporadic abuse issue discussed earlier.

First, it does not avoid the cross-jurisdictional variation problem because it is wedded to sovereign countries' legal authorities. Recall the torture example from earlier. In places where torture is legally permitted, it is not by definition an abuse of public authority. Exposing torture in those places thus does not count as whistleblowing within a strict "public authority" framework. The problem becomes especially apparent when we examine political changes over time. China's government, for example, officially banned torture in 1996. In 1992, a Tibetan Buddhist monk named Palden Gyatso fled China carrying evidence of torture (tools and testimony), which he shared with reporters.[39] Because torture then was not banned in China, his evidence did not reveal abuses of public authority, according to Chinese law. By the logic of the standard, if Gyatso had fled China four years later, the same evidence would have shown such abuses and would therefore have been a justified leak.[40]

A second problem with the formulation is that the focus on public authority excludes whistleblowing about actions in the private sector, and in society more broadly. One easy corrective would involve adding "and private" before authority. Certainly some private actors have authority in their organizations, such as corporate executives. But what does it mean to abuse private authority? We might imagine an executive or manager who embezzled corporate funds. Or perhaps the executive misused his position to exploit subordinates, for instance, by sexually harassing or assaulting them. Both examples appear to be whistleblowing worthy with reference to an abuse of private authority standard.

While useful, the abuse of the private authority construct fails to cover other kinds of whistleblowing-worthy wrongdoings in the private sector, because of the cross-jurisdictional variation problem. Imagine a U.S. pharmaceutical company that takes advantage of a lax legal system in a poor developing country in order to conduct a clinical trial on children that most Americans would deem unethical—something along the lines of John Le Carré's *The Constant Gardener*.[41] A secret-spiller who delivered evidence of that clinical trial to, say, *The New York Times* would not be exposing an abuse of private authority, because the multinational corporation operated in a country where its questionable work was legal. Nevertheless, a leak that revealed the existence of the secret medical experiments would provide useful information to the drug company's customers and shareholders, and it would not unfairly harm the company or its business. The example shows the limits of an abuse of authority standard in the private sphere. More concept development in this area is needed, including in cases involving nonstate actors who lack authority as commonly understood (e.g., warlords or drug cartel bosses).

Clear and Convincing Evidence

Secret-spillers are whistleblowers in Sagar's framework only when their accusations of abuse are supported by *clear and convincing evidence*. While that phrase might seem unassailable and obvious given its opposite (unclear and unconvincing), it has a specific meaning in law. Because of that specificity, as well as its possible influence on would-be whistleblowers' disclosure decisions, it merits scrutiny.

Judges and lawyers work within a hierarchy of burden of proof standards, ranked according to their level of demandingness. Clear and convincing in the United States is the second most demanding burden of proof standard, falling behind "beyond a reasonable doubt," the threshold for criminal convictions. The scale runs from reasonable doubt at the top, followed by clear and convincing evidence, preponderance of the evidence, probable cause, and reasonable suspicion at the bottom. (Other countries' legal systems operate with many of the same concepts, along with others, such as Canada's "air of reality" test.) The lowest burden of proof standard, reasonable suspicion, is not used in U.S. courts but in other areas of governance, such as intelligence collection. The NSA, for example, must show the Foreign Intelligence Surveillance Court that it has a "reasonable, articulable suspicion" that a U.S.-based phone number has links to terrorists' numbers before the agency can legally search its archive to discover the owner's contacts. Preponderance of evidence, ranked just below clear and convincing, requires that a majority (>50 percent) of the evidence supports an allegation about someone's culpability. Clear and convincing, by contrast, requires that "a party must prove that it [i.e., the allegation] is substantially more likely than not [to be] true." In other words, it demands a higher burden proof than preponderance's (not very "substantial") 51 percent of the evidence.[42] (To be clear, Sagar did not define the phrase so legalistically. In *Secrets and Leaks*, something is clear and convincing "when disinterested observers are likely to draw the same inference from it" (131). Still, the phrase comes directly from the law, which shapes how individuals and organizations would interpret it.)

Using a legal burden of proof standard to justify whistleblowing has benefits, and a demanding one underscores the potential costs of leaks. A tough evidentiary standard forces would-be whistleblowers to carefully consider whether their disclosures really do support their allegations. It asks them to consider the real possibility that the evidence is faulty or incomplete. Would it persuade a jury to convict or otherwise sanction the accused?[43]

One likely consequence of the widespread adoption of a strong burden of proof standard is less leaking. If more would-be whistleblowers reflected on the quality of their evidence and the costs of disclosure, fewer of them would probably proceed. To the extent that many leaks are damaging—for instance, to national security—and that the would-be whistleblowers applying the standards make prudent, rational choices, the outcome of less leaking can be positive.[44] On the other hand, it might turn out that too many would-be whistleblowers will be overly prudent. But with a tough standard—or *any* evidentiary standard—at least everyone involved would take more seriously the quality of evidence and the possible harms of disclosure.

Beyond the possible downsides of excessive prudence, the use of the clear and convincing evidence standard in the whistleblowing realm has some drawbacks. First, its use in law is specific, requiring that the vast majority of evidence—well above half of it—supports an allegation. Yet how would would-be whistleblowers estimate something like that with any precision? What if they have only one possibly incriminating document? Or what if they have only fragments of one or more documents? A damning but still cryptic text message? The courtroom analogy, with its stacked file boxes filled with documents obtained through subpoenas and the discovery process, thus might not fit well into the whistleblowing universe. The standard is probably too strict as a general rule.

In some organizations, the would-be whistleblowers' information problem is especially severe. For example, many organizations routinely compartmentalize secrets in order to protect them, as in the military and intelligence agencies. Imagine someone in one of those organizations—say, a mid-level intelligence officer—who one day found an alarming piece of evidence that strongly suggested an abuse of public authority. By virtue of the officer's mid-level security clearance, he or she might find it extremely difficult to find corroborating evidence, and near impossible to find enough to make an allegation that meets the clear and convincing threshold. Even if the officer acquired more evidence, he or she might still lack *enough* information, and the relevant specialized knowledge to make sense of it, that would fit all the pieces together in a clear and convincing way. Would-be whistleblowers often have a big knowledge problem and that should not necessarily preclude disclosure.

Despite the disadvantages of the specific term, Sagar's core idea remains persuasive: would-be whistleblowers should carefully consider the quality of the evidence they plan to reveal. Placing the evidentiary test in a legal framework is probably helpful for secret-spillers and post hoc evaluators alike. It provides a useful way of conceptualizing the costs and benefits of disclosure. The clear and convincing standard is a good place to start, but the common legal understanding of the phrase is disadvantageous because of would-be whistleblowers' information and knowledge problems.

The Two Meanings of 'Made Publicly'

Sagar insists that leaks be "made publicly" in order to be justified and properly described as whistleblowing. Ralph Nader's influential early definition described whistleblowing along similar lines, as "the act of a man or woman who, believing that the public interest overrides the interest of the organization he serves, *publicly* 'blows the whistle' if the organization is involved in corrupt, illegal, fraudulent, or harmful activity."[45] The term in this context has two meanings, both of which are problematic.

One involves self-identification, such that a whistleblower should abjure anonymity. She should show her face and bravely face the music, accepting whatever consequences may come. An expectation that whistleblowers reveal themselves has at least two key benefits. It adds another layer of accountability, by forcing would-be whistleblowers to take personal responsibility for their actions. And it pushes would-be whistleblowers to more carefully weigh the costs and benefits of their unauthorized disclosures. However, a blanket proscription against anonymous disclosures ignores retaliation threats that many would-be whistleblowers face.

Sagar acknowledges those risks and carves out an exception if disclosure would provoke severe retaliation against the individual (e.g., extrajudicial assaults) and if the concealed abuse in question is serious enough that the public must know ("gross wrongdoings").[46] Yet if we look outside of the universe of cases in Sagar's book—national security secrets in rights-protecting democracies—it becomes clear that additional exceptions are needed. For example, individuals in nondemocracies likely face relatively higher retaliation risks, even when they are not severe. Punishment could be arbitrary or, in other ways, unfair. Just because a whistleblower in an authoritarian country does not risk severe punishment does not mean she should reveal her identity. Overall, political context matters. The connection between punishments and unauthorized disclosures is mediated by regime type. The harsh or repressive natures of other environments, such as urban areas with high levels of gang violence, also warrant more anonymous whistleblowing about abuses that occur there.

The second meaning of *made publicly* involves the publication of the secret. In most cases, this condition should be satisfied. Consider the difference between leaking to *The New York Times* versus passing secrets to Russian spies. If someone gave classified details of a U.S. government program to the latter, there is no interpretation of that action in which we would label it whistleblowing, even if the information in question clearly and convincingly showed an abuse of public authority. Passing the same information to the *Times* might provoke debates about whether the act qualifies as an abuse, but the episode is potentially whistleblowing.

Yet here again we have to consider exceptions—not when passing secrets to foreign spies counts as whistleblowing, but when the costs of public disclosure outweigh the benefits. In some cases, whistleblowing should stay within organizations to the extent that there is a fair internal process which adjudicates the conflict and protects the whistleblower from unjust retaliation. Internal whistleblowing of this sort can be cumbersome, but a difficult process is not a sufficient reason for discounting the costs of disclosure. Large, complex organizations often have multiple whistleblowing pathways, so if one becomes a dead end, others are available. If the nearest ombudsman drops the ball, or, from the whistleblower's perspective, makes the wrong decision about how to proceed, other insider recipients with authority might be more agreeable. The bottom line is that *not* going public is sometimes preferable, considering the tradeoffs between the desired consequences of whistleblowing (i.e., stopping abuses or holding perpetrators accountable) and the costs of disclosure (e.g., imperiling public safety, harming national security, violating personal privacy, divulging trade secrets or otherwise unnecessarily destroying economic value, or making career-destroying accusations against possibly innocent persons).

What if Snowden, for example, had gone to Congress or the NSA's inspector general instead of Glenn Greenwald and Laura Poitras? If his primary goal was to stop or reform allegedly unconstitutional NSA domestic programs, he might have achieved that without publicly disclosing operational details about foreign-focused programs, including sources and methods, which adversaries of America could read about, along with its citizens. Had he brought his concerns to one or more of probably hundreds of internal recipients—for example, officials at the NSA and the Office of the Director of National Intelligence, members of Congress on intelligence committees, lawyers at the Office of Special Counsel—then he would have at least shown an awareness of the costs of publicly disclosing a massive trove of documents detailing primarily foreign-focused programs that have nothing to do with domestic surveillance and Americans' privacy rights.

Snowden's defenders and collaborators, Greenwald and Poitras included, have stated (but have not shown) that NSA officials and members of Congress, especially those on the intelligence oversight committees, would not have addressed the problems. Going the internal route would have been a waste of time, they argued, and probably would have just made Snowden vulnerable to retaliation. Besides, they have claimed, he did send an email to supervisors in the NSA's Office of General Counsel (OGC), in which he expressed his misgivings, including about how the NSA interpreted the operative laws. That email, Snowden et al. have claimed, was basically ignored, which proves the futility of the internal route.

Fortunately, the NSA released Snowden's email in 2014 (figure 2.2), as well as an internal evaluation of the email, in the context of a Snowden-focused counterintelligence investigation. According to the NSA's summary,

> On 5 April 2013, Snowden asked about a slide in the USSID 18 training program (OVSC1800) that listed United States legal authorities (Constitution at the top, office policies at the bottom). Snowden argued that Federal statutes should not be on the same level as (i.e., equivalent to) Executive Orders. Snowden also asked which has greater precedence, ODNI [Office of the Director of National Intelligence] or DOD regulations (also listed on the same line). On 8 April 2013, [redacted] responded that E.O.s have the 'force and effects

of laws' but cannot override federal statute. DOD/ODNI conflicts would be settled by date of issuance and subject matter. *It should be noted this is four months after contacting Glenn Greenwald (according to Greenwald) and three months after contacting Laura Poitras (according to Poitras and Greenwald).* So this email is not evidence that he tried to raise concerns about NSA procedures through official channels before turning to the media.[47]

The NSA's point about the timing of Snowden's OGC email is an important one: he sent it months *after* he had already promised Greenwald and Poitras the leaked documents.[48]

The claim that Snowden first tried the insider whistleblower path was also strongly challenged by the House Intelligence Committee, whose two-year investigation found

> no evidence that Snowden took any official effort to express concerns about U.S. intelligence activities—legal, moral, or otherwise—to any oversight officials within the U.S. government, despite numerous avenues to do so. Snowden was aware of these avenues. His only attempt to contact an NSA attorney [i.e., the OGC email] revolved around a question about the legal precedence of executive orders, and his only contact to the Central Intelligence Agency (CIA) inspector general (IG) revolved around his disagreements with his managers about training and retention of information technology specialists.[49]

While the House report likely contained errors, and some statements in the unclassified version are insufficiently supported, none of its critics have supplied evidence beyond Snowden's personal testimony regarding his attempts at internal whistleblowing.[50] (The bipartisan House committee, during a time of high congressional polarization, voted unanimously to approve the report.)

Snowden's backers have made broader arguments about the futility of keeping his whistleblowing inside the government. Greenwald, for instance, has argued that Snowden's public whistleblowing was necessary because the congressional intelligence committees failed in their oversight duties—because even when they knew about the NSA's programs, they did not stop or change them in line with Greenwald's legal interpretations and policy preferences. He has also steeply discounted the risks of disclosure, making the common argument that "Snowden did not tell the terrorists anything they did not already know. The terrorists have known for years that the U.S. government is trying to monitor their communications." Yet this assumes that all U.S. enemies and adversaries knew classified details about all the NSA's sources and methods. They might have suspected some of those, and certainly knew about the risks of communicating with each other, but they did not have the valuable information about sources and methods provided by the leaks. Without that knowledge, they had greater uncertainty, and they were more likely to have made errors or bad communication choices, which might have allowed the NSA to identify their whereabouts, connections, plans, and so on. Giving hostile actors specific

DOCID: 4122161

```
                                                          (b)(3)-P.L. 86-36
   Classification: UNCLASSIFIED//FOR OFFICIAL USE ONLY

   -----Original Message-----
   From:
   Sent: Monday, April 08, 2013 1:37 PM
   To: Snowden Edward J NSA-FHV USA CTR
   Cc:


   Subject: RE: (U) Question for OGC re OVSC1800 Course Content - (U) FW:
   Comments from the D2 General Counsel Email Us Form

   Classification: UNCLASSIFIED//FOR OFFICIAL USE ONLY

   Hello Ed,

   Executive Orders (E.O.s) have the "force and effect of law." That said, you
   are correct that E.O.s cannot override a statute.

   In general, DOD and ODNI regulations are afforded similar precedence though
   subject matter or date could result in one having precedence over another.

   Please give me a call if you would like to discuss further.

   Regards,

                                                          (b)(3)-P.L. 86-36


   Office of General Counsel/D21
   963-3121 NSTS/(301) 688-5015 Commercial
   OPS 2B, 2B8134, Suite 6250
   -----Original Message-----
   From: ejsnowd@nsa.ic.gov [mailto:ejsnowd@nsa.ic.gov]
   Sent: Friday, April 05, 2013 4:11 PM
   To: DL gc_web (ALIAS) D2
   Cc: Snowden Edward J NSA-FHV USA CTR
   Subject: Comments from the D2 General Counsel Email Us Form

   Classification: UNCLASSIFIED//FOR OFFICIAL USE ONLY

   SID: ejsnowd

   fullname: Ed Snowden

   Org: FHV

   Affiliation: Contractor

   Secure_Phone: N/A

   Message: Hello, I have a question regarding the mandatory USSID 18 training.
```

Approved for Release by NSA on 05-29-2014, FOIA Case # 78071

FIGURE 2.2 Snowden's Email to the OGC about the NSA's Legal Interpretation. *Source*: Courtesy of the National Security Agency, https://www.nsa.gov/.

details about your intelligence sources and methods reduces your advantage, obviously. Gellman's relatively measured take that "Snowden's disclosures did a lot more good than harm," at least acknowledges harms.[51]

Another common argument about the futility of internal whistleblowing cites historical precedent. Daniel Ellsberg, the argument goes, first went to Congress and was met with shrugs, cowardice, and hostility. Therefore, important

DOCID: 4122161

```
The training states the following:

--------
(U) The Hierarchy of Governing Authorities and Documents is displayed from the
highest authority to the lowest authority as follows:

    U.S. Constitution
    Federal Statutes/Presidential Executive Orders (EO)
    Department of Defense (DoD) and Office of the Director of National
Intelligence (ODNI) Regulations
        NSA/CSS Directives and Policies
            USSIDs
            SID Management Directives and Policies
            Office Policies
----------

I'm not entirely certain, but this does not seem correct, as it seems to imply
Executive Orders have the same precedence as law.  My understanding is that
EOs may be superseded by federal statute, but EOs may not override statute.
Am I incorrect in this?  Between EOs and laws, which have precedence?

Similarly, between DOD and ODNI regulations, which has greater precedence?

Could you please clarify?

Thank you very much,

Ed

Classification: UNCLASSIFIED//FOR OFFICIAL USE ONLY

=========================================================
Classification: UNCLASSIFIED//FOUO

Classification: UNCLASSIFIED//FOR OFFICIAL USE ONLY
```

FIGURE 2.2 (Continued)   Snowden's Email to the OGC about the NSA's Legal Interpretation. *Source*: Courtesy of the National Security Agency, https://www.nsa.gov/.

revelations about government abuses die in Congress, or, by implication, other parts of the government. Yet the argument, and ones like it built upon a single or small number of cases, weakens when we consider the many whistleblowing cases that are taken seriously by legislators, ombudsmen, inspector generals, and the like. That does not mean that all insider whistleblowers make the correct decision when considering the tradeoffs. The argument here is merely one about fully acknowledging risks and benefits and, more broadly, about considering the unintended social consequences of going public. Strong whistleblower protection laws go a long way in guiding scrupulous would-be whistleblowers toward more prudent choices. Whether the United States or other countries have strong enough laws is a separate question.

Limiting the Scale and Scope of Disclosures

Sagar's insistence that prospective whistleblowers limit the scale and scope of disclosures as much as possible mirrors the framework's other consequentialist provisions. In essence, it asks would-be whistleblowers not to release any more than absolutely necessary, given the costs and benefits of every disclosure. Assessing that tradeoff for a single document is hard enough. Doing the same with twelve or sixty or thousands of documents moves from difficult to impossible. Someone who releases secrets in bulk is unlikely to accomplish that task.

No one, except for Snowden and possibly his closest collaborators, knows exactly how many classified documents he took from NSA servers. Estimates given by the government and Snowden's circle differ, but if we believe the former, then he took up to 1.77 million top secret documents and gave Greenwald et al. about 200,000.[52] While we cannot cite a specific number, we do know Snowden misspoke at best when he claimed in June 2013 that "I carefully evaluated every single document I disclosed [to Greenwald et al] to ensure that each was legitimately in the public interest." If the 200,000 estimate is correct, and given the time frame of his data theft and transfer—March 2012 to May 2013, approximately 430 days—then Snowden would have had to "carefully evaluate" about 465 dense, technical, documents every day, on average, without any breaks for illness, weekends, vacations, or holidays.[53]

Nearly two years after his "carefully evaluated every single document" remark, the television comedian John Oliver pointedly asked Snowden, "How many of those documents have you actually read?" Snowden at first reaffirmed his earlier statement. But when pressed by Oliver—"You've read every single one?"—Snowden implied it was good enough that he knew, in general terms, what the unexamined documents contained: "Well, I do understand what I turned over." Once Oliver pointed out the obvious, that "there's a difference between *understanding* what's in the documents and *reading* what's in the documents," Snowden essentially conceded the point (while shifting into third person singular and plural to refer to himself): "I recognize the concerns . . . I think it's fair to be concerned about, did this person do enough? Were they careful enough?" While Snowden finally admitted, albeit obliquely, that he did not read everything, there is no reason to assume without evidence, beyond his testimony, that he adequately understood what he "turned over."[54]

In the years after his disclosures, Snowden demonstrated a keen understanding of the NSA programs that his collaborators had described in publications. But what counts here is his knowledge of them, and the associated legal foundations, at the moment of disclosure. While he clearly knew enough about some of the NSA's work to speak thoughtfully and coherently in his first public interview in June 2013, Snowden's critics with deep knowledge of the NSA's work insisted that he wildly misrepresented the ease with which NSA staffers and contractors could break privacy laws, given the agency's compliance and oversight procedures. Snowden, for instance, controversially claimed that "I, sitting at my desk, certainly had the authorities to wiretap anyone, from you or your accountant, to a federal judge or even the president, if I had a personal email."[55] Moreover, according to his immediate supervisor at Booz Allen Hamilton, Snowden was not in a position to understand the NSA's elaborate procedures for privacy law compliance and oversight.[56] Overall, the evidence strongly suggests that Snowden did not adequately evaluate the costs and benefits of each document that he transferred to reporters, as all would-be whistleblowers should.

Threats to Public Safety

The consequentialist framework's insistence that would-be whistleblowers carefully consider how disclosures might threaten public safety is in line the other standards. The preceding discussion already covered the main questions. The variable as written, however, is limited in that it omits other kinds of threats besides those to public safety, even within Sagar's national security realm. For example, disclosures might unnecessarily harm aspects of national security that go beyond direct threats to public safety, such as the maintenance of international alliances. We could reasonably expand the variable to include other kinds of harms, such as violating personal privacy, divulging trade secrets or otherwise unnecessarily destroying economic value, and making career-destroying accusations against possibly innocent persons. Transforming the variable beyond public safety in this way maintains the consequentialist framework's prudent, evidence-based approach. The key point merits repeating: Would-be whistleblowers should consider all relevant harms before going public.

Conclusion

Evaluating Snowden's disclosures with a slightly amended version of Sagar's consequentialist framework demonstrates its usefulness. It also shows the weak basis for describing Snowden as a whistleblower. While the framework is imperfect, it offers relatively greater conceptual clarity on key procedural and substantive questions—from what constitutes a whistleblowing-worthy offense to whether or not to spill secrets in the first place. At the very least, the five conditions lead to useful starting questions with which to evaluate individual cases. My proposed amendments and exceptions do expand the framework but do not sacrifice its prudential, cost-benefit rationalism. Overall, while acknowledging the potential benefits of unauthorized disclosures, the framework encourages aspiring whistleblowers to be more mindful of the negative consequences of leaks. Most definitions of whistleblowing, along with cultural images of whistleblowers, focus almost exclusively on the benefits side of the ledger. The framework, if used widely, would almost certainly reduce the number of damaging leaks, for instance, the post-9/11 revelations about the Terrorist Finance

Tracking Program, the "TSA's [Transportation Security Administration] Secret Behavior Checklist to Spot Terrorists" (as the *Intercept* headlined its leak story), and, as argued in this chapter, the vast majority of NSA and partners' programs from the Snowden cache.[57]

One risk of the amended framework is that it would lead to too little whistleblowing. Would-be whistleblowers might become overly prudent, leaving clear evidence of, for example, corruption concealed with abusers free to continue and free from justifiable punishment. In *Secrets and Leaks*, Sagar recognized the problem and seemed comfortable with the end result of a system with perhaps too few instances of whistleblowing.[58] That outcome may be acceptable in some domains, such as national security and intelligence. In other realms, such as human rights violations, an overly cautious approach would likely be too restrictive, and the default position should be much closer to disclosure.

A framework built to reduce harmful leaks will not work on everyone. Risk-disregarding ideologues will still come to the pertinent questions—about threats to public safety, the quality of evidence, and so on—with all of the scales already tipped toward disclosure. Everyone makes decisions with biases, including those who excessively discount risks.

For example, chapters 6 through 8 feature some activists and ideologues who oppose government secrecy almost completely. Someone like WikiLeaks founder Julian Assange would have no use for the consequentialist definition. Snowden's ideological beliefs are less overtly radical than Assange's, although he has a well-documented libertarian worldview, albeit a more common American version compared with Assange's libertarian-inflected cyber anarchism. Snowden's libertarianism transformed over time, as reflected by his preleak chat room posts as TheTrueHOOHA. He was then in favor of a limited, but strong, government. One chatroom post in 2009 had him arguing that national security leakers "should be shot." In 2013, after the first leaks, he claimed his experience working in the U.S. intelligence community darkened his view of his country's government. "Much of what I saw in Geneva [while working for the CIA, before the NSA,] really disillusioned me about how my government functions and what its impact is in the world. I realized that I was part of something that was doing far more harm than good."[59] While we cannot know the full extent of Snowden's thinking, he arrived at his leak decision with the cost-benefit scale already heavily tipped toward leaking—in general, the United States was doing "more harm than good." That probably figured into his decision not to read the hundreds of thousands of classified documents and not to blow the whistle inside the government before giving them to Greenwald et al.

The harms that might or might not come from determined ideologues, vengeful employees, or anyone else with rigid prejudices, however, is not the fault of any reasonable, normative whistleblowing framework. None of them could reliably prevent risk-denying leakers from making unauthorized disclosures. To prevent insiders from spilling necessary secrets, there is no match for top notch employment and security clearance screening, continuous monitoring (of one form or another, depending on the nature of the organization, and with appropriate privacy protections), and, in the intelligence community, interagency communication. If the CIA had properly marked Snowden as a red-flagged "derog" in the interagency system—his boss in Geneva filed a "derogatory report" after detecting changes in his "behavior and work habits," and "suspect[ing] that [he] was trying to break into classified computer files to which he was not authorized to have access"—then the NSA's screeners would probably not have approved him for his work with Dell and Booz Allen Hamilton, jobs he took specifically to steal NSA secrets about foreign-focused operations and capabilities (e.g., "My position with Booz Allen Hamilton granted me access to lists of machines all over the world the NSA hacked. That is why I accepted that position about three months ago," Snowden told the SCMP).[60]

One of the biggest challenges going forward will be to figure out how to best configure the consequentialist framework to alternative policy spaces, organization types, and regime types discussed in this book and others. Perhaps it will be easy enough to adjust some of the knobs in light of a case's context. For instance, we might change the burden of proof standard to "reasonable suspicion" in human rights cases that emerge in repressive nondemocracies. The point is that assessments about a disclosure's costs and benefits are endogenous to the political environment in which an alleged abuse occurred.

The next chapter elaborates on some of the broader claims made so far. First, it reexamines the claim that both organizational insiders and outsiders can be whistleblowers. Then, it revisits and extends the argument about the importance of observing and identifying what happens within whistleblowing networks, rather than the actions of isolated, "lone wolf" whistleblowers. The arguments together lead to some interesting and unusual places covered in later chapters, including the *Chronicle of Current Events* (the Soviet samizdat journal), Amnesty International's information extraction networks, "I Paid a Bribe" and other online crowdsourced whistleblowing sites, and the Citizen's Commission to Investigate the FBI, among other information burglar-whistleblowers.

Notes

[1] Glenn Greenwald, Ewen MacAskill and Laura Poitras, "Edward Snowden: The Whistleblower behind the NSA Surveillance Revelations," *The Guardian*, June 9, 2013, http://www.theguardian.com/world/2013/jun/09/edward-snowden-nsa-whistleblower-surveillance.

[2] Different versions of the drama include: Glenn Greenwald, *No Place to Hide: Edward Snowden, the NSA, and the US Surveillance State* (New York: Macmillan, 2014); *Citizenfour* film, Directed by Laura Poitras, HBO Films, Participant Media, Praxis Films, 2014; Edward

Jay Epstein, *How America Lost Its Secrets: Edward Snowden, the Man and the Theft* (New York: Vintage, 2017).

3 "Treason," FindLaw, accessed January 16, 2019, https://criminal.findlaw.com/criminal-charges/treason.html.

4 "CIA Whistleblower Philip Agee Dies at 72," *Democracy Now!* January 9, 2008, https://www.democracynow.org/2008/1/9/headlines/cia_whistleblower_philip_agee_dies_at_72; Scott Shane, "Philip Agee, 72, Dies; Exposed Other C.I.A. Officers," *The New York Times,* January 10, 2008, A28 [comment by William H. Schaap]. On Agee's Cuban and Soviet ties, see Christopher Andrew and Vasili Mitrokhin, *The World Was Going Our Way. The KGB and the Battle for the Third World* (New York: Basic Books, 2005), 103–4; Christopher Andrew and Vasili Mitrokhin, *The Sword and the Shield: The Mitrokhin Archive and the Secret History of the KGB* (New York: Basic Books, 2000), 230–4; Oleg Kalugin, *Spymaster: My Thirty-two Years in Intelligence and Espionage Against the West* (New York: Basic Books, 2009), 219–20; Christopher Moran, "Turning against the CIA: Whistleblowers during the 'Time of Troubles,'" *History* 100, no. 340 (2015): 251–74. Note the comparable case of NSA cryptologists William Martin and Bernon Mitchell, who appeared in Moscow in 1960 to lambaste and reveal NSA policies, claiming they did so in order to prevent nuclear war. David Barrett, "NSA Secrets Revealed—in 1960," *The Washington Post,* June 21, 2013, 21; *First Unitarian Church of Los Angeles v. National Security Agency,* 3:13-cv-03287 JSW, Amicus Curiae Brief in Support of Plaintiffs' Motion for Partial Summary Judgment, "Experts in the History of Executive Surveillance: James Bamford, Loch Johnson, and Peter Fenn" (Northern California District Court, 2013); Conor Friedersdorf, "Experts on the NSA's History of Abuses: There They Go Again," *The Atlantic,* November 21, 2013, http://www.theatlantic.com/politics/archive/2013/11/experts-on-the-nsas-history-of-abuses-there-they-go-again/281703.

5 While many of the revelations have contained truths, false narratives of the FBI and CIA's Cold War–era work continue to be believed and disseminated. Church Committee. "Final Report of the Senate Select Committee to Study Governmental Operations with Respect to Intelligence Activities: Book II: Intelligence Activities and the Rights of Americans." USS 94d (1976); Arthur Herman, "The 35-Year War on the CIA," *Commentary* 128, no. 5 (December 2009): 9–22; Tim Weiner, *Legacy of Ashes: The History of the CIA* (New York: Anchor, 2008); Tim Weiner, *Enemies: A History of the FBI* (New York: Random House, 2012); David Robarge, "CIA in the Spotlight: The Central Intelligence Agency and Public Accountability," *Journal of Intelligence History* 9, nos. 1–2 (2009): 105–126.

6 Glenn Greenwald, "NSA Collecting Phone Records of Millions of Verizon Customers Daily," *The Guardian,* June 6, 2013, https://www.theguardian.com/world/2013/jun/06/nsa-phone-records-verizon-court-order; Siobhan Gorman, Evan Perez, and Janet Hook, "U.S. Collects Vast Data Trove," *The Wall Street Journal,* June 7, 2013, https://www.wsj.com/articles/SB10001424127887324299104578529112289298922; Barton Gellman and Laura Poitras, "US Intelligence Mining Data from Nine U.S. Internet Companies in Broad Secret Program," *The Washington Post,* June 6, 2013, http://www.washingtonpost.com/investigations/us-intelligence-mining-data-from-nine-us-internet-companies-in-broad-secret-program/2013/06/06/3a0c0da8-cebf-11e2-8845-d970ccb04497_story.n.html; Nick Hopkins, "UK Gathering Secret Intelligence via Covert NSA Operation," *The Guardian,* June 7, 2013, https://www.theguardian.com/technology/2013/jun/07/uk-gathering-secret-intelligence-nsa-prism; Adam Gabbatt, "'Nobody Is Listening to Your Calls': Obama's Evolution on NSA Surveillance," *The Guardian,* August 9, 2013, http://www.theguardian.com/world/2013/aug/09/obama-evolution-nsa-reforms Greenwald, *No Place to Hide.*

7 Greenwald et al., "Edward Snowden."

8 Greenwald, *No Place to Hide*; Poitras, *Citizenfour*; Epstein, *How America Lost Its Secrets.*

9 Epstein, *How America Lost Its Secrets.*

10 The City Council of New York City re-classified public urination from a criminal to civil offense in 2016. See Matt Flegenheimer and J. David Goodman, "A Street Crime Tests Attitudes on How to Fight Minor Offenses," *The New York Times,* July 16, 2015, A18; Erin

Durkin, "City Council Approves Plan to Ease Punishments for Minor Offenses," *New York Daily News,* May 25, 2016.

[11] David Stout, "Ex-Rep. Jefferson Convicted in Bribery Scheme," *The New York Times*, August 5, 2009, A14.

[12] A posthumous disclosure would tarnish his historical reputation but obviously that would be materially inconsequential to him, although it could harm his descendants.

[13] Donald E. Brown, *Human Universals* (New York: McGraw-Hill, 1991); Steven Pinker, *The Blank Slate: The Modern Denial of Human Nature* (New York: Penguin, 2003).

[14] 18 U.S. Code § 1821, https://www.govinfo.gov/content/pkg/USCODE-2011-title18/pdf/USCODE-2011-title18-partI-chap89-sec1821.pdf, accessed March 27, 2019; Sean Gorman, "A Crime to Transport Dentures across State Lines? Goodlatte's Claim Has Teeth," Politifact Virginia, December 7, 2015, https://www.politifact.com/virginia/statements/2015/dec/07/bob-goodlatte/goodlattes-says-clim/; Paul Larkin, "Spring Cleaning for Needless Criminal Laws," Heritage Foundation, March 9, 2016, http://www.heritage.org/research/commentary/2016/3/spring-cleaning-for-needless-criminal-laws.

[15] If everyone agreed on how to read a law, and specifically whether or not an act violated a law or not, we would have far fewer competitive debates in courtrooms and law reviews. Indeed, the United States would probably have fewer trials, lawyers, and law schools. (No comment on whether that would benefit America.) We would also have fewer debates about statutory interpretation in executive branch agencies. Obviously, courtroom and law review debates turn on other issues, such as how to evaluate evidence and how to ascertain an accused person's motivation. On the issue of statutory interpretation in the context of the judiciary, see Robert A. Katzmann, *Judging Statutes* (Oxford: Oxford University Press, 2014). In the executive branch: Cass R. Sunstein, "Interpreting Statutes in the Regulatory State," *Harvard Law Review* (1989): 405–508.

[16] Anyone who looked beyond the headlines at the actual leaked documents saw that the NSA linked each program to congressional statutes. For instance, the main heading of one of the leaked PRISM PowerPoint slides says "FAA702 Operations," which referred to the FISA Amendments Act of 2008's Section 702. Some programs were authorized by FAA 702, while others fell under the Patriot Act and Executive Order 12333. Reasonable observers disagreed about whether the NSA programs comported with those rules, as a result of their different legal interpretations. The strength of their competing arguments led to divergent Snowden-related court rulings. Neither side had an open-and-shut case about whether the NSA programs complied with the law. The legality of the metadata program rested upon the Patriot Act (Section 215), the Supreme Court's decision in *Smith v. Maryland* (442 U.S. 735, 99 S. Ct. 2577, 61 L. Ed. 2d 220 (1979)), and the FISA Amendments Act of 2008 (Section 702). See Charlie Savage and Jonathan Weisman, "N.S.A. Collection of Bulk Call Data Is Ruled Illegal," *The New York Times*, May 7, 2015, A1. Most of the legal memos supporting the NSA programs have remained classified, which has made full analysis of government lawyers' interpretations impossible. Still, the disclosures and subsequent investigations revealed fragments of the NSA's reasoning, which along with independent analysis, made for a debate with multiple, reasonable perspectives about the application of the laws.

[17] Peter B. Jubb, "Whistleblowing: A Restrictive Definition and Interpretation," *Journal of Business Ethics* 21, no. 1 (1999): 77–94, at 78; Janet P. Near and Marcia P. Miceli. "Organizational Dissidence: The Case of Whistle-blowing," *Journal of Business Ethics* 4, no. 1 (1985): 1–16, at 4. See also Janet P. Near, Michael T. Rehg, James R. Van Scotter, and Marcia P. Miceli, "Does Type of Wrongdoing Affect the Whistle-Blowing Process?" *Business Ethics Quarterly* 14, no. 2 (2004): 219–242.

[18] Jesslyn Radack, "High-Level Confirmation That Snowden's a Whistle-Blower," *The New York Times,* December 20, 2013, http://www.nytimes.com/roomfordebate/2013/12/19/has-snowden-been-vindicated/high-level-confirmation-that-snowdens-a-whistle-blower; "Whistleblowing" [flyer], U.S. Office of Special Counsel, https://osc.gov/Resources/post_wb.pdf; Stuart Dawson "Whistleblowing: A Broad Definition and Some Issues for Australia," Victoria University of Technology, 2000, http://www.bmartin.cc/dissent/documents/Dawson.html.

19   While some products did cost more than typical hardware store models, such as the toilet seat covers for P-3 patrol planes that had to be "lightweight, seamless and corrosion resistant," some of the reported sums that had to be "lightweight, seamless and corrosion resistant," some of the reported sums in newspapers' procurement "horror stories" actually resulted from misinterpretation of the bureaucracy's accounting books. They were, in short, "accounting artifacts." See Sydney J. Freedberg Jr., "The Myth of the $600 Hammer," *Government Executive*, December 7, 1998, http://www.govexec.com/federal-news/1998/12/the-myth-of-the-600-hammer/5271/; Steven Kelman, *Unleashing Change: A Study of Organizational Renewal in Government* (Washington, DC: Brookings Institution Press, 2005), 54; James O'Shea, "It Cost $600, But It's Not Just Any Toilet Seat," *Chicago Tribune*, February 5, 1985.

20   Anyone who has ever taught a college course understands the perils of making rounding-up exceptions. If you give B's to students with 79.5 percent to 79.9 percent, how do you explain to the student with a 79.4 percent that he does not deserve a B?

21   Another example of a "reasonable belief" standard in U.S. law is *Graham v. Connor*, 490 U.S. 386 (1989). See also "Whistleblowing and America's Secrets: Ensuring a Viable Balance," Panel discussion at the Secrecy, Openness and National Security: Lessons and Issues for the Next Administration Conference (Mark Zaid, Bob Litt, Steve Vladeck, Ken Dilanian, Gabriel Schoenfeld), Johns Hopkins University Center for Advanced Governmental Studies, April 27, 2015, http://advanced.jhu.edu/jhu-event/secrecy-openness-and-national-security-lessons-and-issues-for-the-next-administration/ (audio available at http://www.lawfareblog.com/2015/05/the-lawfare-podcast-episode-121-striking-a-balance-whistleblowing-leaks-and-security-secrets).

22   According to St. Augustine, "offenses against nature are everywhere and at all times to be held in detestation and should be punished. Such offenses, for example, were those of the Sodomites; and, even if all nations should commit them, they would all be judged guilty of the same crime by the divine law, which has not made men so that they should ever abuse one another in that way. For the fellowship that should be between God and us is violated whenever that nature of which he is the author is polluted by perverted lust." Augustine of Hippo, *Confessions*, 2007 [398], Book 3, chapter 8, translated Albert C. Outler. That interpretation until recently had support from the laws of some liberal societies—for instance, in the United States until the Supreme Court's 2003 decision (6-3) in *Lawrence v. Texas*. The United Kingdom did not begin to decriminalize homosexual acts between consenting adults until the 1960s, with amendments continuing into the 2000s.

23   One tradition that would not work at all is deconstructive postmodernism.

24   In the United States, for instance, since approximately President Franklin Roosevelt's reign, and perhaps specifically at the moment of his "Second Bill of Rights" speech, a large number of liberals began to conceive of and advocate for economic rights, including a worker's guaranteed right to "a useful and remunerative job in the industries or shops or farms or mines" and a "right of every family to a decent home." Not all liberals then or now have lined up behind Roosevelt's vision, but his agenda and New Deal policy initiatives still stand at the center of contemporary American liberalism. Many other Americans, who have identified with the classical, pre-Rooseveltian version of liberalism, have stridently disagreed that such alleged "rights" should be welcomed into the liberal tradition. On the "Second Bill of Rights," see President Franklin Roosevelt's State of the Union Address, January 11, 1944.

25   John Rawls, *Political Liberalism* (New York, NY: Columbia University Press, 2005).

26   Rahul Sagar, *Secrets and Leaks: The Dilemma of State Secrecy* (Princeton, NJ: Princeton University Press, 2014). Although Sagar doesn't use the term "consequentialism" in the book, the approach is clearly driven by consequentialist thinking. Indeed, Sagar generally describes his work this way: "I do problem-driven political theory, from a consequentialist perspective, employing realist methods." "About," Rahul Sagar, accessed June 2, 2015, www.rahulsagar.com/.

27   Sagar, *Secrets and Leaks*.

28   Another analysis that takes the costs of disclosure seriously is Candice Delmas, "The Ethics of Government Whistleblowing," *Social Theory and Practice* 40, no. 1 (2015): 77–105. C. Fred Alford's conception of "responsible followers" of the organization's principles suggests that potential whistleblowers might consider the potential costs of disclosure—that is, by being

"responsible." However, the idea of responsibility in the definition tilts toward disclosure. Alford's point was to illustrate that people often seen as disloyal by organization insiders are perhaps the most loyal, because they care deeply about the organization's integrity and stated mission. C. Fred Alford, *Whistleblowers: Broken Lives and Organizational Power* (Ithaca, NY: Cornell University Press, 2002).

29 Authority means rightful or legitimate rule—the rightful, legitimate use of power. A common definition of "legitimate" centers on adherence to existing laws. David A. Lake, "Rightful Rules: Authority, Order, and the Foundations of Global Governance," *International Studies Quarterly* 54, no. 3 (2010): 587–613, at 591; John A. Simmons, "Political Obligation and Authority," in Robert L. Simon, ed., *The Blackwell Guide to Social and Political Philosophy* (Malden, MA: Blackwell, 2002).

30 For example, see Radack, "High-Level Confirmation"; "Whistleblowing," U.S. OSC.

31 PRGICT, *Liberty and Security in a Changing World*; Peter Baker, "Moves to Curb Spying Help Drive the Clemency Argument for Snowden," *The New York Times*, January 5, 2014, A16; Michael S. Schmidt, "Snowden Faults N.S.A. on Oversight," *The New York Times*, July 20, 2014, A4; Greenwald, *No Place to Hide*, 19.

32 Congressional majorities in December 2012 and January 2018 reauthorized Section 702 of the Foreign Intelligence Surveillance Act of 1978 Amendments Act of 2008, which governs the handling of U.S. persons data in a way that civil libertarians believe prioritizes security over liberty and privacy. On incidental data and 702, see Gellman, "NSA Broke Privacy Rules"; Edgar, *Beyond Snowden*; Jennifer Stisa Granick, *American Spies: Modern Surveillance, Why You Should Care, and What to Do* (New York: Cambridge University Press, 2017); Jennifer Granick and Jadzia Butler, "Correcting the Record on Section 702: A Prerequisite for Meaningful Surveillance Reform," *Just Security*, September 15, 2016, https://www.justsecurity. org/32916/correcting-record-section-702-prerequisite-meaningful-surveillance-reform/; Ashley Gorski and Patrick C. Toomey, "Unprecedented and Unlawful: The NSA's 'Upstream' Surveillance," *Just Security*, September 19, 2016, https://www.justsecurity.org/33044/unprecedented-unlawful-nsas-upstream-surveillance/; Christopher Sprigman, "The NSA's Culture of 'Legal Compliance' Still Breaks the Law," *Just Security*, February 24, 2014, https://www.justsecurity.org/7485/nsas-culture-legal-compliance-breaks-law/; Cindy Cohn, "Word Games: What the NSA Means by 'Targeted' Surveillance Under Section 702," *Deep Links* (ElectronicFrontier Foundation), August 24, 2016, https://www.eff.org/deeplinks/2016/08/nsa-word-games-mass-v-targeted-surveillance-under-section-702.

33 The former NSA director Michael Hayden provided the sixty-one million number for the denominator, but he referred to the three-month period used in a separate part of the audit (related to the types of errors). Thus, we might say that the denominator for the twelve-month period was likely in the ballpark of 244 million (61 million for each quarter year, on average). Andrea Peterson, "Former NSA Chief: 'Morally Arrogant' Snowden Will Probably Become an Alcoholic," *The Washington Post*, September 17, 2013, https://www.washingtonpost.com/news/the-switch/wp/2013/09/17/former-nsa-chief-morally-arrogant-snowden-will-probably-become-an-alcoholic/; Barton Gellman, "NSA Broke Privacy Rules Thousands of Times Per Year, Audit Finds," *The Washington Post*, August 15, 2013, http://www.washingtonpost.com/world/national-security/nsa-broke-privacy-rules-thousands-of-times-per-year-audit-finds/2013/08/15/3310e554-05ca-11e3-a07f-49ddc7417125_story.html.

34 Rebecca J. Richards, NSA Civil Liberties and Privacy Office, "Review of U.S. Person Privacy Protections in the Production and Dissemination of Serialized Intelligence Reports Derived from Signals Intelligence Acquired Pursuant to Title I and Section 702 of the Foreign Intelligence Surveillance Act," October 11, 2017; Timothy H. Edgar, *Beyond Snowden: Privacy, Mass Surveillance, and the Struggle to Reform the NSA* (Washington, DC: Brookings Institution Press, 2017).

35 Lana Lam, "EXCLUSIVE: NSA Targeted China's Tsinghua University in Extensive Hacking Attacks, Says Snowden," *South China Morning Post*, June 22, 2013, https://www.scmp.com/news/china/article/1266892/exclusive-nsa-targeted-chinas-tsinghua-university-extensive-hacking; Lana Lam and Stephen Chen, "EXCLUSIVE: Snowden Reveals More US Cyberspying

Details," *South China Morning Post*, June 22, 2013, http://www.scmp.com/news/hong-kong/article/1266777/exclusive-snowden-safe-hong-kong-more-us-cyberspying-details-revealed.

36 Janet Reitman, "Snowden and Greenwald: The Men Who Leaked the Secrets," *Rolling Stone*, December 4, 2013.

37 The SCMP leak story was conspicuously absent from this otherwise comprehensive list: "NSA Primary Sources," *Electronic Frontier Foundation,* https://www.eff.org/nsa-spying/nsadocs, accessed on February 10, 2016, and February 17, 2017. The SCMP story was also missing from another purportedly complete archive: Snowden Digital Surveillance Archive, Canadian Journalists for Free Expression, https://snowdenarchive.cjfe.org/greenstone/cgi-bin/library.cgi, accessed on February 17, 2017 [in archive, click on "Publishing Source"]. As noted earlier, there has been much disagreement about the harmfulness of the metadata leak. See, for example, Steven Aftergood, review of Rahul Sagar's "Secrets and Leaks: The Dilemma of State Secrecy," *Lawfare,* April 3, 2014, http://www.lawfareblog.com/2014/04/secrets-and-leaks-the-dilemma-of-state-secrecy.

38 Fred Kaplan, *Dark Territory: The Secret History of Cyber War* (New York: Simon and Schuster, 2016), 229; Lorenzo Franceschi-Bicchierai, "Meet Babar, a New Malware Almost Certainly Created by France," *Motherboard*, February 18, 2015, https://motherboard.vice.com/en_us/article/8qxkyg/meet-babar-a-new-malware-almost-certainly-created-by-france; Greg Miller, Julie Tate, and Barton Gellman, "Documents Reveal NSA's Extensive Involvement in Targeted Killing Program," *Washington Post*, October 16, 2013, https://www.washingtonpost.com/world/national-security/documents-reveal-nsas-extensive-involvement-in-targeted-killing-program/2013/10/16/29775278-3674-11e3-8a0e-4e2cf80831fc_story.html. See also Jeremy Scahill and Glenn Greenwald, "The NSA's Secret Role in the U.S. Assassination Program," *The Intercept*, February 10, 2014, https://theintercept.com/2014/02/10/the-nsas-secret-role; Morgan Marquis-Boire, Glenn Greenwald, and Micah Lee, "XKEYSCORE: NSA's Google for the World's Private Communications," *The Intercept*, July 1, 2015, https://theintercept.com/2015/07/01/nsas-google-worlds-private-communications; "The Black Budget," *The Washington Post,* accessed December 13, 2016, http://www.washingtonpost.com/wp-srv/special/national/black-budget; "Inside the 2013 U.S. Intelligence 'Black Budget,'" *The Washington Post,* accessed February 10, 2016, http://apps.washingtonpost.com/g/page/national/inside-the-2013-us-intelligence-black-budget/420.

39 Palden Gyatso, *Fire under the Snow* (London: The Harvill Press, 1997); Tim McGirk, "Tibetan Tells of Chinese Torture; Monk's 24 years of Electric Shocks," *The Independent*, February 26, 1995, 16.

40 A related problem involves the use of secret laws or secret interpretations of public laws. What constitutes an abuse of public authority in those situations is not clear to citizens. See Jason Ross Arnold, *Secrecy in the Sunshine Era* (Lawrence: University Press of Kansas, 2014).

41 John Le Carré, *The Constant Gardener* (London: Hodder and Stoughton, 2001).

42 "Clear and Convincing Evidence," Legal Information Institute, Cornell University Law School, https://www.law.cornell.edu/wex/clear_and_convincing_evidence; "Preponderance of the Evidence," Legal Information Institute, Cornell University Law School, https://www.law.cornell.edu/wex/preponderance_of_the_evidence; Charlie Savage, "Appeals Court Is Urged to Strike Down Program for Collecting Phone Records," *The New York Times,* November 4, 2014, A12.

43 The evidence test is not only about showing a document's authenticity, although that is necessary. No one in the U.S. government denied the authenticity of Snowden's disclosures.

44 Gabriel Schoenfeld, *Necessary Secrets: National Security, the Media, and the Rule of Law* (New York: W. W. Norton & Company, 2010).

45 Ralph Nader, "Preface," in Ralph Nader, Peter J. Petkas, and Kate Blackwell, eds. *Whistleblowing: The Report of the Conference on Professional Responsibility* (New York: Grossman Publishers, 1972), emphasis added.

46 Sagar, *Secrets and Leaks,* 137–8.

47 Jason Leopold, "NSA Emails About Snowden's Concerns," Freedom of Information Act release, *Scribd*, https://www.scribd.com/doc/314796284/NSA-Emails-About-Snowden-s-Concerns#, accessed March 27, 2019, emphasis added.

[48] Jason Leopold, Marcy Wheeler, and Ky Henderson, "Snowden Tried to Tell NSA About Surveillance Concerns, Documents Reveal," *Vice News,* June 4, 2016, https://news.vice.com/article/edward-snowden-leaks-tried-to-tell-nsa-about-surveillance-concerns-exclusive.

[49] U.S. Congress, House Permanent Select Committee on Intelligence (HPSCI), *(U) Review of the Unauthorized Disclosures of Former National Security Agency Contractor Edward Snowden,* 114th Cong., 2d session, September 15, 2016.

[50] Leopold et al., "Snowden Tried"; Barton Gellman, "The House Intelligence Committee's Terrible, Horrible, Very Bad Snowden Report," The Century Foundation, September 16, 2016, https://tcf.org/content/commentary/house-intelligence-committees-terrible-horrible-bad-snowden-report.

[51] Glenn Greenwald tweet, September 15, 2016, https://twitter.com/ggreenwald/status/776528091053191168; Mike Masnick, "House Intel Committee Says Snowden's Not A Whistleblower, 'Cause He Once Emailed His Boss's Boss," *Techdirt,* September 16, 2016, https://www.techdirt.com/articles/20160915/17000035532/house-intel-committee-says-snowdens-not-whistleblower-cause-he-once-emailed-his-bosss-boss.shtml; Glenn Greenwald, "Why the CIA Is Smearing Edward Snowden after the Paris Attacks," *Los Angeles Times,* November 25, 2015, http://www.latimes.com/opinion/op-ed/la-oe-1126-greenwald-snowden-paris-encryption-20151126-story.html; Gellman, "The House Intelligence Committee's."

[52] The estimate apparently does not include the 900,000 files he allegedly stole from U.S. Defense Department servers. But it appears to include documents detailing programs by the NSA's "Five Eyes" partner agencies (Britain's Government Communications Headquarters (GCHQ), Australia's Signals Directorate, Canada's Communications Security Establishment, and New Zealand's Government Communications Security Bureau). On the 1.7 million estimate, see Mark Hosenball, "NSA Chief Says Snowden Leaked up to 200,000 Secret Documents," *Reuters,* November 14, 2013, http://www.reuters.com/article/2013/11/14/us-usa-security-nsa-idUSBRE9AD19B20131114; Michael B. Kelley, "The Pentagon Thinks Snowden Took a LOT of Documents that Had Nothing to Do with Surveillance," *Business Insider,* June 4, 2015, http://www.businessinsider.com/snowden-and-defense-department-files-2015-6; Jason Leopold, "Exclusive: Inside Washington's Quest to Bring Down Edward Snowden," *Vice News,* June 4, 2015, https://news.vice.com/article/exclusive-inside-washingtons-quest-to-bring-down-edward-snowden; David Ignatius, "Edward Snowden Took Less than Previously Thought, Says James Clapper," *The Washington Post,* June 5, 2014, https://www.washingtonpost.com/opinions/edward-snowden-took-less-than-previously-thought-says-james-clapper/2014/06/05/054cb9f2-ecee-11e3-93d2-edd4be1f5d9e_story.html; Glenn Greenwald, "Keith Alexander Unplugged: On Bush/Obama, 1.7 Million Stolen Documents and other Matters," *The Intercept,* May 8, 2014, https://firstlook.org/theintercept/2014/05/08/keith-alexander-unplugged-bushobama-matters/. The bipartisan House Intelligence Committee report claimed the number was 1.5 million. U.S. Congress, House (HPSCI), *(U) Review of the Unauthorized Disclosures,* 2016.

[53] Greenwald et al., "Edward Snowden."

[54] "Government Surveillance" (emphases added) [John Oliver's interview with Edward Snowden], *Last Week Tonight,* https://www.youtube.com/watch?v=XEVlyP4_11M; Harrison Jacobs, "The Most Interesting Part of John Oliver's Uncomfortable Interview with Edward Snowden," *Business Insider,* April 6, 2015, http://www.businessinsider.com/heres-john-olivers-uncomfortable-interview-with-edward-snowden-2015-4#ixzz3cCUAfvmd.

[55] Laura Poitras and Glenn Greenwald, "NSA Whistleblower Edward Snowden: 'I Don't Want to Live in a Society that Does These Sort of Things'—video," *The Guardian,* June 9, 2013, https://www.theguardian.com/world/video/2013/jun/09/nsa-whistleblower-edward-snowden-interview-video. An exceptionally fair-minded analysis is Timothy H. Edgar, *Beyond Snowden: Privacy, Mass Surveillance, and the Struggle to Reform the NSA* (Washington, DC: Brookings Institution Press, 2017).

[56] Mackenzie Weinger, "Snowden's Boss Shares Lessons Learned," *The Cipher Brief,* September 13, 2016, https://www.thecipherbrief.com/article/exclusive/first-cipher-brief-snowdens-boss-shares-lessons-learned-1095.

57 *The New York Times* published the terrorist financing program's details, along with *The Los Angeles Times* and *The Wall Street Journal*. The *Times* editors justified the publication in a way that resembled Greenwald's defense cited earlier, essentially "C'mon! The terrorists already know we look for these kinds of things!" However, as the U.S. Treasury Secretary and other officials argued, the reports of the program were specific and not general, and they featured secret sources and methods. The officials also insisted that many terrorists used relatively conventional, and thus trackable, financing systems, despite knowing that some general program of terrorism financing existed. "Letter to the Editors of *The New York Times* by Treasury Secretary Snow," June 26, 2009, https://www.treasury.gov/press-cent er/press-releases/Pages/4339.aspx; Eric Lichtblau and James Risen, "Bank Data Is Sifted by U.S. to Block Terror," *The New York Times*, June 23, 2006, A1; "Patriotism and the Press," *The New York Times*, June 28, 2006, A20; Jana Winter and Cora Currier, "TSA's Secret Behavior Checklist to Spot Terrorists," March 25, 2015, *The Intercept*, https://theintercept. com/2015/03/27/revealed-tsas-closely-held-behavior-checklist-spot-terrorists. Another questionable leak also involved the *Times*, which published an article about allegedly weak congressional oversight over CIA's overseas drone strike operations. The article revealed the identities of three covert officers, justifying the move with the argument that "the individuals have leadership roles in one of the government's most significant paramilitary programs, and their roles are known to foreign governments and many others." There are many problems with the revelations, and the argument in defense—outlined elsewhere. See Mark Mazzetti and Matt Apuzzo, "Deep Support in Washington for C.I.A.'s Drone Missions," *The New York Times*, April 26, 2015, A1; Yishai Schwartz and Sebastian Brady, "DNI General Counsel Robert Litt: 'The New York Times Disgraced Itself,'" *Lawfare*, April 27, 2015, http://www.lawfareblog.com/2015/04/dni-general-counsel-robert-litt-the-new-york-times -disgraced-itself.

58 Sagar, *Secrets and Leaks*, 182.

59 Greenwald, MacAskill, and Poitras, "Edward Snowden"; Joe Mullin, "In 2009, Ed Snowden Said Leakers 'Should Be Shot.' Then He Became One," *Ars Technica*, June 26, 2013, http:// arstechnica.com/tech-policy/2013/06/exclusive-in-2009-ed-snowden-said-leakers-should-be- shot-then-he-became-one/; Eric Schmitt, "C.I.A. Noted Its Suspicions Over Snowden," *The New York Times*, October 11, 2013, A1; James Bamford, "The Most Wanted Man in the World," *Wired*, August 2014, https://www.wired.com/2014/08/edward-snowden.

60 Lana Lam, "Snowden Sought Booz Allen Job to Gather Evidence on NSA Surveillance," *South China Morning Post*, June 24, 2013, https://www.scmp.com/news/hong-kong/article/ 1268209/snowden-sought-booz-allen-job-gather-evidence-nsa-surveillance; Schmitt, "C.I.A. Warning"; Luke Harding, "How Edward Snowden Went from Loyal NSA Contractor to Whistleblower," *The Guardian*, February 1, 2014, http://www.theguardian.com/world/2014/ feb/01/edward-snowden-intelligence-leak-nsa-contractor-extract; Michael Morrell interview with Elliot Gerson, Aspen Institute, December 13, 2015, https://www.youtube.com/watch?v= 1TL5lmBXvlY.

Chapter 3

Who Blows Whistles?
Insiders, Outsiders, and Their Networks

Most academic and popular conceptions of whistleblowing involve an organizational insider who decides to tell the outside world about some offense committed by others inside the organization. Sagar's conceptual framework, analyzed in chapter 2, presumes an insider. Near and Miceli's whistleblowing requires "disclosure by organization members (former or current)." Jubb's features the protagonist's disloyalty to an organization, which implies an official attachment to it. Alford points to "anyone who speaks out in the name of the public good within the organization," even if they wind up as "poison to the unity of the organization." Bowie's normative framework assumes whistleblowers are by default insiders, by insisting that taking the information outside should occur only after they have "exhausted all internal channels for dissent." Sissela Bok similarly assumes whistleblowers come "from within" and risk accusations of organizational disloyalty.[1]

Perhaps most whistleblowers have been insiders. However, a simple thought experiment illustrates the folly of excluding outsider whistleblowers. Imagine a poultry processing plant in which some workers abused chickens, even "routinely punching, beating, throwing, and tormenting animals for fun."[2] A worker in the plant could not stomach the abuse any longer, and used his smart phone to secretly videotape it. After finding internal reporting channels for complaints worthless—the human resources and legal counsel people discounted the allegations, referring to a "few bad apples"—the worker gave a local journalist the videos and some anonymous testimony. A local television station featured the news story that night at the top of the hour.

Now imagine the same factory with the same abusive practices, but replace the worker with a non-worker who jumped the perimeter fence in order to look into the slaughterhouse's window. (Assume for the sake of argument that a factory of this sort would have such a window.) Our interloper stood right outside the window, 15 feet from the hook line. Like the worker, the outsider recorded the gruesome scene with her smart phone, and passed the evidence to the same reporter, whose TV station featured the news story that night at the top of the hour.

Everything in the two cases is identical except the protagonists' employment status and physical location (i.e., standing inside vs. outside, and slight differences in distances from the window). We have the same secret extraction of the same evidence, with very small differences in captured images, due to the different camera positions. The news program featured the stories in the same way, with the same potential legal and/or commercial consequences for the poultry company. Despite all of those similarities, only the worker would count as a whistleblower, according to many definitions.

Fortunately, some whistleblowing theorists have recently come to the same insight. Miceli et al. seem to believe the conceptual differences between insiders and outsiders are large enough to call the latter "bell-ringers" instead of whistleblowers.[3] While bell-ringers is an evocative term that happens to be rooted in whistleblowing history—"By the ringing of bells, we call the living to the funeral of all that is decrepit, obsolete, disgraceful, servile, ignorant in Russia!" (Alexander Herzen, 1857; see chapter 4)—I doubt the term will catch on outside the academy. Nor should it. The word whistleblower is culturally meaningful. It carries with it noble virtues like public-spiritedness, self-sacrifice, and honor. Why deprive outsider whistleblowers of the social and psychological benefits that come with the label? Besides, their actions are fundamentally similar to those of insider whistleblowers. The descriptive adjective *outsider* already works well as a discriminating device, and a way to add illustrative detail to case histories.

One objection to placing outsiders into the same conceptual category as insiders—that is, calling them outsider whistleblowers—involves their potentially biased approach to one of the consequentialist framework's main planks. Outsiders might by default discount the costs the offending organization might bear from a disclosure, such as reputational costs. After all, an outsider who lacks personal connections to an organization is less likely to care about those costs. But it is also true some individuals inside organizations are disgruntled, even vengeful. Their experiences could generate biases that shape their disclosure decisions, including their discounting of costs. Plus, outsiders can have meaningful indirect connections with organizations, through friends and family, or from business relationships, or from an organization's broader importance to a community. Maybe the poultry plant outsider places a high value on the slaughterhouse business because it is the economic engine of her small town, and she believes it needs to "clean up its practices" in order to be competitive.

Thus, outsiders might have an interest in organizations that involves wanting them to survive; they are not necessarily hostile or indifferent. In any case, would-be whistleblowers who follow the consequentialist framework as fairly and objectively as possible should arrive at appropriate decisions about disclosure, whether or not they are insiders or outsiders. If bias clouds their decision-making, the public can use the same framework to judge the protagonists' actions.

A similar objection involves the knowledge outsider whistleblowers have relative to insiders. Outsiders, the argument goes, likely operate with less information about an organization than insiders, which could make weighing the costs and benefits of disclosure more difficult. But as we have seen, insiders also lack perfect knowledge, including about their organizations, because of strategic compartmentalization and other forms of information access restrictions. Moreover, not all of the relevant information for boundedly rational choices resides within organizations.[4]

Outsider Whistleblowers and Retaliation: The Cases of Ka Hsaw Wa and Harry Wu

Another likely objection to letting outsiders *be* whistleblowers involves the often serious costs the secret-spillers themselves must bear because of their actions. That is, only insiders suffer retaliation. Only they, the argument goes, have to cope with the legal, financial, and social consequences caused by their whistleblowing. The lawsuits and pink slips. The loss of workplace friends and acquaintances. Isolation from a community. The huge obstacles to future employment. Who wants to hire the guy who ratted out his organization, who risked destroying its reputation, along with the reputations and livelihoods of its employees? Compare the slaughterhouse worker with the woman standing outside, these critics might say. Unless the worker remained anonymous, he would almost certainly face the wrath of his supervisors, and probably his colleagues as well. If the firm cannot fire him for legal reasons, they would likely make his work there even more unpleasant than before. By contrast, the woman with the iPhone standing outside the window would avoid the same consequences.

But it is not true that only insider whistleblowers suffer from retaliation. The woman outside the slaughterhouse window, for instance, might be subject to criminal charges if the action occurred in one of six American states with "Ag-Gag" laws, the name given by animal welfare activists to statutes targeting covert filmmakers inside or outside meat, egg, and dairy factories (chapter 8). She might also receive death threats, or letters from corporate lawyers promising years of costly trials. Retaliation comes in many forms, and is not targeted just at organizational insiders.

Moreover, there is nò reason to assume that insiders categorically suffer more retaliation than outsiders. Take, for example, the experience of Ka Hsaw Wa, a Burmese human rights and environmental activist. His life in politics began in the late 1980s, when he joined the burgeoning pro-democracy movement, which demanded that Burma's authoritarian rulers open the political system. During one protest in Rangoon in 1988, agents of the military junta arrested and then tortured Ka Hsaw Wa, along with many others. Once released from detention, he fled Rangoon, first to the jungle outside the city, where he encountered people from his own persecuted Karen ethnic group. State repression forced the democracy movement into hibernation, and Ka Hsaw Wa escaped Burma by crossing into Thailand. Once safely out of the junta's clutches, he developed a plan: he would sneak back into Burma with a fake identity and recording equipment in order to document the regime's human rights violations against the Karen people and others. He also sought to document rights abuses that he believed Unocal and other multinational corporations had committed with the Burmese government. He would then sneak back out, evidence in hand, to show the world.[5]

Other human rights organizations had by then published reports about the regime's abuses, which included forced labor, property destruction, village destruction, assault, torture, and rape. But the junta's level of repression had grown severe enough to prevent most organizations from entering Burma to investigate. Ka Hsaw Wa's undercover work broke that shield. But it came with very high risks. If the regime tracked him down, they would likely have gone well beyond the harsh treatment their thugs meted out in 1988, after his arrest at a protest. For that reason, and because he knew that torture sessions might have eventually forced him to identify and thus endanger people who assisted him, Ka Hsaw Wa always carried a gun during his Burmese journeys. He planned to shoot himself in the head when the regime found him.[6]

Harry Wu's outsider whistleblowing to expose Chinese government abuses also carried great risks of retaliation. Wu's conflict with the Chinese Communists began during Chairman Mao Tse-Tung's first Stalinist purge, 1956's infamous Hundred Flowers Campaign. Mao's invitation to citizens to raise constructive criticisms of the seven-year old Communist regime was a trap. As Mao confided to his doctor, "We want to coax the snakes out of their holes. Then we will strike. My strategy is to let the poisonous weeds grow first and then destroy them one by one. Let them become fertilizer." Wu fell into the trap when he expressed sharp, but not radical, anti-system criticisms. Party officials, including those at the university he was attending, placed him on a watch list.[7]

In 1960, Communist officials arrested Wu on trumped up charges, and sent him to one of China's forced labor camps (*laogai*). For the next nineteen years, Wu endured near-starvation conditions doing grueling work in several *laogai*.

One consequence of Mao's death in 1976 was his successor Deng Xiaoping's (very limited) *laogai* reform program. The government freed Wu in 1979—although millions of others remained prisoners in *laogai*, and many others were sent there in subsequent years. After his release, Wu stayed in China for six years, living in what felt like purgatory. In 1985, he seized an opportunity to move to the United States.[8]

It did not take long for Wu to realize what he needed to do: show the world the horrors of the *laogai*. Yet soon he realized that telling his story in the United States would only go so far. He needed more than testimony; he needed documentary evidence. So he sneaked back into China and talked his way into *laogai*, claiming to be a foreign investor. (One of the focal points of his activism had been multi-national corporations' use of *laogai* slave labor.) Once inside, he used spare moments to steal documents and take photos and videos. His hidden camera lenses peered out of small holes in his knapsack. Each time he went, he gathered clear and incriminating evidence of human rights violations. CBS News's *60 Minutes* found his story and work so compelling that journalist Ed Bradley joined him on one excursion. Because of his whistleblowing work, Wu regularly appeared in the U.S. media and before congressional committees. By going public, he willingly became an enemy of the Chinese state. When Wu worked undercover in China, he usually managed to evade the authorities, knowing that his whistleblowing and anti-*laogai* activism made a return to the ghastly labor camps a very real possibility. When the Chinese did track him down, he saved himself with considerable powers of persuasion plus his recently acquired U.S. citizenship and a network of supporters around the world.[9]

Both Harry Wu and Ka Hsaw Wa blew the whistle on human rights violations. Neither one did so as an organizational insider, but both faced high risks of retaliation—indeed, higher than many insider whistleblowers face. The nature of retaliation may differ depending on whether a whistleblower is an insider or outsider, but the latter can also experience real and potential costs, whether financial, legal, and physical. If whistleblowers, per Alford, are "defined by the retaliation he or she received," then outsiders like Harry Wu and Ka Hsaw Wa certainly deserve the label.[10]

Four Types of Whistleblowing

Figure 3.1 sketches the basic information extraction and dissemination processes of insider and outsider whistleblowing. The figure also makes clear the inherent relational aspect of whistleblowing. Much of the discussion so far has focused on information transfers from organizational insiders or outsiders to outside recipients, such as journalists who publish the evidence. The slaughterhouse worker relied on a local reporter to complete the whistleblowing process. So did the animal rights activist standing outside the slaughterhouse window

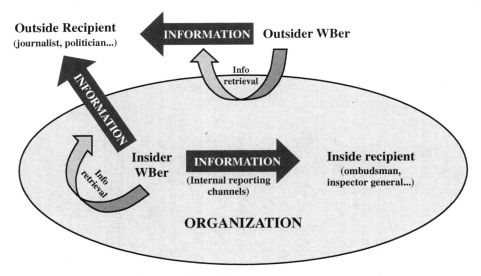

FIGURE 3.1 Insider and Outsider Whistleblowing.

with her iPhone. We can consider the former an example of insider-outsider whistleblowing (from the organization insider to the outside recipient), and the latter an example of outsider-outsider whistleblowing.

Another type, as illustrated in figure 3.1, is that of insider-insider whistleblowing. Insiders sometimes choose to keep the entire process an internal matter, for a variety of reasons, including their sense of loyalty and their rational fear of retaliation. So they choose internal reporting channels. Some go no further than their supervisors. Others go to offices headed by inspectors general, ombudsmen, and ombudswomen, among others. While some insider whistleblowers never go beyond internal recipients, others move on to outsider recipients.

Altogether, when we incorporate both the organizational locations of each type of whistleblower, as well as their recipients, we have four categories, shown in table 3.1. Probably the least common type is that of *outsider-insider* whistleblowing, in which individuals outside an organization extract secrets

TABLE 3.1 Whistleblower Types

		Location of recipient	
		INSIDE	**OUTSIDE**
Location of whistleblower	**INSIDE**	Insider-insider	Insider-outsider
	OUTSIDE	Outsider-insider	Outsider-outsider

from it, and then transfer the information to an inside recipient. While most outsiders are unlikely to choose insider recipients, it is not an inconceivable choice. Imagine a "patriot hacker"—a real phenomenon—finding unmistakable evidence of corruption within a government agency's computer system. While concluding that those responsible for the corruption must face justice, the hacker recognizes that the evidence contains classified information, and concludes that disclosure would unnecessarily harm national security. Wanting to fix the problem while also remaining loyal to and protective of his country, the hacker might choose to quietly relay the information to the agency's inspector general. Another example of an outsider-insider whistleblowing system is that of South Africa's corruption-reporting hotline, in which citizens are encouraged to report government-linked corruption to government insiders hired to investigate allegations and hold perpetrators accountable.[11]

While most cases of whistleblowing can be relegated to one of the four categories, in some contexts the insider/outsider dichotomy breaks down. For example, in some of the human rights cases discussed in chapter 5, the whistleblowers at first glance seem like typical organizational outsiders. Imagine a citizen who observes a human rights violation by a military commander, and then shares the evidence with someone in Amnesty International's network. While not a part of the commander's military unit, or the military in general, the citizen whistleblower belongs to the same broader political unit—the country—that employs the commander. She might also serve the government in a different capacity, say, as a public sector employee. It is not unreasonable to view her as an insider, with the state as the operative organization.

Harry Wu's story further illustrates the permeability of the boundary. Recall Wu's clandestine efforts to expose the horrors of Chinese *laogai*, after being released from 19 years of confinement. Some of his work occurred after he attained U.S. citizenship. While technically no longer a Chinese citizen or prisoner, Wu's relationship with the country and the *laogai* system remained central to his life—on top of his activism and whistleblowing, he founded the Laogai Research Foundation, a global human rights organization, which he directed until his 2016 death.

We can also imagine cases in which the whistleblower/recipient binary breaks down. Whistleblowers might in effect act as their own recipients, by, say, displaying evidence of abuse at a press conference, or self-publishing a pamphlet or newsletter. Or they might set up a public website and publish all the evidence there, interacting with nothing but machines until the information reaches the public. We also have cases in which journalists have acted as whistleblowers and recipients simultaneously; they witness an atrocity, or independently find a smoking-gun document, and then publish it like they normally do. But most of the time, whistleblowers and recipients are different people, a team of collaborators who form the core of a whistleblowing network.

Concept Stretching?

With this inclusive conceptualization of whistleblowing types, do we run the risk of unacceptable "concept stretching," which Giovanni Sartori described as "cover[ing] more . . . only by saying less, and by saying less in a far less precise manner?" Brady and Collier similarly caution against turning an established concept into something "vague [and] amorphous." Does the concept developed in this chapter, with its insiders and outsiders, "inappropriately apply established concepts and theories to new contexts"? Does it ruin our existing idea of whistleblowing by tossing aside essential "prior assumptions about the meaning of some components of the concept, and about the interrelations among those components"?[12]

The answer is no, for all questions, for two reasons. First, whistleblowing is not at all an "established concept" (Brady and Collier), as chapter 2 clearly demonstrated. Second, while the analysis in this book has challenged "prior assumptions" (Brady and Collier) from earlier definitions, it also established why those assumptions were not worth keeping. Recall the poultry slaughterhouse example: there was no good reason why only the insider-outsider earned the whistleblower designation. Similarly, Harry Wu and Ka Hsaw Wa documented human rights violations perpetrated by government agency officials, just as a government or corporate insider-outsider might do. Overall, the concept of whistleblowing, as sketched here and in the chapters that follow, is not stretched beyond recognition and rendered useless. Instead, the revised conceptualization helps us better understand a wide range of whistleblowing activities not typically seen as such.[13]

Burden-Sharing by Whistleblowers and Recipients

The consequentialist framework appears to place the burden of weighing a disclosure's costs and benefits entirely on the would-be whistleblower. Yet there is no reason to relieve recipients of that responsibility, both at the time of their decisions and in our post hoc evaluations of their choices. Let's say a whistleblower did her best to carefully consider the costs of disclosure, but the recipient did not. The disclosure decision would seem to have been vetted already. But because would-be whistleblowers make decisions under uncertainty, with limited knowledge, their choices are not necessarily optimal. Scrupulous, risk-sensitive, knowledgeable recipients can reexamine whistleblowers' decisions and arrive at wiser choices. Since we should not expect—or hope for—anything beyond boundedly rational choices from whistleblowers, we have no reason to let recipients off the hook. They should share the burdens of weighing costs and benefits. And if they have collaborators, those individuals also have a responsibility to contribute to the collective decision-making process.

Whistleblowing Is a Collective Enterprise in Networks

Figure 3.1's depiction of whistleblowers and recipients captures some of the relational nature of whistleblowing: someone inside or outside an organization extracts information and passes it to someone who publicizes it. Sometimes, whistleblowing proceeds like that, essentially as a one-shot affair involving two people. But focusing only on two individuals obscures the many others who often contribute to the process. Chapter 1 illustrated this with the partial network map of Snowden's collaborators (figure 1.1). The birds-eye view showed the dozens of others who facilitated Snowden's secret-spilling, including reporters, editors, and publishers across the world, all of whom handled and publicized some of the NSA's classified secrets. (Although chapter 2 found that Snowden's actions by and large did not meet the whistleblowing framework's standards, the model is useful for the present analysis.) Clearly the social process driving whistleblowing does not always stay within a dyadic network. It incorporates people we would not identify as whistleblowers or recipients.

For example, Glenn Greenwald's partner David Miranda traveled from Germany to Britain in 2013 with part of the Snowden cache in hand. Britain's Heathrow Airport was supposed to be only a layover before his final destination, his home in Rio de Janeiro, Brazil. But because Miranda agreed to ferry documents from Laura Poitras in Berlin to Greenwald in Rio, British authorities detained him in London for nine hours, after questioning him and seizing the stolen NSA and U.K. Government Communications Headquarters (GCHQ)

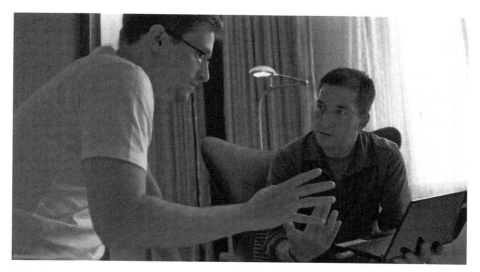

FIGURE 3.2 Snowden and Greenwald in Hong Kong, June 2013. *Source*: Pictorial Press Ltd / Alamy Stock Photo.

documents. While this particular contribution to the network failed in a direct sense—the Brits seized files that Snowden's network needed at that moment—Miranda's work with it continued beyond that single episode. He was neither a whistleblower nor a recipient, but a *facilitator* (again, assume for the sake of the argument that Snowden and his network engaged in whistleblowing).[14] Beyond Miranda, the network encompassed dozens of other facilitators, including lawyers, computer security experts, agents of nongovernmental organizations, diplomats, heads of state, and possibly others, including foreign intelligence agents and Snowden's associates at Dell, Booz Allen Hamilton, and the NSA. Until Snowden was safely ensconced in Russia, he probably had only met a few of the facilitators and recipients.

Miranda's case also shows that all nodes in a network can suffer retaliation. The secret-spiller at the center might suffer the most, although that is not assured. Reporter-recipients might well benefit professionally from publishing valuable secrets, but they might also face, as Greenwald did, death threats, treason accusations, and coordinated character attacks hatched by security firms (see chapter 8). Others in Snowden's network also suffered negative consequences. British authorities, for example, forced *Guardian* editors to let government agents smash company computers because they were thought to contain classified GCHQ files.

The network around Snowden survived for years. That is quite a feat, given all of the heat from two of the world's most powerful governments. The U.S. government charged Snowden with three felonies, including theft of government property, unauthorized communication of national defense information, and willful communication of classified intelligence information to an unauthorized person. Although protected by the Russian government, Snowden remains a sought-after fugitive, who has refused to cooperate with U.S. law enforcement officials, unless Congress or the Supreme Court changes the Espionage Act to accommodate a "public interest" defense argument. Yet even if he surrendered to U.S. authorities, the wider network still has the NSA's secrets in hand, and could continue publishing them for decades to come.

The next chapter tells the tale of another network that endured for an even longer period in Soviet Russia, despite even greater odds. The human rights movement in the Soviet Union sprang up after dictator Josef Stalin's death in the 1950s. At the core of that movement was a secret-spilling network of individuals in the underground who published and circulated homebrewed underground newspapers, known as *samizdat*. The history of the evolution and survival of the *Chronicle of Current Events*—the most important human rights *samizdat*—illustrates one of the unusual places the revised whistleblowing concept can take us. The case also lends itself well to the use of social network analysis in the context of whistleblowing. Which network type works best for an underground network's survival? Which structure best facilitates information flows? It is to human rights activists and ordinary Russians who contributed to the *Chronicle*—unheralded heroes of the Cold War—that we now turn.

Notes

1 Janet P. Near and Marcia P. Miceli. "Organizational Dissidence: The Case of Whistleblowing," *Journal of Business Ethics* 4, no. 1 (1985): 1–16; Peter B. Jubb, "Whistleblowing: A Restrictive Definition and Interpretation," *Journal of Business Ethics* 21, no. 1 (1999): 77–94; C. Fred Alford, *Whistleblowers: Broken Lives and Organizational Power* (Ithaca, NY: Cornell University Press, 2002), 238–41; Norman Bowie, *Business Ethics* (Englewood Cliffs, NJ: Prentice Hall, 1982); Terry Morehead Dworkin and Melissa S. Baucus, "Internal vs. External Whistleblowers: A Comparison of Whistleblowing Processes," *Journal of Business Ethics* 17, no. 12 (1998): 1281–98; Sissela Bok, *Secrets: On the Ethics of Concealment and Revelation* (New York: Vintage, 1989), 214; Myron Peretz Glazer and Penina Migdal Glazer, *The Whistleblowers: Exposing Corruption in Government and Industry* (New York: Basic Books, 1989), 4; cf. Michael Davis, "Rewarding Whistleblowers: A Conceptual Problem?" *International Journal of Applied Philosophy* 26, no. 2 (2012): 269–7.
2 Colleen Curry, "Activists Claim Footage Shows Slaughterhouse Workers 'Tormenting Frightened Animals for Fun,'" *Vice News*, October 28, 2015, https://news.vice.com/article/activists-claim-footage-shows-slaughterhouse-workers-tormenting-frightened-animals-for-fun.
3 Marcia P. Miceli, Suelette Dreyfus, and Janet P. Near, "Outsider 'Whistleblowers': Conceptualizing and Distinguishing 'Bell-Ringing' Behavior," in A. J. Brown, David Lewis, Richard E. Moberly and Wim Vandekerckhove, eds., *International Handbook on Whistleblowing Research* (Northampton, MA: Edward Elgar Publishing, 2014), 71–94.
4 Herbert Alexander Simon, *Models of Bounded Rationality: Empirically Grounded Economic Reason*, Volume 3. (Cambridge, MA: MIT Press, 1982); Gerd Gigerenzer and Reinhard Selten, *Bounded Rationality: The Adaptive Toolbox* (Cambridge, MA: MIT Press, 2002).
5 "Ka Hsaw Wa," 1999 Goldman Prize Recipient (Asia), 1999, http://www.goldmanprize.org/1999/asia; "Ka Hsaw Wa," in Kerry Kennedy, ed., *Speak Truth to Power: Human Rights Defenders Who are Changing Our World* (Brooklyn, NY: Umbrage, 2000); Milena Kaneva, "Total Denial" (film), MK Production, 2007; "Oil Giant Chevron Urged to Cut Ties with Burmese Military Junta," *Democracy Now!*, October 12, 2007, http://www.democracynow.org/2007/10/12/oil_giant_chevron_urged_to_cut.
6 Anita Ramasastry. "Corporate Complicity: From Nuremberg to Rangoon—An Examination of Forced Labor Cases and Their Impact on the Liability of Multinational Corporations," *Berkeley Journal of International Law* 20 (2002): 91.
7 Interview with Harry Wu, Laogai Research Foundation, Washington DC, June 24, 2013; Harry Wu and George Vecsey, *Troublemaker: One Man's Crusade Against China's Cruelty* (New York: Newsmax Media, 2002); John Lewis Gaddis, *The Cold War: A New History* (New York: Penguin, 2005), 111; Li Zhi-Sui, *The Private Life of Chairman Mao* (New York: Random House, 2011), 201.
8 Interview with Harry Wu; Wu and Vecsey, *Troublemaker*; Sarah Henry, "Harry's War," *Los Angeles Times*, November 17, 1996, 12.
9 Interview with Harry Wu; Wu, *Troublemaker*; "A Prisoner's Journey," September 22, 1991, *Newsweek*, http://www.newsweek.com/prisoners-journey-203504. Wu's later years before his 2016 death was clouded with allegations of financial mismanagement and worse. See Isaac Stone Fish and Melissa Chan, "The Complicated and Contradictory Legacy of Harry Wu," *Foreign Policy*, May 25, 2016, http://foreignpolicy.com/2016/05/25/the-complicated-and-contradictory-life-of-harry-wu-china-yahoo.
10 Wu was once a *laogai* prisoner, but that did not make him an organizational insider, especially 15-some years after the fact. Alford, *Whistleblowers*.
11 "Government Call Centres and Help Lines," South African Government, accessed June 9, 2015, http://www.gov.za/about-government/government-call-centres-and-help-lines.

12   Giovanni Sartori, "Concept Misformation in Comparative Politics," *American Political Science Review* 64, no. 4 (1970): 1033–53, at 1034–5; Henry E. Brady and David Collier, *Rethinking Social Inquiry: Diverse Tools, Shared Standards* (Lanham, MD; Rowman and Littlefield, 2005).

13   Brady and Collier, *Rethinking Social Inquiry.*

14   Owen Bowcott, "David Miranda Lawyers Argue that Heathrow Detention Was Unlawful," *The Guardian,* November 6, 2013, http://www.theguardian.com/world/2013/nov/06/david-miranda-lawyers-heathrow-detention-high-court.

Chapter 4

Dark Networks That Shed Light

The Case of *A Chronicle of Current Events*

"By the ringing of bells, we call the living to the funeral of all that is decrepit, obsolete, disgraceful, servile, ignorant in Russia!"

—Alexander Herzen, 1857[1]

"It is because of people like Natalya Gorbanevskaya, I am convinced, you and I are still alive and walking around on the face of the earth."

—Joan Baez, 1976[2]

The first issue of *A Chronicle of Current Events* did not reach many readers when it appeared in the Soviet Union in the spring of 1968. The odds that an illegal newspaper reporting on the Communist regime's human rights violations would gain a wide readership, let alone survive to publish another issue in the repressive environment, were understandably low. But the *Chronicle* eventually did find a wide audience, and it persisted despite great risks, not least the regime's fourteen-year quest to imprison its contributors and smash to pieces the underlying social network.

Indeed, after just a few issues, the *Chronicle* became a formidable political force in the Soviet Union, and the wider Cold War, despite having to fight for air in the underground, and for readers' eyeballs in the increasingly competitive black publishing market. It became a centerpiece of the burgeoning human rights movement. Soviet nuclear physicist turned dissident Andre Sakharov— the "father of the Soviet hydrogen bomb," whose later activism earned him a Nobel Peace Prize—called the *Chronicle* "the best in the human rights movement, its principles and highest achievements." Vladimir Bukovsky, another prominent dissident, praised the *Chronicle* and other underground journals for their work promoting democracy, human rights, and the fall of Communism.

To honor the democracy movement's achievements, "I would erect a monument to the typewriter" instead of any individual, Bukovsky once said.[3]

That it took the KGB (Komitet Gosudarstvennoy Bezopasnosti), the Soviet government's secret political police force, fourteen years to bring down the *Chronicle* underscores the network's resilience, along with the regime's steely determination. No matter how many key figures the KGB identified and arrested, new issues would appear, usually without much of a delay in its bimonthly schedule (about six issues a year). The Communist regime usually did not have such difficulty with its political enemies. Something about the *Chronicle*'s network kept it safe, albeit bruised, from the KGB's relentless efforts, which must have felt like an eternal whack-a-mole game.

What was the secret of the *Chronicle*'s success?

Part of the explanation has to focus on the courage, tenacity, resourcefulness, and adaptiveness of the *Chronicle*'s contributors. They were a part of something strong and righteous, and they knew it. They operated quietly, covertly, and prudently but recognized the enormous risks they faced, in many cases sacrificing their lives to the cause. At any moment, they realized, the KGB could arrive, banging on their doors, destroying their futures. They persevered nevertheless.

While the character of its contributors mattered, much of the *Chronicle*'s robustness came from the largely decentralized structure of its network, which as one contributing editor observed, "spread out silently and invisibly . . . like mushroom spores." That winning formula emerged from the astute choices of the *Chronicle*'s founders and later participants, all of whom operated in the hostile environment of a re-Stalinizing Soviet Union. The *Chronicle* was not the only *samizdat* (self-published, uncensored text) in the Soviet empire. But it was probably the most consequential samizdat periodical, with a dry, just-the-facts style, and an "utter lack of melodrama" that veiled its ability to rattle the Kremlin and keep liberal democratic hopes alive.[4]

A Brief History of Samizdat in Russia

The Soviet government claimed a monopoly on all forms of publishing, but its repressive apparatus could not always eliminate the black market for highly demanded texts. The regime kept printing presses out of private hands, and it dominated all media and publishing companies. The only thing writers and editors could do was surreptitiously publish their ideas themselves, using whatever materials they could get their hands on.[5]

Historians credit the poet Nikolay Glazkov with the first use of the word *samizdat*, and his story highlights the procedural side of the definition. (The word refers to self-published texts, as well as the underground, self-publishing process.) Writing during the Stalin era, Glazkov had grown frustrated with the drawn-out process of getting his works published by state officials. So, in 1952, he scraped together rudimentary printing resources—pens and unused school notebooks—to laboriously publish his own poetry collection. In the front matter, he wrote *"samesbyaizdat,"* which means "publishing house for oneself" (or "I-self-pub"), in the place reserved for publishers' names. Samizdat, the acronym of *samesbyaizdat,* carried the original word's self-publishing meaning, while also offering its users a satisfying moment of defiance with every writing or utterance. Samizdat rhymed with *Gosizdat,* the name of the official Soviet state publisher, along with its offshoots *Politizdat* (for political works), *Voyenizdat* (military works) and *Yurizdat* (legal works), among others.[6]

Glazkov had not invented self-publishing. He pinned his witticism to an existing, but dormant, tradition in Russia. Alexander Herzen's nineteenth-century newspaper *Kolokol* ("The Bell") evaded the tsars' censors and regularly reported on political corruption and other abuses of power, along with radical political commentary. *The Bell's* secrets section, *Pravda-li?* ("Can it be true?"), was such a hit with readers that Herzen published thirteen issues of the supplementary journal, *Pod sud!* ("On trial!"), to satisfy their demand.[7]

Russian radicals after Herzen followed *The Bell's* model of an "uncensored" newspaper. Vladimir Lenin began circulating his *Iskra* in 1900, publishing it abroad but smuggling copies into Tsarist Russia. After Lenin and the Bolsheviks' 1917 revolution, a new set of authoritarians picked up from where the tsars left off. In fact, the Communist regime made information control an even greater governing priority than under the tsars. Printing presses became contraband, which forced dedicated, independent writers to hand copy their manuscripts on their kitchen tables, a process they sometimes called "overcoming Gutenberg." Many of these self-publishers of the 1920s loosely identified with the Underwood movement—named not for an individual but a typewriter brand. Even dedicated Communists had to resort to samizdat. After Stalin outmaneuvered Trotsky for the top spot after Lenin died, Trotskyists went underground. Trotsky recalled how his minions circulated his 1927 "Letter to the Bureau of Party History" inside and outside of the country: "It circulated from hand to hand in the USSR. In hundreds of copies, either retyped or copied by hand. Single copies, often inexact, filtered abroad. Translation of them appeared in several languages."[8]

The harsh Stalinist repression of the 1930s and 1940s persuaded even the bravest writers who somehow escaped the Great Terror and the Gulag that the risks of self-publishing were too great. Nothing resembling a samizdat movement reappeared until after Stalin's death in 1953. However, we know from Glazkov's case from 1952 that the tradition had not completely gone into hibernation.

The Rise of the Post–Stalinist Samizdat Movement

Stalin's unexpected 1953 death caused a lot of private joy, and even more uncertainty. Everyone knew that the tools and institutions of Stalinist repression would survive his death, but it remained unclear whether the next leader would be as tyrannical. It took some time, but after a while, many Soviets sensed a slight opening, a foreshadow of the coming "thaw." But it remained risky to test the waters, and the new government's continued control of information flows still made it difficult and dangerous to share ideas about the new political climate. As Soviet dissident Lyudmila Alexeyeva recounted, although "Stalin's death . . . marked the end of total terror, society remained in a half-awake state of shock" that lasted for years.

> The awakening was also slow because new awareness had to be hidden, not only because of fear—there have always been brave people among us—but because of the complete monopoly and control of the flow of information and ideas by the [Communist] Party and the government. Literature of all kinds was controlled by the State: scientific as well as artistic, contemporary editions, reprints, and translation, cinematography, the theater painting (from the individual canvas to matchbox labels), records and radio (from political to musical broadcasts), and the education system—from nursery school to doctoral programs.

A turning point came in 1956 with new Soviet leader Nikita Khrushchev's 1956 "secret speech," "On the Cult of Personality and Its Consequences," in which he sharply criticized Stalin's leadership. The circulation of the leaked speech sent a shock wave through Soviet society and the rest of the Communist bloc. For Alexeyeva and millions of others, the speech seemed to deliver a fatal blow to any lingering remnants of Stalinist terror.[9]

The leak of the speech itself became a sign of the government's inability to completely control information flows. Officials in Moscow had sent copies of Khrushchev's speech to senior Communist leaders, who passed it on to lower-level functionaries and their comrades. A copy of the speech soon fell into the lap of Israel's domestic intelligence service (Shin Bet), thanks to a defector from Communist Poland. Newspapers in the West published the speech in full, which attacked Stalin's personality cult as well as his government's violations of socialist, Communist Party, and revolutionary "legality," including "cruel and inhuman tortures" to force confessions, often resulting in the "death of innocent people." To reach Soviet citizens who had not heard Khrushchev's denunciations of Stalin, the CIA used shortwave signals to break through the heavily jammed Soviet airspace to broadcast a Russian reading of the speech. Radio Free Europe reported on the speech to listeners across the Eastern bloc.[10]

The speech itself, of course, did not transform Soviet society overnight, and Khrushchev later that year mercilessly crushed the pro-democratic uprising in

Hungary, which added to the lingering uncertainty about how things would develop in the post-Stalin era. At the same time, Khrushchev's government did not deny reports about the speech, and Soviet citizens gradually began to notice tangible evidence of what became known as the "thaw." Some long-gone political prisoners started returning from the Gulag. Loyal Stalinist leaders in the Communist satellite states were replaced. Later moves by Khrushchev to loosen the state's control over information reaffirmed the reality of the thaw, such as his 1963 reversal of Stalin's policy of jamming foreign radio broadcasts, with the exception of Radio Liberty, the station run by CIA front groups who beamed its signals into Soviet territory. For a while, many things once prohibited were suddenly tolerated.[11]

The thaw created just enough warmth for *Kolokol* variety seeds to grow. People finally felt comfortable enough again to interact and exchange ideas. As Alexeyeva recounted (while generalizing liberally from her own experience):

> After the fear of the mass arrests had passed, people threw themselves at each other, deriving satisfaction from merely being together. A normal Moscow circle numbered forty to fifty "close friends." Although divided into smaller subgroups, the entire group regularly gathered for parties that were held on the slightest excuse, and everyone knew everything about everybody else. All these circles were connected with other similar circles and the links led to Leningrad, Novosibirsk, and other cities.

By contrast, "under Stalin, when informing [on each other to the regime] had become the norm, unofficial contacts between people had been reduced to a bare minimum. As a rule, two or three families would associate only among themselves, and there were very few homes where many people gathered." In the time of the thaw, they could enjoy some of the small pleasures of life outside the clutches of the state, such as socializing in their apartment buildings' communal kitchens without worrying as much about informers. For old timers, it was a return to normalcy. Younger generations, who had only known Stalinism, experienced the private sphere for the first time. Little of the new socializing was self-consciously political. They "sang, danced, and listened to music." They passed unauthorized songs around largely for the love of music, although by doing so they unintentionally had experimented with underground distribution systems.[12]

Some of the new relationships deepened and evolved along political lines. People realized they shared beliefs about the problems of the Soviet system, and about possible solutions, from incremental reforms to more radical alternatives. There were still real risks in spreading these subversive ideas. Khrushchev had not abandoned totalitarian Communism nor did he dismantle the regime's fearsome political police force, the KGB. But over time in the *khrushchevka* kitchens, and the nearby bedrooms, people began to trust each other. Social circles developed. "It was very small-town, very close, gossipy, everyone knowing one another, everyone privy to the others' thoughts," Alexeyeva recalled. Friend groups became a "family unto themselves, not without other associations, but they all saw and knew enough of one another that they could tell the strengths and weaknesses of each, and they knew whom to trust." With time and experience, some of the networks developed strong ties, which incentivized more risky talk—and later, action—which in turn strengthened the trust relations. It was out of these trust networks that the human rights movement grew.[13]

The Khrushchevian thaw thus begat relatively small groups of like-minded trust networks. Some of them were especially attuned to their political environment. They sensed an opportunity. They tested the waters.

They knew from the crackdowns in Budapest and Poznań (Poland) that street protests would likely be treated as illegal, subversive, anti-Soviet actions, despite the thaw. Discounting the risks, activist leaders Vladimir Bukovsky, Alexander Esenin-Volpin, and others planned and executed protests, circulated leaflets, and otherwise poked at the Kremlin's hornet nest. They were promptly arrested and deposited into *Gulag* labor camps and psychiatric prison hospitals.[14] However, their struggles, along with the many daily injustices and aggravations of life under Communist rule, produced discussion fodder and inspiration for the dissident networks, more and more of them jumping onto the revived samizdat bandwagon.

Although the content of samizdat grew more diverse over time, most from 1956 until about 1962 focused on literature, in particular poetry and literary fiction, as table 4.1 illustrates. This literary focus mirrored trends in book self-publishing, Boris Pasternak's *Doctor Zhivago* being the most prominent example. The early samizdat focus on poetry and fiction makes sense for at least two reasons.

First, Soviet society remained for the most part locked down. Any aspiring reporters interested in politics, public policy, economics, and crime still faced an information vacuum. The government was as transparent as electrical tape. Independent (i.e., illegal) journalists who asked around for information or approached officials for interviews knew that would guarantee a one-way ticket to the Gulag. Soaking and poking around totalitarians and their offices and dungeons is not permitted. Even above-average interest in political goings-on would set off KGB alarm bells.

Second, Russia had a long and rich literary tradition: Chekhov, Dostoevsky, Gogol, Tolstoy, and beyond. But it had virtually no history with a free press. Except for the occasional *Kolokol* or Underwood weekly, Russians had learned by necessity to communicate their political ideas through fiction rather than reported nonfiction. Major works of (usually samizdat) fiction in the 1950s and 1960s often had a distinctive political character. Pasternak,

TABLE 4.1 Soviet Samizdat, 1956–1967

	Start	End		Subject 1	Subject 2	Subject 3	Subject 4	Subject 5
Fresh Voices	1956	1956	St. Petersburg	Literature				
Heresy	1956	1956	St. Petersburg	Literature				
The Free Word	1956	1956	Irkutsk	Literature				
Information	1956	1957	St. Petersburg	Economy	Socio-political issues			
White Nights	1956	1958	St. Petersburg	Literature				
A Small Voice	1957	1957	St. Petersburg	Literature				
One Step Forward, Two Steps Backward	1957	1957	Kazan'	Literature	Socio-political issues			
Irtysh Waves	1957	n/a	Omsk	Literature				
Five Rivers	1958	1959	Mordovia (Republic)	Literature				
Extinguished Intention	1959	1959	Barnaul	Literature				
Syntax	1959	1960	Moscow	Literature				
Boomerang: Literary-Artistic and Cultural Monthly	1960	1960	Moscow	Literature	Art			
Optima: Literary Manuscript Journal	1960	1962	St. Petersburg	Literature				
The Beginning	1960	1962	Novosibirsk	Literature				
Literary Almanac	1961	1961	Moscow	Literature				
The Second Year	1961	1961	Novosibirsk	Literature				
Collections	1961	1962	St. Petersburg	Literature				
Phoenix	1961	1966	Moscow	Literature	Religion/ Philosophyl	Socio-political issues		

TABLE 4.1 (Continued)

	Start	End		Subject 1	Subject 2	Subject 3	Subject 4	Subject 5
Fikkiwers if Girshfel'D	1962	1962	Krasnoyarsk	Literature				
The Siren	1962	1962	Moscow	Literature				
Art of the Commune	1962	1963	Moscow	Literature	Art	Socio-political issues		
Fraternal Leaflet	1962	1986	s.l.	Religion/Philosophy	Socio-political issues			
Lamp	1962	n/a	Moscow	Literature	Art			
Crocus	1963	1964	Minsk	Literature	Belarussia			
Neck	1964	1964	Moscow	Literature				
Freedom and Homeland	1964	1966	L'viv, Morshyn	Economy	National culture	History	Socio-political issues	Ukraine
Political Diary	1964	1970	Moscow	Literature	Economy	History	Socio-political issues	
Herald of Salvation	1964	1975	St. Petersburg	Religion/Philosophy				
Avant-Garde	1965	1965	Moscow	Literature	Art			
Notebook of Social Democracy	1965	1965	Moscow	Socio-political issues				
Sphinxes	1965	1965	Moscow	Literature	Art			
The Bell	1965	1965	St. Petersburg	History	Socio-political issues			
Almanac	1965	1966	St. Petersburg	Literature	Socio-political issues			
Sail	1965	1966	St. Petersburg	Literature				

				Religion/ Philosophy	Socio-political issues	
Storm-Tossed	1965	1970	Novosibirsk			
Number	1965	1974	Yekaterinburg; Rostov	Literature	Art	
Information: Bulletin of the Crimean Tatars	1965	1985	Moscow; Tashkent; Samarqand	Human Rights	National culture	Crimean Tatars
The Square	1965	1987	St. Petersburg; Novosibirsk	Music		
Fioretti	1965	n/a	St. Petersburg	Literature		
Old Believer	1966	1966	St. Petersburg	Literature		
The Russian Word	1966	1966	Moscow	Literature		
In the Name of the Homeland	1966	1982	Yerevan	Socio-political issues	Armenian	
Beat-Echo	1967	1967	Kharkiv	Music		
Fiction	1967	1971	Moscow	Art		
Beacon	1967	n/a	Yerevan	Socio-political issues	Armenian	

Source: Ann Komaroni, Soviet Samizdat Periodicals, University of Toronto Library, accessed January 18, 2017, https://samizdat.library.utoronto.ca/.

Alexander Solzhenitsyn, and Vladimir Dudintsev, among others, dealt with the Soviet political system head on, channeling their strong critiques of the Gulag, the stultifying bureaucracy, Stalin's purges, and so on, through fictional narratives rather than reporting or analysis.[15] Overall, the literary focus, while not predetermined, was not surprising.

While uncensored literature dominated most samizdat pages of this era, one-third (15/45) of the journals launched between 1956 and 1967 published nonfiction, whether about the economy, human rights, other social/political issues, or local/regional problems. Most of the nonfiction samizdat emerged after 1962 (table 4.1). *Information* and *Phoenix*, for example, featured reasoned commentaries and fiery polemics, along with cartoons, manifestos, biographies, and memoirs, sometimes with a few rumors thrown in to stir the pot (other publications threw in pornography to stir other things). Because of the roadblocks to information access, readers during this first decade of samizdat could get little investigative journalism or even "straight news." Some of that reader demand was met with published translations of foreign news and broadcast transcripts, a derivation of samizdat called *radizdat*. Foreign radio broadcasts, when available, also scratched that itch. But, by and large, most samizdat before 1968 focused only obliquely on politics. Dissenting voices tended to be "prepolitical," even if they often presented alternative ways to think about societies and governments. As Aleksandr Solzhenitsyn, probably the most widely circulated samizdat author, put it in his Nobel Prize speech, fiction and other "works of art . . . scoop [up the truth and present] it to us as a living force."[16]

The Origin of the *Chronicle*
The End of the "Thaw" and the Sinyavsky-Daniel Trial

In 1965, a year after he deposed Khrushchev in a palace coup with the KGB's help, Leonid Brezhnev and his allies struck hard against the incipient human rights movement, including the emerging corps of dissident writers.[17] Khrushchev's KGB had also worked hard to track "anti-Soviet" writers hiding behind pseudonyms and working with publishers at home (in samizdat) and abroad (in *tamizdat*—"published over there" and brought back). However, dissidents through experience had learned ways to better hide their tracks and to evade and deceive KGB agents. An example of the latter came, courtesy of Andrei Sinyavsky, a gentile who chose the pen name Abram Tertz, which led the KGB on a confused chase for a Jewish man. When the regime eventually figured it out, state newspapers angrily denounced Sinyavsky's "squalid provocation."[18]

Brezhnev led a willful, resourceful regime, whose KGB agents' dogged, shoe-leather intelligence work eventually let them track their prey. By mid-1965, they had enough intelligence to identify Sinyavsky and another tamizdat writer close to him, Yuli Daniel, whose pseudonym was "Nikolai Arzhak." Agents arrested the men in September 1965 on charges of "Anti-Soviet Agitation and Propaganda," because they had intentionally produced and disseminated texts that "slandered" the Communist system, which Soviet law considered a "grave crime." That Khrushchev's government created that law in 1960 (in Article 70 of the criminal code) suggests the limits of the thaw concept, although the evidence is abundant and clear that many people, including liberal activists, perceived one.[19]

News of Sinyavsky and Daniel's arrests reverberated through the movement's growing network of writers, students, academics, professionals, and sundry urbanites. The regime had gone after writers before. Khrushchev's government, for instance, had attacked Boris Pasternak after his *Doctor Zhivago* was published abroad. But Brezhnev's more serious moves against Sinyavsky and Daniel for writing unapproved allegorical and mildly satirical fiction signaled a potential return to Stalinist totalitarianism.[20] It also came at a time when the dissident network had ripened, with members ready for a fight.

On December 5, 1965—Soviet Constitution Day—the poet and mathematician Alexander Esenin-Volpin led about 200 placard-waving brave souls right into the belly of the beast: Pushkin Square, Moscow, about a mile from the Kremlin. The public protest was something most Soviet citizens, and their rulers, had never seen before—an "action so daring that it was almost inconceivable." It was not spontaneous, as Esenin-Volpin and other organizers had passed out detailed fliers announcing the protest on local college campuses. The protesters, before they were swiftly grabbed and handcuffed by a beefed-up KGB battalion (their bosses had also seen the fliers) and then thrown into ghastly prisons and psychiatric hospitals, loudly demanded that authorities "Respect the Soviet Constitution!" and open the Sinyavsky-Daniel trial to the public. While the protesters were in some ways sincere in their professed fealty to the Constitution, which Stalin had cynically inscribed with civil rights and liberties protections, the protest frame was nevertheless a clever one.[21] The movement would have had a more difficult time influencing fairer-minded officials and mobilizing other Russians if they had been overtly subversive and had openly challenged the legitimacy of the entire system.

It came as a surprise when Brezhnev's regime announced that it would make the trial "open," the protesters' core demand. Yet it soon became clear that Brezhnev's concession was a cynical one. He had decided to resurrect an old Stalin favorite: show trials. The Kremlin planned to stage-manage the proceedings, obsessively directing every scene and point of access. They would squeeze self-incriminating confessions out of the writers, block access to the courtroom to nonloyalists, and control every channel of communication that would carry reports of the trial. The swift reappearance of show trials signaled to dissidents that Khrushchev's thaw was over, full stop. Whatever remained of Khrushchev's "ideologically more relaxed atmosphere" had been sucked back into the Kremlin's black hole.[22] Brezhnev wanted to demonstrate strength and intolerance; dissidents needed to be deterred. But after tasting a few freedoms, however diluted and circumscribed they were, the activists were not willing to relinquish them without a fight. They were ready to push for more.

During the February 1966 Sinyavsky-Daniel hearings, the regime made every pretense of following due process procedures. The *New York Herald Tribune* reported that the regime publicly trumpeted the defendants' legal rights, while flouting them inside the restricted courtroom: "Those rights included the right to be laughed at by a hand-picked audience of 70 persons . . . [and] the right to have only the prosecution side of the case reported in some detail to those who cannot claim access to the 'open' trial because they have no passes." That *Herald Tribune* correspondents were able to report those observations from such a restricted trial was an indication that Brezhnev's regime did not have complete control.[23]

On top of the leaks, there was another way the show trial deviated from Stalin era trials: the defendants refused to play along. Sinyavsky and Daniel denied that they intended to foment "ideological struggle against the USSR" or to slander the state with "anti-Soviet propaganda." When the judge asked whether he was guilty, Sinyavsky replied, "not at all." Daniel concurred, "No. Neither in part nor in full." Brezhnev's plan had backfired. He could not publicize the dissidents' coerced confessions, and their courtroom defiance would almost assuredly be leaked. Sinyavsky and Daniel had refused to follow the show trial script, despite not knowing whether Brezhnev would also resurrect Stalin's punishment preferences, such as firing line executions.[24]

Fortunately, the writers were spared the firing line, although both had to suffer the horrors of the Gulag. Sinyavsky got seven years of hard labor. Daniel got five.

Galanskov-Ginzburg and the White Book

Sinyavsky and Daniel's courtroom defiance was not the regime's only unforeseen trial-related problem. Although the Kremlin controlled how the state press covered the proceedings, it did not take long for the transcript to appear in samizdat form. Yuri Galanskov and Alexander Ginzburg published the samizdat *White Book*, which included the trial transcript along with many dissidents' letters criticizing the spectacle and the Gulag sentences. Sinyavsky and Daniels's wives, Maria Rozanova and Larisa Bogoraz, respectively, had launched the letter-writing campaign.[25]

The widely circulated *White Book* changed the political dynamic. First, it—like the trial and its aftermath—fortified the dissident movement, by showing weaknesses of the regime. Dissidents knew they faced a very hostile, repressive regime. However, the regime clearly stopped short of full-blown Stalinism. If Stalin had been in charge, Sinyavsky and Daniel would not have survived. Furthermore, when the *White Book* defiantly published the trial transcript and the accompanying letters, the regime's inability to control sensitive information was on full display. Such things did not occur under Stalin. How many sympathizers lurked within official Sovietdom, dissidents and their foreign supporters wondered?

Second, Western reporters with dissident connections in Russia got copies of the *White Book*. Some of those journalists convinced their editors to publish excerpts of the trial abroad, which inaugurated a collaborative process between dissidents and Western publishers that would be crucial to the later success of the *A Chronicle of Current Events*. The publication of the unfiltered transcripts of the Sinyavsky-Daniel trial also awakened human rights activists in the West to the deteriorating situation in the Soviet Union. They too began to recognize that the thaw had ended. The circulation of the *White Book* set into motion new efforts to forge transnational links between human rights activists in the West and East, which would also prove significant in the history of the *Chronicle*.[26]

A third consequence of the samizdat/tamizdat *White Book* was the arrest of its publishers. For their work on the *White Book*, as well as the literary samizdat *Pheonix-61*, *Pheonix-66*, and *Syntax*, authorities in 1967 tracked down and arrested Galanskov and Ginzburg, along with their assistants Alexei Dobrovolsky and Vera Lashkova. The arrests themselves sparked another protest, organized by Bukovsky.

The January 1968 "trial of the four" in many ways resembled the earlier Sinyavsky-Daniel trial. The regime again touted its openness, while working hard to keep the trial closed and stage-managed. The defendants again refused to play along, disputing the "anti-Soviet" charges leveled against them and defiantly proclaiming their innocence. Despite even greater efforts at information control, Soviet authorities again could not plug all leaks, from basic trial details to delicious moments of insubordination, such as Ginzburg's quip that "it is patriotic to die, but not to lie, for one's country." And despite the obvious end to the thaw, protesters again converged in Moscow, a couple of hundred of them, similar to the number in late 1965 in Pushkin Square. But these protests lasted longer, in part because of the relatively larger foreign news contingent, whose cameras reduced the regime's viciousness. Those protesters also seemed to have bootlegged a crop of the global "Spirit of '68." *Time* magazine reported that "crowds gathered outside the courtroom, yelling, shoving and needling security guards," despite the "50 below zero" weather. They "crowded against police barricades and dashed from door to door . . . only to be turned away because they lacked official passes." They forced court officials to let Galans-kov's father inside. They stood up and let themselves be identified:

> One of the main protesters was a balding but erect Soviet general in his 60s who circulated petitions among the assemblage, brandished his cane at a policeman who took his picture. "I'm not afraid of little boys!" shouted Major General Pyotr Grigorenko, who was fired by ex-Premier Khrushchev for protesting "lack of freedom" in the Soviet Union. "I shed blood for this country."[27]

Scenes like that would have been unthinkable under Stalin's reign and probably Brezhnev's two years earlier.

The protest raged outside the courtroom in Moscow, and around the world. Bogoraz, who had organized the letter-writing campaign featured in the *White Book*, worked with Pavel Litvinov, the grandson of Stalin's foreign min-ister, to circulate an "Appeal to World Public Opinion" to "everyone in whom conscience is alive and who has sufficient courage," but "in the first place to Soviet public opinion." The London *Times* published it on January 11, 1968. Writing from Russia, Bogoraz and Litvinov denounced the rigged proceedings, comparing them to "witch trials" and Stalin's show trials. The Kremlin's hand-picked courtroom audience jeered at the defendants and witnesses, they wrote. The prosecutors presented false evidence. And the judge pressured Galanskov and Ginzburg to plead guilty and corroborate the government's claims. Bogoraz and Litvinov demanded immediate "public condemnation of this shameful trial and the punishment of those guilty of perpetrating it . . . [T]he release of the accused from arrest . . . [and a] new trial with the observance of all legal norms and with the presence of international observers." Their "Appeal" included their names and Russian addresses, which essentially put bulls' eyes on their heads.[28]

The publication of the letter in London as the five day trial proceeded in Moscow was a testament to how well developed the human rights activists' links with foreign journalists already were. Another link, between Western and Soviet human rights activists, was starting to develop, helped by tamizdat and international communications like Bogoraz and Litvinov's, as well as the emergence of global human rights organizations, whose agents were beginning to peek behind the Iron Curtain.

Indeed, Bogoraz and Litvinov's decision to write their letter appears to have been partly inspired by the presence in Moscow of an Amnesty Inter-national investigator, I. A. Soerheim, who tried but failed to gain access to the trial. He froze outside with the other activists who had somehow evaded arrest. While the weather was unpleasant, the circumstances proved useful for network-building. Back in London, prominent Westerners, unaffiliated with Amnesty, but affiliated with the human rights cause, were moved to action by Bogoraz and Litvinov's claims in their *Times* piece. Some were given the opportunity by *Times* editors to publish a "Telegram to Moscow" just below the dissidents' letter: "We, a group of friends representing no organisation, support your statement, admire your courage, think of you and will help in any way possible." The sixteen signatories included W.H. Auden, Bertrand Russell, Igor Stravinsky, and "Mrs. George Orwell."[29]

Despite all of the organization and effort, the domestic and foreign protesters were no match for Brezhnev's regime. The court in Moscow delivered guilty verdicts against Galanskov and Ginzburg, who received seven- and five-year Gulag sentences, respectively. But the growing movement would not be deterred. Activists flooded government offices with letters, at least 700 of them, according to the *Chronicle's* estimate in its first issue. While the regime had received letters and petitions before, such as the petition 116 citizens had sent to the Moscow City Court in November 1967, the human rights movement was clearly growing, despite—and in part because of—all of the repression. The 700-plus letter-writers after the trial demanded justice for Galanskov, Ginzburg, and other political prisoners and framed their arguments in the language of constitutional rights (e.g., 1936 Constitution: Chapter 9, Article 111; Chapter 10, Articles 124 and 125). When their arguments appeared in samizdat, the legalistic, officially Soviet themes would help neutralize the Kremlin's propaganda offensive, carried out in *Pravda* and other state outlets, which featured sneering, snarling articles portraying the activists as criminals at best, treasonous subversives at worst.[30] It is remarkable how many individuals chose to identify themselves, given the circumstances.

The Need to Publish a "Bulletin": There Were "Hundreds of Sentences Just Hanging in the Air"

The *Chronicle of Current Events* emerged in early 1968 from the clash of political currents roiling Moscow. The actual decision point came nonchalantly, unceremoniously, even somewhat forgettably. As the *Chronicle's* first editor Natalya Gorbanevskaya (Figure 4.1) later recounted the story, she and a group of Muscovite activists and samizdat dabblers had an informal social club. While all of them were politically conscious, they usually just discussed "whatever was interesting at the time."[31]

Like others in the burgeoning human rights movement, Gorbanevskaya's group had begun compulsively collecting data about rights violations—anything they could find, such as trial information, conditions in the Gulag, and the increasing use of punitive psychiatry. Through the process of actively collecting data, the human rights network forged links with victims and witnesses of rights violations, as well as insiders, such as Gulag guards, who helped them ferry messages and care packages to prisoners.[32]

FIGURE 4.1   Natalya Gorbanevskaya. *Source*: MS Russ 78 Box 2: 436, Houghton Library, Harvard University. From the library's Peter Reddaway photograph collection.

Sometime in February or March 1968, Gorbanevskaya and some friends met in an apartment deemed KGB free (i.e., no surveillance bugs) in Dolgoprudny, about 15 miles from central Moscow. Joining Gorbanevskaya were Grigorenko, the fearless major general who helped lead the protests outside the Galanskov-Ginzburg trial; Litvinov, the coauthor of the "Appeal to World Public Opinion"; Pyotr Yakir; Victor Krasin; and Ilya Gabai. Two others were likely there: Galina Gabai and Larisa Bogoraz, Yuli Daniels's wife and the coauthor of the "Appeal."[33]

Someone at the meeting argued the time had come "to organize regular information," as Gorbanevskaya recalled. It was time to put out a samizdat with all of the information they had collected about "trials, arrests, labor camps, searches, [and] interrogations." As Litvinov recalled, there were "hundreds of sentences just hanging in the air," waiting to be published. The talk turned to the idea of a "bulletin," a repository for news about human rights violations. Gorbanevskaya agreed to take on the initial "blue collar" work of putting it together. She was a poet, prose writer, librarian, bibliographer, and translator, but at the moment her pregnancy left her with extra time at home. That twist of fate, plus her courage, led to Gorbanevskaya becoming the

Chronicle's inaugural editor. Alexeyeva volunteered as well, lending her time and typing skills. Together, they and their network would lead the samizdat community from a "prepolitical or literary" phase to a political phase that placed human rights front and center.[34]

The *Chronicle*'s Early Years

The first issue of the *Chronicle* hit the streets on April 30, May Day eve, its liberal, rights-based message a counterpoint to the Communists' annual celebration of individual rights-trampling authoritarian egalitarianism (Figure 4.2). The banner headline, "Year of Human Rights in the Soviet Union," captured the *Chronicle*'s substantive focus and signaled its international influences. The first clause was an explicit reference to the United Nations' declaration of 1968 as the "International Year of Human Rights."[35]

Unlike many literary samizdat, which brimmed with passion and colorful imagery, the *Chronicle* exhibited a restrained, dry writing style. Gorbanevskaya was a literary writer and could have easily made its prose lively and lovely. But what Soviet citizens needed more than that, she and the others decided, was dispassionate reporting—straight news—to clearly depict the repressive nature of the regime. Thus, the first issue was thick with details about the Galanskov-Ginzburg trial, along with the associated protests and "repressive measures in response to the protests," with descriptions of dozens of cases. It reported on a February 1967 arrest of Valentin Prussakov, a Soviet Jew who had written about Soviet anti-Semitism. It updated readers on the depredations of the Gulag, focusing on a hunger strike "in Camp 17 of the Mordovian camps (Mordovian ASSR, Potma, Ozerny post office, postbox 385/17a)" staged by Yuli Daniel, Boris Zdorovets, Victor Kalnins, Sergei Moshkov, Valery Ronkin, and Yury Shukhevych. It provided all known details about "The Leningrad Trial" against seventeen members of the illegal All-Russian Social-Christian Union for the Liberation of the People. It reached outside of the Soviet Union, with an "Appeal to the Budapest Conference of Communist and Workers' parties."[36]

The size of the *Chronicle*'s first "printing"—really just kitchen-table typing on black-market typewriters—did not augur its later circulation and influence. "The first issue was small," Gorbanevskaya recalled, "twenty-something pages on a typewriter. I made seven copies. I gave six of them away and kept the seventh to make new copies from it." She gave one to a Western reporter in Moscow for foreign coverage, and five to close friends who retyped and carbon copied Alexeyeva's original. The *Chronicle*'s circulation quickly grew after that issue, but the process of passing copies hand to hand, with legions of kitchen table typists quietly making their own batches to pass on, would stay constant for in-country production. Tamizdat versions of the *Chronicle* (published outside the country) proliferated from modern printing machines.[37]

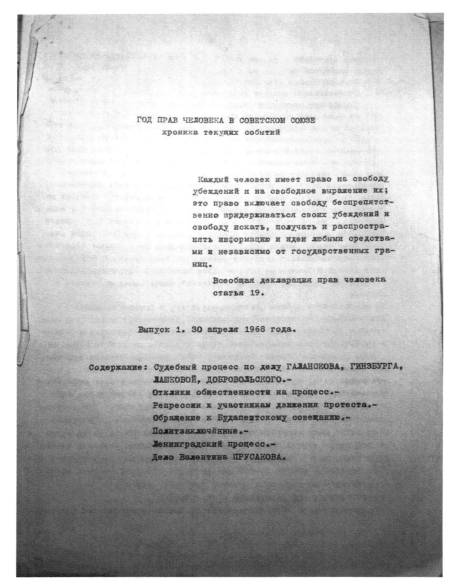

FIGURE 4.2 The First Page of the First Issue of the *Chronicle*. *Source*: "Soviet Samizdat Periodicals" database, Project for the Study of Dissidence and Samizdat, Edited by Ann Komaromi, Toronto: University of Toronto Libraries, 2015, samizdatcollections.library.utoronto.ca, based on an original held at the Archive of the History of Dissidence in the USSR, International "Memorial" Society, Moscow, Russian Federation.

In its first year of publication, the *Chronicle's* geographic coverage rapidly extended beyond Moscow and Leningrad. Copies began to pop up across the Soviet Union's massive expanse, and cases of rights violations from outside the two biggest cities increasingly began to appear in the *Chronicle*'s pages. Gorbanevskaya et al. featured trials, torture, and self-immolations in far-flung places, including Crimea, Gorky, Kharkov, Kiev, Perm, Riga, and Simferopol. An analysis Alexeyeva later completed in exile quantified the geographic spread during and after that first year. For example, Issue 1 covered cases from Moscow and Leningrad (including Gulag reports about dissidents from those cities); Issue 7 (April 1969) covered cases from thirty-four places; and Issue 11 (December 1969) featured thirty-two places. Though the *Chronicle*'s network of contributors and copiers remained underground, its size and geographic breadth grew rapidly over time.[38]

The first major shock to the network came in December 1969, when the KGB arrested Gorbanevskaya and locked her in a psychiatric hospital/prison (*psikhushka*) until 1972. The *Chronicle* lost its first editor, along with case files in her apartment, the information in her head, and any isolated network links she may have had for idiosyncratic reasons. Her arrest clearly hurt the network. The next issue's (Issue 12) geographic coverage shrunk to eighteen locations (from thirty-two), which resulted in part from her arrest and from the network's scramble for a new editorial team.[39]

But the disruption was temporary; it did not hobble the network for long. Indeed, the *Chronicle* published that next issue (Issue 12) in February 1970, just two months after Gorbanevskaya's arrest. Despite the KGB's tactical victory, the *Chronicle* continued its regular publishing schedule and demonstrated its geographic reach, first under the new editor Galina Gabai and then Anatoly Yakobson.[40]

The *Chronicle's* Sources, Information Flows, and Network Security

How did information move across the clandestine network? While the *Chronicle*'s underground nature shielded its specific, daily operations from Brezhnev's KGB—and, unintentionally, from present-day scholars—its editors and contributors occasionally revealed how it worked. In Issue 5 (December 31, 1968), a piece by Gorbanevskaya describes how readers from Volgograd to Vladivostok could bring cases of human rights violations to the editors' attention. Given that "the *Chronicle* cannot . . . give its postal address on the last page," she explained,

> anybody who is interested in seeing that the Soviet public is informed about what goes on in the country, may easily pass on information to the editors of the *Chronicle*. Simply tell it to the person from whom you received the *Chronicle*, and he will tell the person from whom he received the *Chronicle*, and so on. But do not try to trace back the whole chain of communication yourself, or else you will be taken for a police informer [by others in the chain, including the editors].

Geoffrey Hosking described the two-way communication links succinctly: "distribution channels functioned in the reverse direction as channels of information."[41]

An even more difficult challenge for analysts is identifying the people who contributed, those who actually "pass[ed] on information to the editors." Early contributors to the young publication probably came from the human rights movement's activist core, the intellectuals, students, artists, and professionals, who were already reading samizdat and perhaps taking notes about worrisome local cases. They were the ones who wrote the letters of protest about the Galanskov-Ginzburg trial. One tally estimated that self-identified "workers" wrote or signed only 6 percent of those, suggesting that most came from movement activists.

Yet we do know that the Muscovites who founded the *Chronicle*, along with their friends and family, had already started making connections with government sources, such as Gulag guards. As the *Chronicle*'s distribution grew, and its coverage expanded geographically, it encompassed larger and more diverse portions of Soviet society. With that growth came more clandestine "chains of communication" moving through state organizations where human rights violations were commonly observed. Contributors assumed great risks, KGB-flagged political prisoners even more so. One Gulag inmate described how he smuggled out poetry for another journal:

> In minute letters, I write out my latest poem on four centimeter-wide strips of cigarette paper . . . These strips of cigarette paper are then tightly rolled into a small tube (less than the thickness of your finger) sealed and made moisture proof by a method of our own devising, and handed on when a suitable opportunity presents itself.

Prisoners passed notes to visitors in the facilities that allowed them. The gambit sometimes succeeded because of Gulag guards' well-deserved reputation for bribe taking. Over time, the *Chronicle*'s network learned more about guards' particular preferences, such as new cigarette lighters and other scarce goods, which contributors stockpiled. Sometimes Gulag visitors hid the goods outside the prison walls and would whisper the secret locations to guards once inside. The guards would then fade into the countryside to find the buried goodies, like spies checking dead-drops.[42]

The *Chronicle*'s founders were deadly serious about protecting the network, and the enterprise, from the KGB. Recall Issue 5's warning to contributors and readers: "Do not try to trace back the whole chain of communication yourself, or else you will be taken for a police informer." Readers probably, and properly, interpreted that message about "the whole chain" as applying to smaller sections of the chain as well. People who were caught poking around would be eyed warily and flagged. Alerts about a potential interloper, and his identity, would spread.

While most contributors stayed cautious, following their rationally paranoid instincts, the founders took risks that may have unnecessarily endangered themselves and their project. For instance, while they did not identify themselves as *Chronicle* editors and contributors, they published their names and, in some cases, their addresses, alongside those of other activists who signed petitions. For example, the first issue named Gabai, Gorbanevskaya, Grigorenko, Krasin, Litvinov, and Yakir. The *Chronicle* also reported on the founders' own cases, when appropriate. Gorbanevskaya, for instance, reported on her experience being "forcibly interned in [a] psychiatric hospital" in February 1968. The passage from that first issue described her and Esenin-Volpin—another psychiatric prisoner—as "two of the most active participants in the protests" after the Galanskov-Ginzburg trial. Alexeyeva also typed her own name and circumstances in the first and second issues, in reporting related to her expulsion from the Communist Party for signing letters protesting the regime's treatment of the Ginzburg-Galanskov trial and its critics. And in the first issue's report on the "Appeal to Budapest Conference of Communist and Workers' Parties," six of the *Chronicle's* eight founders named themselves and provided their home addresses (Litvinov, Yakir, Krasin, Gabai, Grigorenko, and Bogoraz), for example, "Larissa BOGORAZ—Philologist; Moscow V-261, 85 Leninsky prospekt, apartment 3" and "Pavel LITVINOV—Physicist; Moscow K-1 8 Alexei Tolstoy St, apartment 78." The full list of signatories contained only twelve names and addresses.[43] Sometimes they made it too easy for the KGB.

Why did the founders take such risks? First, while they were careful, they were also deeply principled, almost to a fault. Many of them refused to imitate the regime they despised. Thus, unless it was necessary, they "shunned conscious, planned secrecy," or more broadly "the Leninist concept of a political movement."[44]

Second, all eight founders knew that the KGB already had files on them. They probably expected that the KGB would inevitably arrest them. Indeed, the KGB by June 11, 1968, already had solid intelligence that Gorbanevskaya, Litvinov, and Yakir were running the *Chronicle*. KGB Chairman Yuri Andropov's classified report to the Central Committee of the Communist Party of the Soviet Union states that

> operational information available makes it clear that LITVINOV, GOR-BANEVSKAYA, YAKIR, and certain other like-minded individuals have prepared and are disseminating a document entitled "The Year for Human Rights in the Soviet Union" (copy enclosed herewith) that contains slanderous accounts of trials [for activists] in Moscow and Leningrad, along with summaries of letters and statements discrediting Soviet authorities.[45]

It is likely that Gorbanevskaya et al. calculated that if they did *not* include them-selves—major activists all—in the *Chronicle*'s pages, the KGB would suspect them even more. The omissions would become red flags. Thus, the founders' seemingly reckless idealism might have been tempered by realism, a kind of steely pragmatism.

When KGB agents did come knocking, the *Chronicle* crew proved their shrewdness. One morning in the fall of 1969, about ten officials appeared at Galina Gabai's door. She grabbed a stack of *Chronicle* files and stuffed them into her bathrobe before letting the agents in. While they prowled her two room apartment, she managed to sneak the papers into a boiling pot of borscht on the stove that her mother had earlier prepared. Luck intervened and kept the papers submerged in the borscht pot during the KGB's visit. The agents left without arresting Gabai. The *Chronicle* source material she fished out of the borscht was stained red.[46]

Alexeyeva also had her Hollywood moments, even if they were relatively more clichéd than Gabai's borscht trick. (To be fair, one doesn't always have a boiling pot of dark red soup nearby.) Faced with approaching state agents who wanted to question her, she pulled the old stuff-eight-copies-of-the-*Chronicle*-in-the-brassiere trick.[47]

At least as important as the *Chronicle* founders' ability to think on their feet in dangerous situations were their decisions that structured the network, which would keep the samizdat in business for nearly fifteen years despite the Communist regime's unrelenting hostility.

The *Chronicle's* Structural "Wisdom"

In a smuggled out forward to a 1983 book about the *Chronicle*, Andrei Sakha-rov, the nuclear scientist and Nobel Peace Prize winner, argued that "the very fact of the almost uninterrupted publication of the *Chronicle* for [14] years is a miracle of self-denial, of wisdom, of courage and intellectual integrity." But the journal's robustness was hardly a miracle. Its founders, editors, and all other contributors made smart decisions about the network's structure, its "chain of communication." Gorbanevskaya's instructions for contributors in the fifth issue—"Simply tell it [i.e., provide your information] to the person from whom you received the *Chronicle*, and he will tell the person from whom he received the *Chronicle*, and so on"—demonstrates that she and her collaborators had the right instincts for building a robust, decentralized, dark network, glued together by shared principles and localized trust.[48]

Decentralization

As Gorbanevskaya indicated in her instructions for contributors, the chain of communication had a final destination: the editors and assistants in Moscow ("pass on information to the editors of the *Chronicle*"). Contributors lived all across Soviet territory, but the Muscovite editors occupied a more central network location than some occasional contributor in Gorky or a copier/distributor in Crimea. They had more network *centrality*, or more precisely, they had greater degree centrality, with more "ties to other actors." If we had data on all contributors and distributors to create a complete network map—an impossibility given the *Chronicle*'s clandestine, underground nature—we would also likely see that the Muscovites had greater closeness centrality. As nodes in the network they were "closer . . . to all other actors than others [were]." Moreover, taking into account all of the network nodes, the Muscovite publishers were likely located on average "on the shortest path . . . between any two actors," reflecting their greater betweenness centrality. Finally, they probably had more "ties to actors who [were] highly central," a sign of their greater eigenvector centrality.[49]

Given all of that centrality, one might reasonably argue that the *Chronicle* network had a *centralized* structure. Indeed, Paul Baran's model of a centralized network (figure 4.3) evokes Gorbanevskaya's chains of communication construct, with all chains ending in Moscow with the editors.[50] Certainly the fact that some nodes had more centrality kept the network from being *distributed*, a structure with nodes more or less evenly dispersed with roughly the same number of links. However, there are several reasons why the network structure probably resembled something closer to Baran's *decentralized* model.

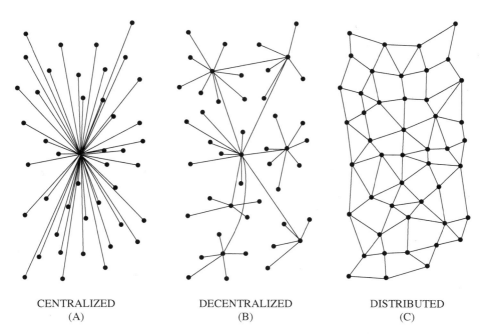

CENTRALIZED   DECENTRALIZED   DISTRIBUTED
(A)   (B)   (C)

FIGURE 4.3 Models of Centralized, Decentralized, and Distributed Networks. *Source*: Paul Baran, On Distributed Communications, RAND report RM-3420-PR, https://www.rand.org/pubs/research_memoranda/RM3420.html.

Although the editors clearly had greater centrality, the *Chronicle's* modus operandi prevented the network from developing too far in a centralized direction. First, we have the crude mechanics of samizdat production, in which self-selected nodes all across the network reproduce and distribute copies. The *Chronicle's* editors in Moscow began by making large batches, but they came nowhere close to printing the full circulation of an issue. There were *Chronicle* publishing nodes of varying centrality across the Soviet Union's vast territory, each one with multiple links, some of which made their own copies for ever wider distribution. Each one of those well-connected nodes was the center of a major network section, much like those in Baran's decentralized structure. Not every *Chronicle* reader was a copier, but plenty were. One analysis estimated that the *Chronicle's* duplicators together distributed up to 10,000 copies of each issue in the early 1980s, with each copy reaching up to ten separate readers.[51] By that point, just before its demise, the KGB had already depleted much of its network. The number could well have been higher years earlier.

If the *Chronicle* had a centralized structure, its chains of communication would have resembled separate lines jutting out from the center linked to single, peripheral nodes (figure 4.3). Or, each chain would have had multiple nodes, but each relationship would have still been dyadic, where some source A transferred information to B, who gave it to C, who passed it to D, who delivered it to editor E (or some more elaborate variant of that):

$$A \rightarrow B \rightarrow C \rightarrow D \rightarrow E$$

In a network like that, with multiple segregated chains stretching from a peripheral node to the center, each node would have only one (e.g., A or E) or two (e.g., B, C, D) links. Yet the isolated chains model does not fit a network like the *Chronicle's*, with its multiple centers of publication and distribution, each one serving as a bridge for disseminating copies *and* collecting source material to send back to other section centers and eventually to some unknown editorial team in Moscow, whose identity and location changed over time. Overall, the *Chronicle's* network was vast and decentralized, with multiple branches that clustered around semicentral nodes, each one of those loosely clustered around the most central nodes in Moscow. As Alexeyeva described it, its jagged, irregular "channels spread out silently and invisibly . . . like mushroom spores."[52]

The network developed in a decentralized structure in large part for security reasons. A centralized structure would have quickly led to the *Chronicle's* collapse. If the KGB knocked out the central node, it would have demolished the network in one fell swoop. Yet each time the KGB arrested editors and other nodes with relatively high centrality, new *Chronicle* issues continued to appear, usually on schedule. Recall that the KGB arrested Gorbanevskaya on December 24, 1969, about twenty months after the *Chronicle*'s launch. They also snagged Krasin four days earlier. Despite the regime's success in knocking out those important network nodes, it failed to disrupt the *Chronicle*'s publishing schedule. Issue 11, which Gorbanevskaya had mostly completed, appeared a week after her arrest on December 31, 1969. It contained a detailed section about her arrest and prior activism—except for her *Chronicle* involvement—all of which was obviously written by someone else who eluded the regime's grasp:

> On 24 December 1969, Natalya Gorbanevskaya was arrested.
>
> Natalya Gorbanevskaya was born in 1936, and graduated from the philological faculty of Leningrad State University in 1963. A talented poet, she took part in the 25 August 1968 demonstration on Red Square against the sending of troops to Czechoslovakia, and is author of the book *Noon*, which brings together material about the demonstration. A member of the Action Group for Civil Rights in the USSR, she is the mother of two young children (the elder is eight years old, and the younger one year seven months).
>
> On 24 December a search was made of Gorbanevskaya's flat. The search warrant was signed by L.S. Akimova, senior investigator of the Moscow Procuracy, and the search was carried out by Shilov, an investigator of the Procuracy. Confiscated during the search were items of samizdat, the manuscript "Free Medical Aid" and a copy of Anna Akhmatova's *Requiem* with a handwritten dedication from the author.
>
> A search was made of the persons of the friends who were present in Gorbanevskaya's flat during the search.
>
> Natalya Gorbanevskaya has been charged under Article 190-1 of the Russian Criminal Code. The investigation is being conducted by L.S. Akimova. Gorbanevskaya is at present in Butyrka Prison.
>
> As early as 1968—after the demonstration of 25 August—Gorbanevskaya was declared to be of unsound mind, and now she is threatened with imprisonment in a hospital prison for an unlimited term.

Many people made possible the speedy publication of Issue 11, but it would not have come out if not for Galina Gabai and Anatoly Yakobson, who stepped in as senior editors. Gabai and Yakobson had help: Nadezhda Pavlovna Emel'kina, Gabriel Superfin, Tatyana Velikanova, and Irina Petrovna Yakir served as contributing editors.[53] Overall, while Gorbanevskaya and Krasin's arrests were unwelcome (and unjustified, from a human rights perspective), they were not terribly disruptive.

After Issue 11, the *Chronicle*'s stable publishing schedule continued with Yakobson as senior editor. Gorbanevskaya had actually expected that Vladimir Telnikov would succeed her as editor. She had anticipated her arrest, knowing it was imminent. But Yakobson appears to have taken over without incident, leading the *Chronicle*'s editorial team through Issue 27.[54]

Other books recount the often dramatic history of the *Chronicle*'s editorial successions, replete with KGB visitations and detentions of activists and their typewriters. Despite all of that tumult, the *Chronicle* had a remarkable continuity of publication: sixty-four issues across fourteen years in a repressive environment. Table 4.2 shows the timeline of editorial successions. The incomplete historical record prohibits a list of often equally important contributing editors, of which there were probably more than fifty.[55] The key point is this: when the KGB detained or exiled one editor, new ones always were ready to assume responsibilities, until they too were picked off, and then replaced by others. There were always more human rights activists and samizdat enthusiasts waiting in the wings.

The inability of the KGB to smash the *Chronicle* by arresting its chief and contributing editors—network nodes with high centrality values—is one indication that the network structure was not very centralized. The ability of new editors to take the helm and then survive, sometimes for years, speaks of the network's *robustness*—in that it could still "function (i.e., transmit information) after the 'failure' of a node or its removal from the network."[56] Figure 4.4 shows the number of days that elapsed between issues across the *Chronicle*'s full run between 1968 and 1982. It shows the network's remarkable robustness,

TABLE 4.2 The *Chronicle*'s Chief Editors

Issues 1–10	Natalya Gorbanevskaya
11	Galina Gabai
11–27	Anatoly Yakobson
12	Yelena Smorgunova
12	Yuly Kim
28–30	Tatyana Khodorovich
28–30	Tatyana Velikanova
28–30	Sergei Kovalev
31	Alexander Lavut
32–34	Sergei Kovalev
32–53	Tatyana Velikanova
54–55	Alexander Lavut
56–64*	Yury Shikhanovich

Source: The list of senior editors was compiled by Alexander Daniel of the Russian nongovernmental organization Memorial: An International Historical, Educational, Human Rights And Charitable Society. The Memorial list is available at Crowfoot and Lipovskaia, "The Editors," The Chronicle of Current Events, accessed April 6, 2016, https://chronicle6883.wordpress.com/the-chronicle-in-russian/the-editors/.
*The KGB confiscated Issue #59 and related materials before it could be published.

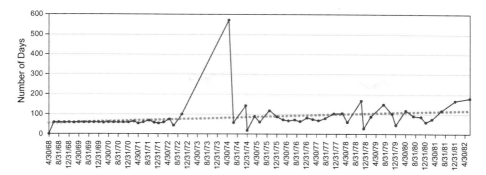

FIGURE 4.4 Days between *Chronicle of Current Events* Issues. *Three issues from 1972 and 1973 (12/31/72, 7/31/73, 12/31/73), which were prepared but not distributed because of KGB repression, were finally released at the same time as the 5/17/74 issue. The gray dotted line is a trendline. *Source*: Hopkins; Crowfoot and Lipobskaia.

given that it was an underground newspaper up against a hostile regime and its skillful, well-funded domestic intelligence agency.

Clearly there are exceptions to the overall trend, as figure 4.4 also shows. The most obvious one involves the major gap in publication between late 1972 through early 1974, which appears as a giant mountain against the low plains and rolling hills in the graph. The delay came courtesy of a stepped-up anti-*Chronicle* KGB operation called Case 24, housed in the Fifth Chief Directorate, which the service launched in late December 1971. In early 1972, the KGB snagged Krasin (again) and Yakir. In May, KGB agents raided the homes of key *Chronicle* figures, including (Chief Editor) Yakobson's, who in 1973 managed to flee to Israel. It took until May 1974—after 572 days—for Khodorovich, Velikanova, and Kovalev to publish another issue, with Kovalev shouldering a disproportionate share of the responsibilities. In the issue marking the *Chronicle*'s comeback, Kovalev et al. described that the KGB had made "repeated and unequivocal threats to respond to each new issue of the *Chronicle* with new arrests—arrests of people suspected by the KGB of publishing or distributing new or past issues."[57]

During the interim, the editors continued their work, but they chose not to release Issues 28 through 30 when they were ready for release in December 1972, July 1973, and December 1973, because of the KGB's renewed assault. Yet even during that exceptionally difficult period, a new crop of editors quietly filled Yakobson et al.'s shoes and managed to collect enough publishable material to keep preparing issues. That is, as Case 24 operatives attempted to break apart all of the "chains of communication" leading back to the still large group in Moscow, individuals with evidence about Soviet human rights violations continued to pass information "to the person from whom you received the *Chronicle*, and he will tell the person from whom he received the *Chronicle*, and so on," just as Gorbanevskaya instructed in 1968. By 1972, there were too many hidden branches for the KGB to dismantle. They snaked through the underground with a size and complexity that could withstand the regime's strongest arsenal. The turning point came in May 1974, when Kovalev et al. decided they would no longer play along with the KGB's "tactic of hostages," which they argued was "incompatible with justice, morality and human dignity. Therefore, the *Chronicle* is resuming publication and will strive to preserve both the principles and the style of previous issues."[58] It took a little while, but the *Chronicle* network came back with at least as much robustness as before. The KGB could not eradicate it for another eight years. Only five issues during that time hit the streets late.

The *Chronicle* as a "Dark Network"

The *Chronicle*'s underground, clandestine nature was obviously one of its defining features, as with all samizdat in the Communist bloc. Its participants—whistleblowers, facilitators (e.g., Gulag guards), copiers, other distributors, and editorial recipients—operated with deliberate, necessary secrecy in order to escape detection and detention. Networks like the *Chronicle*'s that "try to remain hidden" to sustain themselves and achieve their goals are *dark networks*—"covert and illegal networks" that conceal their activities and node identities from authorities. Social network theorists often use the term when referring to generally harmful groups, like those involved in terrorism and organized crime. However, the concept also applies to generally "benign groups" like Żegota, the underground organization of mostly Polish Catholics who helped persecuted Polish Jews during World War II. Żegota qualifies as a dark network because "it was covert, and, at least from the perspective of the Nazis, illegal."[59] Similarly, the *Chronicle* was covert, and, at least from the perspective of the Communists, illegal. And, like Żegota, it was righteous.

Needing to operate in the dark poses unique challenges to networks and to those who want to study them. One problem with all of the darkness is that we will never comprehend what the *Chronicle*'s network looked like with any real specificity. Even the *Chronicle*'s editors did not know and probably could not have known. At one point they tried to map the network, without success. The best we can do is appreciate the fragmentary knowledge, the nodes and links that show up here and there in the historical record, from participants' testimonies and candid interviews, and from the place-specific information that flowed out of the darkness into Moscow, sometimes including arrest reports of *Chronicle* distributors and carriers. All of the fragments together, like a mosaic, show the *Chronicle*'s geographic reach. Flip randomly through the archives and find fragments of the network in Odessa (Issue 25, May 20, 1972), Tarusa (Issue 46, August 15, 1977), Vorkuta (Issue 57, August 3, 1980), and dozens of other places from the iciest tip of the Far East to Estonia, Moldavia, Armenia, and on to Tajikistan.[60]

The editors encountered practical problems because of the dark network. For example, they had limited opportunities to "fact check," to verify evidence that effectively came out of nowhere through a complex anonymous pipeline. That problem was compounded by the near-medieval communication technologies that network nodes had at their disposal. They rarely used phones or mail, because of all the government surveillance. They had no computers, given the historical era. Instead, the network had to rely on person-to-person transfers across complex, nonlinear chains of communication that sometimes stretched thousands of miles long. Perhaps the only difference between the *Chronicle*'s experience and that of a secret medieval clan's was the availability of Soviet cars and trains, which obviated the need for horses and carrier pigeons.

The fact that the network was dark, decentralized, and technologically restricted made its communication system inefficient. It was inefficient in the economic sense, given all of the transaction costs. It was also inefficient as social network theorists understand that term, in its "[in]ability to transmit information across the network 'quickly,' with speed defined as the number of links between nodes through which a message must travel before reaching its target."[61]

The *Chronicle*'s network structure and environment also made it vulnerable to information corruption. Recall the telephone game (or "Chinese whispers"), when an original message grows increasingly distorted as it passes through successive dyads. When A whispers her message to B, the message might stay unvarnished. But when B whispers it to C, or anywhere down the line—C to D, E to F, and so on—the message likely becomes corrupted, usually because of listening errors, but sometimes because of deliberate bungling. In a very large network where messages have to snake through any number of unseen branches, the problem could become devastating. When networks require constant operational secrecy and node anonymity, the problem compounds, because it becomes difficult if not impossible to go back down the chain of communication to verify a message's veracity. It is surprising that the KGB did not make a greater effort to subvert the *Chronicle* through disinformation from within.

Although a large, scrappy, pretechnological dark network like the *Chronicle*'s cannot hope to eliminate information corruption problems, it did develop mechanisms for limiting their occurrence and influence. For example, the editors asked sources to supply official documentation, whenever possible, which helped to validate claims. They also published corrections, like any good newspaper does. For instance, in Issue 28, the *Chronicle* included these corrections in its characteristic dry style: "Nikolai Kovalenko was mistakenly called Ivan. Lisovoi did not send his letter to the KGB. M. Kholodny's letter was published in *Literaturnaya Ukraina* on 7 June 1972, not 7 July." Also to its credit, the *Chronicle* was upfront with readers about the tentative nature of some reported information. From Issue 7 (April 1969):

> The Chronicle aims at the utmost reliability in the information it publishes. In those instances when it is not absolutely certain that some event has taken place, the Chronicle indicates that the piece of information is based on rumor. But at the same time the Chronicle requests its readers to be careful and accurate in the information they provide for publication.
>
> A number of inaccuracies occur during the process of duplicating copies of the Chronicle. These are mistakes in names and surnames, in dates and numbers. The quantity of them grows as the Chronicle is retyped again and again, and they cannot be corrected according to the context, as can other misprints.

Overall, as analysts of the *Chronicle* observed during and after its run, the journal's "record [was] remarkable," especially but not only "on the crucial question of accuracy."[62]

Shared Principles and Interpersonal Trust as Network Glues

The *Chronicle*'s surprising fourteen-year run had much to do with its contributors' operational security and the adaptability and complexity of its decentralized network structure.[63] But it did have a weak spot. The editors and those close to them were typically Muscovites, and the KGB knew it. That fact narrowed their investigations. Worse, given the editors' often public, nonanonymous, human rights activism, the KGB probably had a good idea of the likely culprits, as well as their links down the chain. The suspects' specific roles in the movement, and the *Chronicle*, may not have been entirely clear to the regime, but the names were not difficult to find. They sometimes even appeared in the *Chronicle*'s pages, as shown earlier. When the KGB detained suspects, its agents used torture and other forceful means to extract intelligence about the network, such as its more central nodes, recent meeting locations, and internal government collaborators (e.g., Gulag guards who accepted bribes).

Fortunately for the network, the KGB's efforts were often frustrated by strong-willed *Chronicle* detainees who had learned how to survive under constant duress and who had maintained their loyalty to family, friends, and the movement. They knew what to expect from the KGB, from their own prior experiences, from the testimonies of others who had experienced its wrath, and from helpful guides like Krasin's *Legal Instructions*, an important samizdat in its own right. From these various sources, *Chronicle* had learned tips and techniques about how to resist KGB pressure. They bit their tongues during interrogations, with notable exceptions. Most also had an intense commitment to the cause and a stubborn solidarity with the network.[64]

But shared principles and good training alone did not keep *Chronicle* contributors from betraying each other. What kept them from doing so, most of the time, were strong bonds of trust, built from personal interactions as well as the *Chronicle*'s reputation for trustworthiness and resilience. It never published identifying information of its covert operatives, unless those individuals were featured in a story, but even then their *Chronicle* activities were not revealed. And the *Chronicle* editors sometimes emphasized the need for constant vigilance and careful trust judgments about collaborators. Someone who tries to "trace back the whole chain of communication" might be a "police informer" (Issue 5).

Trust worked not only by being abstract and broadly network-directed—the sense that the *Chronicle* and its network were trustworthy—but also by being compartmentalized and personal. It worked at the street-level, facilitating dyadic and small group exchanges by reducing the risks. It enabled individuals to pass what the regime considered subversive information to others in city parks and apartment kitchens. It was based on thousands of separate conclusions that their network partners would not betray them and the movement to the KGB. Positive trust judgments were transitive in that they led participants to others in the network, whom their network partners trusted. If X trusts Y, and Y trusts Z, X will be more likely to take the risk of meeting Z if Y suggests it. Then, the opportunity arises for X and Z to develop their own relationship built on trust. Of course, it was not as if everyone in the large and far-flung network knew and trusted everyone else. Distributors in Leningrad tended not to know contributors in Kuybyshev. A prisoner in a Siberian hell hole knew nothing about the people half a dozen nodes down the line, who dutifully carried reports of his mistreatment back to the editors in Moscow. But information was passed across the network's branches at the dyadic or small group level. It closely approximated what Charles Tilly called a "trust network," held together by "ramified interpersonal connections, consisting mainly of strong ties, within which people set valued, consequential, long-term resources and enterprises at risk to the malfeasance, mistakes, or failures of others." To call it a trust network does not imply that all nodes equally trusted each other. It refers to the thousands of separate links between and among nodes dispersed across the network. *Chronicle* cofounder Alexeyeva believed that was key to its success: "large groups that fostered mutual trust created ideal conditions for the spread of *samizdat*."[65]

Given the KGB's unrelenting focus on editors and their accomplices, trust within their orbits was especially crucial. It was certainly in abundance with the *Chronicle*'s cofounders, who had cultivated strong relationships with each other, and others in the incipient human rights movement in the mid-1960s. Based on his many interviews, Hopkins describes the scene:

> It was small-town, very close, gossipy, everyone knowing one another, everyone privy to the others' thoughts. Galanskov and Ginzburg were friends. Litvinov's

mother knew Ginzburg's mother. Larisa Bogoraz was married to Yuly Daniel. Gorbanevskaya knew Galanskov and Sinyavsky. They were a family unto themselves, not without other associations, but they all saw and knew enough of one another that they could tell the strengths and weaknesses of each, and they knew whom to trust. The close-knit relationship was to prove important later, after the Chronicle became established and the KGB tried to break the organization.

Prudence and comradeship typified those early years of the *Chronicle*. "Tasks were coordinated between friends, and this ensured mutual trust without which organized activities would be impossible under conditions of constant surveillance . . . . Ties of friendship also made penetration by provocateurs difficult." In the movement's earliest years, before the *Chronicle*, and before the shock of Brezhnev's re-Stalinization fully set in, many were not as prudent as they needed to be, Alexeyeva recalled. Once Communist repression came roaring back—and, crucially, once the scale and scope of it was more widely known, thanks in part to the *Chronicle*—more network nodes understood the stakes, and more relied on prudence and their trust judgments. Occasionally, even the editors misjudged new people. For instance, Alexeyeva recalled a woman who volunteered to type for the *Chronicle* but defected to the KGB as soon as she came to grips with what she was asked to do.[66] But she was a rare exception in a dark network robust enough to last fourteen years, in an intensely hostile police state environment.

Dark Networks that Shed Light: Conclusions and Comparisons

The KGB targeted the *Chronicle*'s network because it procured and published illicit information about the Soviet regime's human rights violations against its own citizens. Those violations, the editors liked to point out, contradicted the Soviet Constitution and, later, the Helsinki Accords.[67] A chief purpose of the *Chronicle* was thus to publicize what the network perceived as officials' abuses of public authority. The *Chronicle* also adhered, across its entire run, to strong evidentiary standards, using official documents whenever possible, and printing corrections when previous reports erred. Its reports were surprisingly reliable, given all of the impediments to verifying facts. And while the regime would have disagreed, the information published by the *Chronicle*'s whistleblowing network did not "pose a disproportionate threat to public safety" (chapter 2). Indeed, its reporting relentlessly demonstrated the *regime's* threat to public safety. For that reason, and because the *Chronicle*'s disclosures did not reveal crucial state secrets in bulk, its whistleblowing never exceeded reasonable limits of scale and scope. Indeed, if the *Chronicle* had published ten times as much as it did about torture, the Gulag, political psychiatry, and the like, it still would not have disclosed too many secrets. The *Chronicle*'s work thus fits within the whistleblowing framework discussed in chapter 2. The editors clearly were the recipients, but they also occasionally served as whistleblowers and facilitators, when they wrote about their own run-ins with the regime, or those of their family and friends.

Overall, the network was robust, decentralized, and dark, held together by trust and shared principles. It was robust because it endured the KGB's unrelenting attacks for fourteen years. It was decentralized because contributors passed information to trusted network neighbors, who passed them up branches that snaked through hidden pathways, with nodes of varying centrality, to Moscow. The information eventually arrived to the editors' ramshackle, home-spun, pre-computer center of operations, in grungy kitchens in towering brutalist apartment blocks. It was dark because it needed to conceal itself from the KGB to flourish. Communist Party leaders recognized the *Chronicle* and the wider human rights movement as a threat to its totalitarian regime and utilized a variety of repressive tools to eliminate it. Although *Chronicle* contributors could hold up the Constitution to justify their enterprise, the state had a variety of criminal statutes, such as the "Anti-Soviet Agitation and Propaganda" law, as well as a compliant judiciary. Thus, the *Chronicle* resembled other dark networks like terrorist organizations and drug cartels by being, officially, a criminal enterprise. Yet the *Chronicle*'s particular means and ends made it and similar networks quite different from those other kinds of dark networks. It shares space uneasily in that conceptual category. Most dark networks bring violence and sorrow. The *Chronicle*'s dark network shed light.

So did others across the Communist world. For instance, the samizdat scene in Poland was, in H. Gordon Skilling's account, "mightier than in Czechoslovakia or Soviet Russia," and, we could add, Hungary. Polish samizdat tended to be literary or polemical, but some resembled the *Chronicle*'s fact-based style and approach, most notably *Kommunikat* (Communiqué) and *Biuletyn Informacjny* (Information Bulletin), both published by the multifaceted organization Komitet Obrony Robotnikóws (KOR). They may have not been as robust as the *Chronicle*, but they did survive Polish martial law from December 1981 to June 1983. Future researchers might consider systematically comparing the networks, perhaps starting with Polish samizdat's "looser, more flexible" nature, and KOR's decision to keep its publishing arms "dark" while keeping its charitable and civil society work in the light. In addition, the tamizdat element appears to have been even more vital to the domestic samizdat networks in Poland, Czechoslovakia, and Hungary, compared with those in the Soviet Union, or at least the *Chronicle*. The *Chronicle* did have a very large global readership, thanks to foreign reporters in Moscow as well as Amnesty International, which regularly published tamizdat originals and translations.

But whereas a tamizdat-to-samizdat pipeline was often vital to the domestic distribution in the non-Russian cases, the *Chronicle* network was relatively more self-sufficient.[68]

While this chapter did review some of the *Chronicle*'s international connections, it was not a central feature of the analysis. We saw, for instance, how Amnesty materialized almost right from the onset of the Soviet human rights movement, with a supporting role in the Galanskov-Ginzburg trial protests. And, as noted just above, within a few years, Amnesty would become a key part of *Chronicle*'s international network, smuggling out and then publishing translated versions that reached untold numbers of Westerners. Amnesty also used the *Chronicle* as source material for its reports about the Soviet Union. The two organizations worked together for many reasons, their shared commitment to human rights most important of all. And as the next chapter shows, while Amnesty also developed a powerful whistleblowing network, it did so in a much different way.

Notes

1   Alexander Herzen, *Kolokol*, July 1, 1857, 1, cited in Helen Williams, "Ringing the Bell: Editor-Reader Dialogue in Alexander Herzen's Kolokol," *Book History* 4, no.1 (2001): 115–32, at 120.

2   Joan Baez, "Natalia," *From Every Stage*, 1976.

3   Mark Hopkins, *Russia's Underground Press: The Chronicle of Current Events* (New York: Praeger Publishers, 1983); Andrei Sakharov, Forward to Hopkins, *Russia's Underground Press*, vii; Ann Komaromi, "About Samizdat," Soviet Samizdat Periodicals, University of Toronto Libraries, accessed July 27, 2015, https://samizdat.library.utoronto.ca/content/about-samizdat.

4   H. Gordon Skilling, *Samizdat and an Independent Society in Central and Eastern Europe* (Columbus: Ohio State University Press, 1989), 8 [Alexeyeva quote "mushroom"]; Anthony Lewis, "A Chronicle History," *The New York Times*, February 20, 1971, A27 ["utter lack of melodrama"].

5   Komaromi, "About Samizdat"; Peter Steiner, "Introduction: On Samizdat, Tamizdat, Magnitizdat, and Other Strange Words That Are Difficult to Pronounce," *Poetics Today* 29, no. 4 (Winter 2008): 613–28, at 614 ("information monopoly").

6   Gordon Johnston, "What Is the History of Samizdat?" *Social History* 24, no. 2 (May 1999): 115–33, at 122; Ann Komaromi, "The Material Existence of Soviet Samizdat," *Slavic Review* 63, no. 3 (October 2004): 597–618, at 598; Julius Telesin, "Inside 'Samizdat,'" *Encounter* XL (February 1973): 25; Ann Komaroni, "Samizdat: Material Texts and Extra-Gutenberg Publics," Book Lecture Series on "Samizdat: Material Texts and Extra-Gutenberg Publics," Toronto Review of Books, October 28, 2011 http://www.torontoreviewofbooks.com/2011/10/samizdat.

7   *Kolokol* was first published on July 1, 1857, and continued for ten years. *Pod sud!* issues went out between 1859 and 1862. Although Herzen and his network of writers covered many topics, their initial interests included "Freedom of speech—without censorship!," the abolition of the death penalty, and the emancipation of the serfs. Hopkins, *Russia's Underground Press*, 8, 13, 23; Skilling, *Samizdat and an Independent Society*; Williams "Ringing the Bell"; Friederike Kind-Kovács and Jessie Labov, "Introduction," in Kind-Kovács and Labov, eds., *Samizdat, Tamizdat, and Beyond: Transnational Media during and after Socialism* (New York City: Berghahn Books, 2013), at 4.

8   Hopkins, *Russia's Underground Press*; Skilling, *Samizdat and an Independent Society*; Johnston, "What Is the History of Samizdat?" at 123; George Saunders, *Samizdat: Voices of Soviet Opposition* (New York: Pathfinder Press, 1974), at 8.

9   Ludmilla Alexeyeva, *Soviet Dissent: Contemporary Movements for National, Religious, and Human Rights* (Middletown, CT: Wesleyan University Press), 3–4 ("Half-Awake State of Shock"); Nikita Khrushchev, "Speech to 20th Congress of the C.P.S.U.," February 24–25, 1956, https://www.marxists.org/archive/khrushchev/1956/02/24.htm.

10 Hopkins, *Russia's Underground Press*, 4, 8; John Prados, *Safe for Democracy: The Secret Wars of the CIA* (Lanham, MD: Ivan R. Dee, 2006), 153–5; A. Ross Johnson, *Radio Free Europe and Radio Liberty: The CIA Years and Beyond* (Washington, DC: Woodrow Wilson Center Press, and Stanford, CA: Stanford University Press, 2010).

11 Alexeyeva, *Soviet Dissent*, 4; Hopkins, *Russia's Underground Press*, 8. There were other important parts of the thaw that developed soon after Stalin's death, before Khrushchev took power. Soviet officials released more than a million Gulag prisoners; released the alleged conspirators of the "doctors' plot" against Stalin; executed Lavrentiy Beria, the infamous NKVD chief (and serial rapist), along with five colleagues; and indicted more than sixty senior intelligence officials on charges of treason and espionage. See Robert W. Pringle, "The Intelligence Services of Russia," in Loch K. Johnson, ed., *The Oxford Handbook of National Security Intelligence* (New York: Oxford University Press, 2010), 774–89, at 777.

12 Alexeyeva, *Soviet Dissent, 269–82*; Hopkins, *Russia's Underground Press*, 6–7; Davia Nelson and Nikki Silva, "How Soviet Kitchens Became Hotbeds of Dissent and Culture," *NPR*, April 27, 2014, http://www.npr.org/blogs/thesalt/2014/05/27/314961287/how-soviet-kitchens-became-hotbeds-of-dissent-and-culture.

13 Hopkins, *Russia's Underground Press*, 6–7; Alexeyeva, *Soviet Dissent, 269–82*; Nelson and Silva, "How Soviet Kitchens"; Charles Tilly, *Trust and Rule* (Cambridge University Press, 2005).

14 Peter Steiner, "Introduction: On Samizdat, Tamizdat, Magnitizdat, and Other Strange Words That Are Difficult to Pronounce," *Poetics Today* 29, no. 4 (Winter 2008); Richard J. Bonnie and Svetlana V. Polubinskaya, "Unraveling Soviet Psychiatry," *Journal of Contemporary Legal Issues* 10 (1999): 279.

15 Hopkins, *Russia's Underground Press*.

16 Most works appeared in print, but as the samizdat movement evolved, other forms emerged, including audio tapes of radio broadcasts, speeches, and talks (*magnitizdat*, as is magnetic tape). People also cut and swapped rock and jazz records, often substituting old X-ray film for scarce, costly vinyl (*roentgenizdat*). Ann Komaroni, Soviet Samizdat Database, https://samizdat.library.utoronto.ca/; Johnston, "What Is the History of Samizdat?"; Steiner "Introduction: On Samizdat," 616; Josh Rothman, "Unearthing Russia's X-Ray Records," *Brainiac (Boston Globe)*, March 16, 2011, http://www.boston.com/bostonglobe/ideas/brainiac/2011/03/unearthing_russ.html; Benjamin Nathans, "The Disenchantment of Socialism: Soviet Dissidents, Human Rights, and the New Global Morality," in Jan Eckel and Samuel Moyn, eds., *The Breakthrough: Human Rights in the 1970s* (Philadelphia: University of Pennsylvania Press, 2013), 33–48, at 36; Alexandr Solzhenitsyn, Nobel Lecture, 1970, http://www.nobelprize.org/nobel_prizes/literature/laureates/1970/solzhenitsyn-lecture.html;

17 Pringle, "The Intelligence Services of Russia," 777.

18 Kind-Kovács and Labov, *Samizdat*; Friederike Kind-Kovács, *Written Here, Published There: How Underground Literature Crossed the Iron Curtain* (Budapest, Hungary: Central European University Press, 2014); Christopher Andrew and Vasili Mitrokhin, *The Sword and the Shield: The Mitrokhin Archive and the Secret History of the KGB* (New York: Basic Books, 1999), 307–11.

19 Khrushchev's reform revised earlier "anti-Soviet" laws from the Stalin era, such as Article 58. Some saw the change as evidence of liberalization, but historians of the period tend to interpret it as "linguistic change instead of real change." Article 72 is also relevant here ("Organizational Activity of Especially Dangerous Crimes of the State and Also Participation in Anti-Soviet Organizations"). Anne Applebaum, *Gulag: A History* (New York: Doubleday, 2003), 530; Benjamin Nathans, "The Dictatorship of Reason: Aleksandr Vol'pin and the Idea

of Human Rights under 'Developed Socialism,'" *Slavic Review* 66, no. 4 (December 2007): 630–3; Harold Joseph Berman, *Soviet Criminal Law and Procedure: The RSFSR Codes* (Cambridge, MA: Harvard University Press, 1972), 81–2; Andrew and Mitrokhin, *The Sword and the Shield*, 307–11.

20 Stephen V. Bittner, *The Many Lives of Khrushchev's Thaw: Experience and Memory in Moscow's Arbat* (Ithaca, NY: Cornell University Press, 2008), 175–8.

21 Alexeyeva, who attended the protest, estimated a number lower than 200 participants and argued that the KGB must have known about the protest in advance because of the fliers distributed at local colleges. However, other historians, with data available after the Soviet Union's collapse, estimated a relatively higher number. Soviet Constitution Day was celebrated on December 5 from 1936 until 1977, when officials changed the date to December 7. See Alexeyeva, *Soviet Dissent*, 274–9. See also Bittner, *The Many Lives of Khrushchev's Thaw*, 176 ["action so daring..."]; Andrew and Mitrokhin, *The Sword and the Shield*, 307; Jan-Werner Muller, *Contesting Democracy* (New Haven: Yale University Press, 2011), 228. On social movement framing, see Sidney Tarrow, *Power in Movement: Social Movements and Contentious Politics* (New York: Cambridge University Press, 1998).

22 Steiner, "Introduction: On Samizdat," 615.

23 Andrew and Mitrokhin, *The Sword and the Shield*, 309; Leopold Labedz and Max Hayward, *On Trial: The Case of Sinyavsky (Tertz) and Daniel (Arzhak)* (London: Collins and Harvill Press, 1967), 306.

24 Estimates of total Great Purge executions vary, but scholars have recently circled around the number 680,000 for the years 1937–1938. Robert Conquest, *The Great Terror: A Reassessment* (Cambridge University Press, 2008); Allen C. Lynch, *How Russia Is Not Ruled: Reflections on Russian Political Development* (Cambridge University Press, 2005), 68; Michael Ellman, "Soviet Repression Statistics: Some Comments," *Europe-Asia Studies* 54, no. 7 (2002): 1151–72; Berman, *Soviet Criminal Law*, 81–2; Robert Hornsby, *Protest, Reform and Repression in Khrushchev's Soviet Union* (Cambridge University Press, 2013), 280–1; Vladislav Zubok, *Zhivago's Children: The Last Russian Intelligentsia* (Cambridge, MA: Belknap Press, 2009), 259–96; Andrew and Mitrokhin, *The Sword and the Shield*, 309; Reuters, "2 Soviet Writers Deny Slander Charge in Trial," *Toledo Blade*, February 10, 1966; Alexeyeva, *Soviet Dissent*, 277.

25 Alexeyeva, *Soviet Dissent*, 274–9; Fred Coleman, *The Decline and Fall of the Soviet Empire: Forty Years That Shook the World, from Stalin to Yeltsin* (New York: Macmillan, 1997), 97. One of several individuals at the trial who compiled and then distributed the transcript was Boris Vakhtin, who was affiliated with the Union of Writers. Bittner, *The Many Lives of Khrushchev's Thaw*, 201.

26 Geoffrey Hosking, "The Twentieth Century: In Search of New Ways, 1953–80," in Charles Moser, ed., *The Cambridge History of Russian Literature* (Cambridge University Press, 1989), 520–94, at 536.

27 Bukovsky worked with two co-organizers, Vadim Delaunay and Evgeny Kushev, to stage a protest in Pushkin Square in January 1967. They focused on the arrests, as well as illiberal Soviet statutes. [These references support the linked and previous paragraphs.] Alexeyeva, *Soviet Dissent*, 280; Pavel Mikhaĭlovich Litvinov, *The Demonstration in Pushkin Square: The Trial Records with Commentary and an Open Letter* (Boston, MA: Gambit, 1969); Pavel Mikhaĭlovich Litvinov, *The Trial of the Four* (New York: Viking Press, 1972), 227; Bohdan R. Bociurkiw, "The Voices of Dissent and the Visions of Gloom," *The Russian Review* 29, no. 3 (July 1970): 328–35; Jerry F. Hough and Merle Fainsod, *How the Soviet Union Is Governed* (Cambridge, MA: Harvard University Press, 1979), 283; "Off with the Mask," *Time*, January 19, 1968; Kind-Kovács, *Written Here, Published There*; Gerd-Rainer Horn, *The Spirit of '68: Rebellion in Western Europe and North America, 1956–1976* (Oxford University Press, 2007).

28 "Telegram from Moscow," *The Times* (London), January 13, 1968, reprinted in *Index of Censorship* 31, no. 2 (2002): 6–7.

29 The full list of "Telegram" signatories, in the order they were published: Cecil Day-Lewis, Yehudi Menuhin, W. H. Auden, Henry Moore, Stephen Spender, A. J. Ayer, Bertrand Russell,

Julian Hartley, Mary McCarthy, J. B. Priestley, Jacquetta Hawkes, Paul Scofield, Igor Stravinsky, Stuart Hampshire, Maurice Bowra, and Mrs. George Orwell. "Telegram from Moscow"; Peter Reddaway, ed., *Uncensored Russia: Protest and Dissent in the Soviet Union: The Unofficial Moscow Journal, A Chronicle of Current Events* (American Heritage Press, 1972); Peter Reddaway, commentary on *Chronicle of Current Events*, Issue 1, April 30, 1968, *A Chronicle of Current Events*, John Crowfoot and Tanya Lipovskaia, trans., eds., A Chronicle of Current Events, accessed March 23, 2016, https://chronicle6883.wordpress.com/2013/09/26/commentary-no-1.

30   According to one translation of the first Chronicle issue, "After sentence was passed and the trial had ended, a series of collective and individual letters was addressed to Soviet judicial, government and Party authorities as well as to organs of the press (mainly in reply to articles which had appeared in certain newspapers). The total number of people who have signed such letters, up to the present, amounts to some seven hundred." The dissident and scholar Andrei Amalrik in 1970 wrote that the actual number was 738. Andrei Amalrik, *Will the Soviet Union Survive until 1984?* (New York: Harper and Row, 1970), 15; Marshall S. Shatz, *Soviet Dissent in Historical Perspective* (Cambridge University Press, 1980), 138; "1.2 Protests about the Trial," *Chronicle of Current Events*, Issue #1, April 30, 1968, available at Crowfoot and Lipovskaia, eds., *A Chronicle of Current Events*, https://chronicle6883.wordpress.com/2013/09/25/1-2-protests-about-the-trial; Alexeyeva, *Soviet Dissent*, 280; Bittner, *The Many Lives of Khrushchev's Thaw*. The Soviet Constitution of 1936 promised Soviet citizens a plethora of civil rights and liberties, including freedom of conscience, freedom of religious worship, freedom of speech, freedom of the press, freedom of assembly, freedom of street processions and demonstrations, the right to unite in public organizations, the inviolability of the person, the inviolability of the homes of citizens, and privacy of correspondence. Moreover, if the state had kept its commitments, it would have provided the samizdat crowd with "printing presses, stocks of paper, public buildings, the streets, communications facilities and other material requisites for the exercise of these rights." Of course, if the state had kept its commitments, there would have been no need for an underground publishing movement.

31   Hopkins, *Russia's Underground Press*, 7–12, 39–40; Sakharov, "Foreword," vii.

32   Hopkins, *Russia's Underground Press*, 7–12, 39–40.

33   Ibid.

34   Reflecting on the fortieth anniversary of the first issue, Alexeyeva allowed herself some bombast: "I have done a lot in the human rights movement. But I think perhaps the most important thing I did was that I typed out the first issue of the 'Chronicle.' It was an epoch-making thing." "Russia: Chronicling a Samizdat Legend," *Radio Free Europe Radio Free Liberty*, May 3, 2008, http://www.rferl.org/content/article/1109670.html; Hopkins, *Russia's Underground Press*, 1, 2, 7–12; Nathans, "The Disenchantment of Socialism," 36; Douglas Martin, "Natalya Gorbanevskaya, 77, Soviet Dissident and Poet," *The New York Times*, December 2, 2013, A31.

35   The Soviet Union abstained from the United Nations (UN) General Assembly vote and forced the other Communist countries to follow. UN General Assembly, 2081 (XX), International Year for Human Rights, December 12, 1963.

36   *Chronicle of Current Events*, Issue #1; Google Translate provides a slightly different version of the original Russian from http://www.memo.ru/history/diss/chr/index.htm.

37   "'Going to That Demonstration Was a Selfish Move: I Wanted to Have a Clean Conscience': Natalia Gorbanevskaya in Her Own Words," Institute of Modern Russia, December 4, 2013, http://imrussia.org/en/society/614-going-to-that-demonstration-was-a-selfish-move-i-wanted-to-have-a-clean-conscience-natalia-gorbanevskaya-in-her-own-words; Geoffrey A. Hosking, *The Awakening of the Soviet Union* (Cambridge, MA: Harvard University Press, 1991), 46.

38   Hopkins, *Russia's Underground Press*, 12–13, 24–5, 169–171; Alexeyeva, *Soviet Dissent*, 286; Hosking, *The Awakening of the Soviet Union*, 46.

39   Alexeyeva, *Soviet Dissent*, 286.

40   Ibid.; Hopkins, *Russia's Underground Press*.

41   Hopkins, *Russia's Underground Press*, 12–13, 24–5, 169–171; "5.6 Human Rights Year Continues," *Chronicle of Current Events*, Issue 5, December 31, 1968, ed., trans., Crowfoot

and Lipovskaia, A Chronicle of Current Events, accessed January 25, 2017, https://chronic
leofcurrentevents.net/2013/09/21/5-6-human-rights-year-continues; Alexeyeva, *Soviet Dissent*,
286; Hosking, *The Awakening of the Soviet Union*, 46.

[42] It is worth noting that some of the information that appeared in the *Chronicle* came from
other *samizdat*. This is not too different from how news sources operate in democratic societies. For example, U.S. publications utilize information from other publications. Shatz, *Soviet
Dissent*, 138; Amalrik, *Will the Soviet Union Survive*; Applebaum, *Gulag*, 30–31; Hopkins,
Russia's Underground Press, 12–13, 24–5, 169–171; Chronicle, issue #5; Alexeyeva, *Soviet
Dissent*, 286; Hosking, *The Awakening of the Soviet Union*, 46.

[43] Recall Bogoraz was a probable founder. "Repressive Measures in Response to Protests about
Trial," *Chronicle of Current Events*, April 30, 1968, ed., trans., Crowfoot and Lipovskaia,
accessed January 20, 2017, https://chronicleofcurrentevents.net/2013/09/28/1-3-repression-in
-response-to-protests-about-trial; *Chronicle of Current Events*, June 30, 1968; Hopkins, *Russia's Underground Press*, 24–5, 169–171.

[44] Hopkins, *Russia's Underground Press*, 12–13.

[45] Committee for State Security [KGB] report #1372-A, June 11, 1968, trans. George Sklyar,
Vladimir Bukovsky Soviet Archives, accessed January 20, 2017, http://bukovsky-archives.
net/pdfs/dis60/dis6814a.pdf, http://bukovsky-archives.net/pdfs/dis60/0030_dis6814a-Eng-
Sklyar.pdf.

[46] Hopkins, *Russia's Underground Press*, 39–40.

[47] Ellen Barry, "Tested by Many Foes, Passion of a Russian Dissident Endures," *The New York
Times*, January 12, 2010, A1.

[48] Sakharov, "Foreword," vii; *Chronicle of Current Events*, December 31, 1968 (op. cit.).

[49] Sean F. Everton, *Disrupting Dark Networks* (Cambridge University Press, 2012), 12–13, 398;
Charles Kadushin, *Understanding Social Networks: Concepts, Theories, and Findings* (New
York: Oxford University Press, 2012).

[50] Paul Baran, "On Distributed Communications Networks," *IEEE Transactions on Communications Systems* 12, no. 1 (1964): 1–9.

[51] Hosking, *The Awakening*, 46.

[52] Alexeyeva, *Soviet Dissent*, 284.

[53] Gorbanevskaya was arrested under Article 190-1 ("continuous sluggish schizophrenia,"
"unsound mind"). Hopkins, *Russia's Underground Press*, 40–44; Alexeyeva, *Soviet Dissent*, 282–3, 311–12; Komaromi, Samizdat collection, University of Toronto, accessed April
6, 2016, http://samizdat.library.utoronto.ca/content/khronika-tekushchikh-sobytii; Joshua
Rubenstein, "The Enduring Voice of the Soviet Dissidents," *Columbia Journalism Review*,
September–October 1978, 32–9; "11.9 The Arrest of Natalya Gorbanevskaya," *Chronicle
of Current Events*, Issue #11, December 31, 1969, trans. Crowfoot and Lipovskaia, The
Chronicle of Current Events, January 25, 2017, https://chronicleofcurrentevents.net/2013/10/
07/11-9-the-arrest-of-natalya-gorbanevskaya.

[54] Telnikov was a well-connected activist, a friend of Bukovsky, and a Soviet Jew who was able
to move to Israel after facing years of repression. See Hopkins, *Russia's Underground Press*,
42; Colin Shindler, "Vladimir Bukovsky's Fight for Harassed Jews," *Jewish Observer*, March
1, 1977; "15.1 The Trial of Natalya Gorbanevskaya," *Chronicle of Current Events*, Issue #15,
August 31, 1970, trans. Crowfoot and Lipovskaia, The Chronicle of Current Events, January
25, 2017, https://chronicleofcurrentevents.net/2014/05/01/15-1-the-trial-of-natalya-gorban
evskaya-2/; "News in Brief," *Chronicle of Current Events*, Issue #16, October 31, 1970, trans.
Crowfoot and Lipovskaia, The Chronicle of Current Events, accessed January 25, 2017, https
://chronicleofcurrentevents.net/2014/05/16/16-10-news-in-brief.

[55] As far as I can tell, the only compilation of contributing editors' names appears on Wikipedia's
entry on the *Chronicle*, which counts forty-nine names. It is likely incomplete, and possibly
erroneous, given Wikipedia's format (e.g., I could add my name to the list without anyone
noticing for a while). That is why I chose not to publish that list, even if it includes many verified contributing editors like Alexeyeva, Yakir, and others.

[56] David A. Lake and Wendy H. Wong, "The Politics of Networks: Interests, Power, and Human
Rights Norms," in Miles Kahler, ed., *Networked Politics: Agency, Power, and Governance*
(Ithaca, NY: Cornell University Press, 2009), 127–50, at 129.

[57] *Chronicle* editors, as well as connected journalists from the London *Times* and *The New York Times*, concluded that the KGB changed its anti-*Chronicle* strategy on December 30, 1971. See Reddaway, *Uncensored Russia*, available athttps://chronicleofcurrentevents.net/2016/03/30/24-2-searches-and-arrests-in-january/; Emma Gilligan, *Defending Human Rights in Russia: Sergei Kovalyov, Dissident and Human Rights Commissioner, 1969-2003* (London: Routledge, 2004), 31; Shatz, *Soviet Dissent*, 132. On case 24, see *Chronicle* issue 28 and issue 29.

[58] "28.0 To Readers of the Chronicle," *Chronicle of Current Events*, Issue 28, December 31, 1972, published on May 17, 1974, The Chronicle of Current Events., trans. Crowfoot and Lipovskaia, The Chronicle of Current Events, accessed January 25, 2017, https://chronicleofcurrentevents.net/2013/09/27/28-0-to-readers-of-the-chronicle.

[59] Everton, *Disrupting Dark Networks*, xxv, 399; Jörg Raab and H. Brinton Milward, "Dark Networks as Problems," *Journal of Public Administration Research and Theory* 13, no. 4 (2003): 413–39; H. Brinton Milward and Jörg Raab, "Dark Networks as Organizational Problems: Elements of a Theory 1," *International Public Management Journal* 9, no. 3 (2006): 333–60; Michael Kenney, "Turning to the 'Dark Side': Coordination, Exchange, and Learning in Criminal Networks," in Kahler, ed., *Networked Politics*, 79–102; Miles Kahler, "Collective Action and Clandestine Networks: The Case of Al Qaeda," in Kahler, ed., *Networked Politics*, 103–26.

[60] Hopkins, *Russia's Underground Press*, 26–7; Vladimir V. Kara-Murza, Interview with Vladimir Bukovsky, *They Chose Freedom: The Story of Soviet Dissidents*, Episode One: The Awakening, http://imrussia.org/en/project/534-they-chose-freedom-the-story-of-soviet-dissidents; Hosking, *The Awakening*, 46; *Chronicle of Current Events*, May 20, 1972, Issue #25, trans. Crowfoot and Lipovskaia, The Chronicle of Current Events, accessed January 25, 2017, https://chronicleofcurrentevents.net/no-25-20-may-1972; *Chronicle of Current Events*, August 15, 1977, Issue #46, trans. Crowfoot and Lipovskaia, The Chronicle of Current Events, accessed January 25, 2017, https://chronicleofcurrentevents.net/no-46-15-august-1977; *Chronicle of Current Events*, August 3, 1980, Issue #57, trans. Crowfoot and Lipovskaia, The Chronicle of Current Events, accessed January 25, 2017, https://chronicleofcurrentevents.net/no-57-3-august-1980.

[61] Lake and Wong, "The Politics of Networks," 129.

[62] Chronicle issue 28, 35, in *A Chronicle of Current Events: Numbers 28-31*, original Russian translated by Amnesty International, London, May 1975, Amnesty International Publications; Chronicle issue #7 April 30, 1969, translated https://chronicle6883.wordpress.com/2013/09/21/7-14-on-the-reliability-and-accuracy-of-information-in-the-chronicle; Reddaway, *Uncensored Russia*, available at https://chronicle6883.wordpress.com/2013/09/26/commentary-no-7.

[63] Everton, *Disrupting Dark Networks*, xxvi.

[64] As with any human enterprise, other motivations for participation beyond ideology, shared principles, and a sense of solidarity—such as ambition, domination, profit, and so on—were present but were either nonexistent or non-interfering. If more narrowly self-interested motivations did appear, they were probably ignored or shunned enough to stop their recurrence, given the amount of unity in the movement overall. Andrew and Mitrokhin, *The Sword and the Shield*, 311–17; Anatoly Koryagin, "Toward Truly Outlawing Torture," *Science* 241, no. 4871 (September 9, 1988): 1277; Gordon B. Smith, *Reforming the Russian Legal System* (Cambridge University Press, 1996), 65; Darius Rejali, *Torture and Democracy* (Princeton University Press, 2009), 394; Alexeyeva, *Soviet Dissent*, 282–3, 311–12; Hopkins, *Russia's Underground Press*, 47–65.

[65] Tilly, *Trust and Rule*, 41; Everton, *Disrupting Dark Networks*, 35; Alexeyeva, *Soviet Dissent*, 269–70.

[66] Hopkins, *Russia's Underground Press*, 6–7; Alexeyeva, *Soviet Dissent*, 269–70, 283–5.

[67] On the importance of the Helsinki Accords, see John Lewis Gaddis, *The Cold War: A New History* (New York: Penguin, 2006). See also Reddaway, *Uncensored Russia*, https://chronicle6883.wordpress.com/2013/09/26/commentary-no-7/; Hopkins, *Russia's Underground Press*, 13.

[68] On Polish samizdat, see Skilling, *Samizdat and an Independent Society*, 13–4 ["mightier"]; Johnston, "What Is the History of Samizdat?" 122; Barbara J. Falk, *The Dilemmas of*

Dissidence in East-Central Europe: Citizen Intellectuals and Philosopher Kings (Budapest: Central European University Press, 2003), ch. 2; Steiner, "Introduction: On Samizdat," 615. On the fact-based nature of early Polish samizdat, Stöcker writes that editors "initially focused on informing the domestic public of the brutality of the regime's police forces and the arbitrariness of the courts." Fredrik Lars Stöcker, "The Baltic Connection: Transnational Samizdat Networks between Émigrés in Sweden and the Democratic Opposition in Poland," in Kind-Kovács and Labov, eds., *Samizdat, Tamizdat, and Beyond*, 51–69, at 58. On Hungarian samizdat, see Johnston, "What Is the History of Samizdat?"; Falk, *Dilemmas*, ch. 4; Bill Lomax, "Independent Publishing in Hungary," *Index on Censorship* 12, no. 2 (1983); Bill Lomax, "Samizdat under Siege," *Labour Focus on Eastern Europe* 6, nos. 1–2 (1983).

Chapter 5

The "Curious Grapevine" in Reverse

Human Rights Organizations' Whistleblowing Networks

Two days before the United Nations approved the Universal Declaration of Human Rights in 1948, Eleanor Roosevelt, the Declaration's principal champion, optimistically predicted that its message would spread across the world, even to the millions trapped under "totalitarian regimes which completely control the means of information." "Though a curious grapevine," she wrote, "this information may seep in even when governments are not so anxious for it."[1] Roosevelt's metaphor was apt in illustrating the norm-spreading social networks that snake through and across countries. It also works well by describing the networks that transmit tips about human rights violations to global human rights organizations (HROs). This chapter focuses on the latter.

How do HROs collect evidence about violations in countries whose "governments are not so anxious for" that kind of work? We have learned already about how some human rights activists have done it. Contributors to the *Chronicle of Current Events* adapted its whistleblowing network to the internal conditions of the Soviet Union and forged links with external groups, including Amnesty International (AI). The challenge now is to probe more deeply into the information extraction methods of global HROs who do the lion's share of building and maintaining human rights whistleblowing networks around the world. Research into this subject is complicated in part because HROs conceal some sources and methods to protect vulnerable witnesses and victims. Fortunately, enough information is available to theorize how HRO whistleblowing networks operate.

The chapter proceeds by first contrasting two types of monitoring that global HROs might employ and then showing why they rely on a reactive "fire alarm" approach, rather than a more proactive "police patrol" approach. Second, it outlines the likely structure of an HRO's whistleblowing network, including the official parts of an HRO, as well as the sections that have no formal affiliation. Finally, it shows why some of the more obvious and overt information extraction methods HROs use, such as fact-finding investigations, have ancillary benefits for the mission of learning about and reporting on violations.

Human Rights Monitoring: Fire Alarms and Tips, Not Global Police Patrols and Spies

How do large global HROs like AI and Human Rights Watch (HRW) learn about human rights violations? One possibility is. that they put lots of "eyes on the ground," especially in places more prone to abuses. Not only would monitors, distributed around the world, make information collection direct and widespread, but the presence of monitors would have a beneficial deterrent effect, at least for the set of potential perpetrators who fear sanctions and/or reputational damages.

Global monitoring like that might be ideal, but it is obviously infeasible. First, financing a global army of monitors is expensive. HROs would need countless people for routine, proactive, omnipresent "police patrol" monitoring.[2] Even if HROs restricted the target area to conflict zones, authoritarian regimes, and illiberal democracies, they would still need a huge number of monitors, given how large a portion of the globe that set encompasses.

Second, repressive rulers "are not so anxious for" (Roosevelt) human rights monitors all over their countries. While HROs are unlikely to care about dictators' feelings, inserting monitors into places crawling with "anxious" power holders endangers them. The last thing an HRO wants to do is to *increase* the prevalence of human rights violations. Plus, an influx of conspicuous monitors might exacerbate an already dangerous, delicate political environment, by antagonizing power holders. Besides, repressive regimes would likely turn away the throngs of human rights monitors when they arrived at the international airport's passport control desk.

Sending covert, nonconspicuous monitors—in essence, spies—would in some ways solve that problem. However, HROs probably do not do much spying, in part because of the high costs. To evade capture and to fool anxious dictators, HROs would need to become de facto intelligence agencies, their work consumed by the creation and maintenance of cover stories, the protection of covert agents, and all of the other day-to-day duties of spy services. They would also need to develop good training programs, a costly challenge in and of itself. Plus, people drawn to human rights advocacy and analysis probably differ in important ways from people drawn to espionage. The self-selection problem would make training all the more difficult. Even if HROs could develop competent spies, hostile government officials and other perpetrators have the motivation, and often the capacity, to identify covert operators. Interrogation of a captured HRO spy might endanger others in the network. Furthermore, the work of HROs would become even more difficult and dangerous if government officials knew they used spies. Doing so would certainly inhibit the development of strategic working relationships with repressive regimes (see the argument below). Overall, while some HROs might use spies, there is no evidence that they do, and there are very good reasons they do not.

Although HROs might first receive information about violations from its own staffers, they more often get it from sources who reside outside of the organization's formal structure. The process likely resembles an active "fire alarm" monitoring model, where the HRO "listens" for tips that come through its large and open network, and then responds with an investigation if the information is deemed credible and corresponds with the organization's strategic interests.[3] While an individual who has evidence of a human rights violation might contact an HRO staffer directly, she is at least as likely to share it with others—clerics, lawyers, doctors, labor union leaders, and so on—given the limited accessibility and number of organizational insiders. The recipient of the tip may or may not already be a node in the HRO's network or linked to one personally, professionally, or politically. If all goes well, at some point along a (possibly long) chain of connections, an HRO staffer picks up the information. In general, it is likely that global HROs build and structure their networks in part to maximize tip-reporting opportunities, to hear alarms from individuals who may or may not live where the organization has a formal presence.

The individuals who first sound the alarms, the ones who introduce tips into HROs' sprawling networks, are victims and/or witnesses. The latter is a broad category, including those who observe human rights violations with their own eyes, as they happen, as well as those who encounter evidence of abuse after the fact. For example, a woman might find her fiancée's smart phone in the bushes, which contains a video documenting a militia's rampage through the village before troops abducted him and fled. Or, a doctor in a dictatorship might treat a democracy activist who was just released from jail and see clear signs of torture. Using the rough model from above, we can imagine how that kind of information moves along the grapevine. The doctor treats the torture victim and encounters other patients with similar cuts and bruises. He sends his clinical notes, including pictures of the injuries, to a lawyer friend in the capital. The lawyer then contacts someone she knows at the nearest AI office, who soon consults with colleagues at AI's International Secretariat in London. AI then launches an investigation and later releases a report. All of the individuals who passed the evidence along comprise a branch of AI's "hub and spokes" network.[4] The operative network branch may have already existed, or it may have been constructed spontaneously in response to the incident. It might endure, or it might wither away.

While HROs do not actively monitor the globe in omnipresent "police patrols," tips do sometimes enter the organization's orbit directly. One of the reasons the large HROs have many in-country offices is to create access opportunities. AI, for instance, has nineteen "regional offices" and sixty-four "sections," which operate under the International Secretariat in London. In addition, AI supports its "groups" and "networks," such as the Health Professionals Network and the Legal Support Network.[5] HRW, by contrast, has its headquarters in New York City, and twenty field offices.[6] Those numbers suggest the large HROs' impressive global reach, but the distribution of offices and personnel still leaves most of the world uncovered and unmonitored. Even in the cities and countries in which they reside, their coverage is limited to a specific region. These limitations have remained even as HROs have expanded their reach, as with former AI Secretary-General Salil Shetty's "closer to the ground" initiative.

Individuals working with any of those locations may not perform prototypical police patrol monitoring, but they do get out of the office sometimes. When moving around the country for business or personal reasons, HRO staffers sometimes encounter people with tips, as illustrated in this hypothetical example from the United Nations' Office of the High Commissioner for Human Rights (OHCHR) Training Manual on Human Rights Monitoring:

> This afternoon, whilst visiting a neighbourhood in a town near your office, a young man approaches and asks if he can speak privately with you. You agree to meet him in a few minutes in a more secure location. The young man asks for your help and advises you of the following incident, which has reportedly occurred in his home village a few kilometres away. The young man states that this morning his sister returned home after being missing for five days.[7]

If deemed credible, that kind of tip prompts further investigation, which in turn can yield additional tips.

HROs also routinely monitor the news media for tips or for corroborative information. They also utilize new technologies. For example, AI has used satellite imagery to decipher and then disclose details about North Korea's political prison camps and to analyze Boko Haram attacks on Nigerian villages by comparing before and after images (figure 5.1).[8] In addition, the fast developing field of open source and social media investigations, which use social media platforms (e.g., Facebook and Twitter) and mapping technologies (e.g., Google Maps), will become increasingly useful to HROs.[9]

HROs have also invested in technologies that provide new access opportunities for individuals with tips. AI, for example, released a Panic Button mobile phone app in 2014 (the metaphorical "Fire Alarm" would have been confusing for some users). It ran disguised in the background so that an individual facing hostile forces could press "panic"—that is, the power button repeatedly—which sent an emergency text message with GPS coordinates to trusted contacts saved

13° 6'33.77"N, 13°52'34.98"E   DigitalGlobe False-Color Infrared Imagery, January 2, 2015

13° 6'33.77"N, 13°52'34.98"E   DigitalGlobe False-Color Infrared Imagery, January 7, 2015

FIGURE 5.1 AI Satellite Images Showing the Destruction of a Nigerian Village by Boko Haram. *Source*: Amnesty International, Creative Commons License 4.0.

to the phone's memory. Presumably, the "panic" text (or some version of it) and related data moved upward through AI's hierarchy, giving section staffers new leads to investigate. AI made its app freely available to Android users and invested (with Google support) in training and awareness programs in El Salvador, Philippines, and Sudan, among other places. The app's developer announced its retirement in 2017 due to resource shortfalls.[10]

Tip-reporting technologies can offer victims and witnesses relatively inexpensive and convenient ways of communicating with HROs. But these benefits need to be weighed against any new retaliation risks the technologies pose. While they may offer security features, they probably cannot withstand the surveillance and investigative capabilities of strong, willful state and nonstate actors, who, for whatever reason, might target victims, witnesses, and their allies.

Overall, any new technology offers risks and benefits, and HROs should conduct systematic risk assessments of any new tools. Some of those risks, however, will look like old wine in new bottles. Officials could torture, for example, panic button users for their PIN numbers to access their contact lists, just as they could torture others for similar information stored in their brains. Or, authoritarians might block access to AI's website, much like they could prevent the distribution of AI reports in hard copy.

Other Nodes in the Network

The analysis so far has conceived of HROs as being a part of large networks that afford many access points, including physical offices, email addresses, phone numbers, panic button servers, and so on. While a scarcity of financial and human resources limits how many people and machines can collect and investigate tips, the HROs have an impressive reach. This all remains true, but it is a truncated, incomplete model.

The focus on victims, witnesses, downstream nodes, and HRO employees has provided a too narrow depiction of human rights whistleblowing networks. Missing from the model are other organizations, including not only other HROs but also government agencies, labor unions, political parties, legal organizations, and religious associations. AI notes the importance of these other organizations in its very brief summary of its methodology for collecting and investigating tips:

> Our research teams focus on particular countries and themes and investigate reports of human rights abuses, corroborating information from a wide range of sources and contacts. They monitor newspapers, websites and other media outlets. Amnesty International often sends fact-finding missions to assess matters on the spot. We also receive information from many sources, including from prisoners, human rights defenders and others who suffer human rights abuses; lawyers and journalists; refugees; religious bodies and community workers; diplomats; and humanitarian agencies.

A more complete list would also include individuals, such as police officers, prison guards, customs officers, diplomats, labor union officials, student group leaders, academics, archivists, psychologists, weapons and ballistics experts, environmental toxicologists, DNA analysts, computer modelers, and healthcare workers and medical specialists, which by one tally included "internists, pediatricians, family practitioners, surgeons, trauma specialists, epidemiologists, pathologists, forensic anthropologists, radiologists, odontologists, nurses, and social workers."[11] Some serve the enterprise as sources of new information, while others work as corroborators or other kinds of facilitators.

When all of the interpersonal and interorganizational links a large HRO like AI continuously adds to its network are included, the true number of nodes is probably in the millions. When those organizations' and individuals' links are added, the number of potential whistleblowing contributors grows staggeringly larger. Each organization has its own members, as well as links with other organizations, which have their own members and links. While most nodes are not in constant contact with an HRO, tips can move quickly through the global network—especially so with the Internet but also in the pre-Internet era, as later examples illustrate. If AI USA maintains a link to large organization X, say, a large American labor union which maintains links with Y, a labor union in a small developing country, tips that move from Y to X can be channeled to AI. The AI USA archive contains many letters and telegrams showing this kind of interorganizational correspondence, some of it conveying new information about human rights violations, some of it coordinating multilateral responses.[12]

As the number of NGOs in the developing world mushroomed in the last part of the twentieth century (the developed world was already well covered), the linkage and communication possibilities became enormous. As AI and HRW connected with those NGOs, their networks greatly expanded, incorporating previously excluded locations, where tip-reporting was once very difficult. There were already approximately 35,000 NGOs in the developing world in the late 1990s. Approximately twenty years later, the number had jumped into the millions. India alone had 3.1 million NGOs in 2015, according to a government estimate.[13] Of course, not all NGOs focus on human rights or reside in any permanent way along the human rights grapevine. Still, the thousands of interorganizational links within the HRO/NGO ecosystem, held together with relatively cheap Internet, smart phone, and satellite technologies, has provided HROs with an immensely valuable information resource.

While HROs cannot be everywhere at once, the enormity and connectivity of their larger networks goes a long way toward correcting for biases and resource limitations (e.g., the scarcity of in-country offices and the opportunity costs of focusing on selected problems or countries which keeps HROs from observing others). As the number and global distribution of NGOs continues to increase, and as those NGOs develop and maintain links with each other, the geographic biases in human rights reporting should decrease, and the quantity and reach of tips should increase. Although HROs may not employ as many investigators as they might wish, they have access to an ever-growing network of information providers.

Furthermore, there are countless other individuals, some of them donors or dues-paying members, who funnel information to the HROs and their partners. AI, for example, claimed over two million members in 2016, although that number appeared to merge official members and contributing "supporters." AI also boasted of five million additional "activists who strengthen our calls for justice," presumably all of the people signed up for Urgent Action Network alerts, or affiliates of AI's long-running networks (e.g., the Health Professionals Network). Some members and supporters do little more than send checks and receive newsletters or alerts, such as the Urgent Action Network, which began in 1973. But AI members and supporters have also supplied tips.

For example, a woman from Lakewood, Ohio, sent a letter to AI USA Executive Director David Hawk on May 18, 1975, that begins: "Dear Mr. Hawk, Moved by the story of disorientation, separation, torture of members of Chilean family of five whom I have known for 10 years and whom I have visited in their home in Santiago four years ago, I have sought help from three members of [President Ford's] U.S. Latin American Commission," who recommended AI. She offered the tip, requested AI's help, and promised to provide more details in a subsequent letter.[14] The exact nature of her relationship with AI was not clear, but the letter clearly demonstrates that AI kept its communication channels open to individual tip-providers, including in its early years.

Another example of a tip-providing individual comes from a September 21, 1981, telegram from "JOAN DARBY, AIUSA" to "UGANDAN RESEARCHER" [caps in original], apparently at AI's International Secretariat. The telegram details how she received the tip: "RECVD CALL FROM MAN WHOSE FATHER WAS ABDUCTED. MR. ROKONA WAS COUNTY CHIEF IN MADI DISTRICT. RETIRED 1974. DUE TO RAIDS BY UGANDAN SOLDIERS IN HOME TOWN, MOVED THIS PAST FEBRUARY TO CATHOLIC MISSION AT ADJUMANIA. WAS KIDNAPPED FROM MISSION SEPT. 7TH AND TAKEN TO SUDAN BY 'GUERILLAS [sic] WHO OPERATE ON BORDER BETWEEN THE 2 COUNTRIES.' THIS IS ONLY INFO I HAVE, BUT CAN GET SOME MORE IF YOU WISH. REGARDS."[15]

Overall, AI's huge network contains millions of potential secret-spillers with information about human rights violations, from its members to lawyers, labor leaders, priests, prison guards, diplomats, nurses, and beyond, many of whom may never contact AI directly. The organization itself might have a hub and spokes network structure, but it is embedded within a much larger decentralized network, which is a vital part of its operational success. Technologists and business writers sometimes use the term "network effects" too loosely to describe the increasing value of expanding networks. Here is a case where the term fits well.

Ancillary Benefits of Doing Field Work and Having Close Links with Governments and International Organizations

The human rights reporting process for HROs consists of the three R's: receiving tips, researching them, and reporting the findings via publication of some sort. In some cases, investigating tips yields additional tips. AI investigators on fact-finding missions put themselves in the vicinity of individuals with secrets to tell, who may or may not already be linked into the network. Just by being on the ground—in labor union offices, police stations, prisons, and so on—investigators make themselves available at a low cost to potential secret-spillers. Thus, fact-finding missions have multiple purposes, including unguided networking. For instance, one AI delegation to Mexico in 1975, investigating the abduction of labor union leaders Carlos de Hoyos Perez and Carlos Mendez Trujillo, interviewed "a number of individuals who witnessed the kidnapping" of the men, along with Mexican lawyers contacted by the union, and others, including an elevator operator outside of the union's raided and burgled offices.[16] All of them had unique opportunities to link up with a global HRO, just by being in the right place at the right time.

Investigators on fact-finding missions also build HRO networks more deliberately once on the ground. For example, an AI mission to Chile soon after the 1973 coup met with a large and diverse group of individuals, including the president of the Chilean Colegio de Abogados (the Chilean Bar Association) and fifteen lawyer colleagues; Chilean government officials; three foreign ambassadors, a charge d'affaires, and other diplomats; officials from international organizations, including UNHCR, International Red Cross, Comite Nacional de Ayuda a los Refugiados, Comite de Cooperaction Para la Paz; and "innumerable . . . lawyers, prisoners and ex-prisoners, priests, professors and students, research and welfare workers, journalists, relatives and friends of prisoners, others too."[17]

A more recent example illustrates the large number of individuals HRO investigators can meet during a fact-finding mission, even in countries led by some of the world's most repressive rulers. In 2013, HRW dispatched a team of researchers to Burma to investigate the government-backed ethnic cleansing campaign against Rohingya Muslims by Arakanese Buddhists. The resulting 165-page report drew from the more than 200 interviews conducted in "Burma and Bangladesh in June and July 2012, and in Burma in October and November 2012." Of that total, HRW researchers interviewed 104 individuals—"54 Rohingya, 34 Arakanese, and 9 Kaman, as well as . . . aid workers and others . . . who witnessed or were otherwise directly affected by the violence in June and October 2012." On top of the individual interviews, the researchers conducted ten group interviews, comprising the other half of the approximately 200. Complementing those interviews were an unspecified number of others conducted in the latter half of 2012: "numerous UN and NGO staff members; national, regional, and local politicians; democracy activists, and local and international journalists."[18] Each interview afforded victims and witnesses opportunities to report human rights violations or to suggest additional people to meet.

Overall, case-specific research may be the primary reason for fact-finding missions. Yet every in-country interview, chance meeting, and uncovered document offers potential networking opportunities. New nodes can later send tips, corroborate evidence, and/or expand the network on their own as needs or opportunities arise. Moreover, investigators can discover tips and potential new contacts when digging through archives, such as police, trial, prison, and military records; morgue and cemetery records; and customs and immigration records.[19]

Cooperating with Authoritarians

It might seem surprising that authoritarian rulers allow HROs to enter their countries in the first place. To be sure, many of them do not. North Korea has barred HROs for decades. Venezuela expelled HRW in 2008. And so on. Yet HROs are allowed into relatively closed societies more than we might expect. Why wouldn't those governments stop HRO investigators at their borders?

One reason is that rational authoritarians will understand that blocking HROs from entering, or kicking them out, will generate unwanted press and foreign government attention. When Venezuelan president Hugo Chávez deported HRW executives in 2008, the next day the press buzzed about Venezuela's human rights violations and about Chávez's defensiveness about that topic.[20] Rulers who prefer to avoid the costs of that bad publicity might believe, correctly or not, that they can appear accommodating while their agents can more or less control a HRO delegation's visit with assertive, inflexible restrictions on travel and communications, enforced by minders, troops, and surveillance. But dictators face a dilemma. They want to control HRO delegations as much as possible, but too much control might lead the HRO to declare the visit a farce in its press releases, generating the unwanted publicity, the international discussions about economic sanctions, and the like. Therefore, human rights–violating governments must find a balance between accommodation and control, which gives the HROs a modicum of investigatory discretion as well as networking opportunities.

These windows of opportunity that open as a result of developing strategic, civil relationships with repressive rulers is likely a key reason why the major HROs have followed a generally cooperative approach with regimes they have targeted. To be sure, they do not pull punches when they criticize governments' human rights violations, but they operate more like professionals than agitators (or spies, in the earlier example). This approach by HROs is consistent with their general policy of developing and maintaining relationships with governments and international organizations, which has probably enhanced their credibility, and has definitely proved useful when helping enfeebled local human rights defenders battle their repressive governments.[21]

Conclusion

Human rights reporting is integral to what major HROs do. Surprisingly little previous research has examined how HROs learn about the violations central to that reporting. The major HROs like AI and HRW have offices in many countries, but their resources, while substantial, do not allow for omniscient monitoring. Instead of that kind of "police patrol" monitoring, they employ "fire alarm" monitoring, in which they build and integrate themselves into wider networks, wherein they can receive and respond to tips about violations. This chapter used a variety of sources, including AI's archives, to outline the structure of, and the information flows within, the network of which AI is a part.

Because AI and HRW severely limit access to their records, generally to protect the confidentiality of vulnerable network nodes, outside researchers cannot access the information for a comprehensive analysis of case-specific network sections.[22] A scholar wanting to build a detailed network model of, say, AI's reporting on Argentina's "dirty war" in the late 1970s, would need to wait until the mid- to late twenty-first century for AI to make the relevant records available. Nevertheless, the data fragments available in the AI USA archive and elsewhere in the public sphere provided enough information to construct a somewhat legible mosaic that approximated how information moves through AI's whistleblowing network.

Notes

[1] "Mrs. Roosevelt Reveals Human Rights 'Grapevine,'" *The New York Times,* December 8, 1948, 13; William Korey, *NGO's and the Universal Declaration of Human Rights: A Curious Grapevine* (New York: St Martin's Press, 1998); Amanda Murdie, "The Ties that Bind: A Network Analysis of Human Rights International Nongovernmental Organizations," *British Journal of Political Science* 44, no. 1 (January 2014): 1–27.

[2] Mathew D. McCubbins and Thomas Schwartz, "Congressional Oversight Overlooked: Police Patrols Versus Fire Alarms," *American Journal of Political Science* 1 (1984): 165–179.

[3] McCubbins and Schwartz, "Congressional Oversight Overlooked."

[4] David A. Lake and Wendy H. Wong, "The Politics of Networks: Interests, Power, and Human Rights Norms," in Miles Kahler, ed., *Networked Politics: Agency, Power, and Governance* (Ithaca, NY: Cornell University Press, 2009).

[5] In 2018, the regional offices were in Bangkok, Beirut, Brussels, Dakar, East Jerusalem, France, Geneva, Hong Kong, Jakarta, Johannesburg, Lebanon, Lima, London, Mexico City, Moscow, Nairobi, New York, Tunis, and Washington. For many years AI referred to upcoming, "aspiring" sections as "structures"; however that category, along with pre-structures, has vanished from the organization after 2013.

[6] HRW field offices in 2018 were in Amsterdam, Beirut, Berlin, Brussels, Chicago, Geneva, Johannesburg, London, Los Angeles, Nairobi, Oslo, Paris, San Francisco, São Paulo, Sweden, Sydney, Tokyo, Toronto, Washington, and Zürich. The United Nations' Office of the High Commissioner for Human Rights (OHCHR) maintains an even larger global "field presence," although as a part of an international organization comprised of governments, it is qualitatively different than the HROs analyzed in this chapter.

[7] Office of the High Commissioner for Human Rights, 2001, Training Manual on Human Rights Monitoring, Professional Training Series No. 6, United Nations, chapter 6, Appendix 1 ("Case Study"), http://hrlibrary.umn.edu/monitoring/chapter6-appendix1.html.

8 "North Korea: New Satellite Images Show Continued Investment in the Infrastructure of Repression," Amnesty International, December 5, 2013, ASA 24/010/2013, https://www.amn esty.org/en/documents/ASA24/010/2013/en/; "New Satellite Images Show Scale of North Korea's Repressive Prison Camps," Amnesty International, December 5, 2013, https://www.amnesty.org/en/latest/news/2013/12/new-satellite-images-show-scale-north-korea-s-repress ive-prison-camps/; Christoph Koettl, "The Story Behind the Nigeria Satellite Images," *Human Rights Now Blog* [AI], January 15, 2015, http://blog.amnestyusa.org/africa/the-story-behind -the-nigeria-satellite-images/; Mausi Segun, "Dispatches: What Really Happened in Baga, Nigeria?" Human Rights Watch, January 14, 2015, https://www.hrw.org/news/2015/01/14/ dispatches-what-really-happened-baga-nigeria; "Nigeria: Satellite Images Show Horrific Scale of Boko Haram Attack on Baga," Amnesty International, 2015, https://www.amnestyusa.or g/news/news-item/nigeria-satellite-images-show-horrific-scale-of-boko-haram-attack-on-baga.

9 The work of Bellingcat and its partners is exemplary. See, e.g., Syrian Archive, "Eyes on Aleppo: Visual Evidence Analysis of Human Rights Violations Committed in Aleppo [July–Dec 2016]," Bellingcat, March 29, 2017, https://www.bellingcat.com/news/mena/2017/03/ 29/eyes-aleppo-visual-evidence-analysis-human-rights-violations-committed-aleppo-july-dec-2016/; Emerson T. Brooking and P. W. Singer, *Like War: The Weaponization of Social Media* (New York: Eamon Dolan/Houghton Mifflin Harcourt, 2018).

10 "The Story behind Panic Button," Panic Button, June 17, 2016, https://panicbutton.io/about. html; Tanya O'Carroll, "More than an App: the Panic Button, One Year On," Amnesty International, July 22, 2015, https://www.amnesty.org/en/latest/campaigns/2015/07/panic-button-one-year-on/; Tanya O'Carroll, "Inside the Development of Amnesty's New Panic Button App," Amnesty International Human Rights Now blog, September 2, 2013, http://blog. amnestyusa.org/amnesty/inside-the-development-of-amnestys-new-panic-button-app/; "New 'Panic Button' App Provides Safety Net to Human Rights Activists," Amnesty International, May 1, 2014, https://www.amnesty.org/en/latest/news/2014/05/new-panic-button-app-provides-safety-net-human-rights-activists/; Panic Button Team, "Panic Button: Why We Are Retiring the App," The Engine Room, September 1, 2017, https://www.theengineroom.org/ panic-button-retiring-the-app/. Panic Button was not the first tip-reporting app. Benetech's Mobile Martus appeared in 2013, and was preceded by the same company's desktop platform. Martus was also an early adopter of end to end encryption and other security features. However, its relative obscurity, compared with the major global HROs, has limited its reach. Collin Sullivan, "Introducing Mobile Martus 1.0!" Benetech, October 2, 2013, http://www .benetech.org/2013/10/02/introducing-mobile-martus-1-0/; "About Us," The Martus Project, accessed June 30, 2016, https://www.martus.org/about.html.

11 James Ron, Howard Ramos, and Kathleen Rodgers, "Transnational Information Politics: Human Rights NGO Reporting, 1986–2000," *International Studies Quarterly* 49, no. 3 (2005): 557–88; Navanethem Pillay, "Human Rights Investigations and their Methodology," United Nations High Commissioner for Human Rights, February 24, 2010, http://unispal.un.org/UNI SPAL.NSF/0/C9222F058467E6F6852576D500574710; Julie Mertus, "Considerations for Human Rights Fact Finding by NGOs," accessed January 15, 2019, http://fs2.american.edu/m ertus/www/HR%20fact-finding.htm#_ftn1; The New Tactics in Human Rights Project, *New Tactics in Human Rights: A Resource for Practitioners* (Minneapolis: Center for Victims of Torture, 2004), 37; Geoffrey Robertson, "Human Rights Fact-Finding: Some Legal and Ethical Dilemmas," UCL *Human Rights Review* 3 (2010): 15; Jack H. Geiger and Robert M. Cook-Deegan. "The Role of Physicians in Conflicts and Humanitarian Crises: Case Studies from the Field Missions of Physicians for Human Rights, 1988 to 1993,"*Journal of the American Medical Association* 270, no. 5 (1993): 616–20; "Justice and Forensic Science," Physicians for Human Rights, accessed June 29, 2015, http://physiciansforhumanrights.org/justice-forensic-science/; Physicians for Human Rights, MediCapt, accessed June 29, 2015, http://physicia nsforhumanrights.org/medicapt; National Library of Medicine, "The New Forensic Science," accessed June 29, 2015, https://www.nlm.nih.gov/visibleproofs/exhibition/newscience.html; "Forensic Evidence and Human Rights Reporting," Human Rights Advocacy and the History of Human Rights Standards, University of Michigan, accessed January 15, 2019, http://human rightshistory.umich.edu/research-and-advocacy/forensic-evidence-and-human-rights-reporting/;

Adam Rosenblatt, *Digging for the Disappeared: Forensic Science after Atrocity* (Palo Alto: Stanford University Press, 2015).

12 For an example of interorganizational communication—in this case, a U.S. union and AI USA, see Esteban E. Torres (UAW International Affairs Department Assistant Director) to Ginetta Sagan (AI USA West Coast Director), January 23, 1975, AI USA archive, Columbia University Box II.1 4, Folder 7. The archive's general citation is Amnesty International of the USA, Inc. National Office Records, 1966–2003 [Bulk Dates: 1974-1993], Rare Book and Manuscript Library, Columbia University Library.

13 Ron et al., 2005, "Transnational Information Politics"; Bob Clifford, "Merchants of Morality," *Foreign Policy* 129 (March 2002): 36–45; Jessica T. Matthews, "Power Shift," *Foreign Affairs* (January 1997): 50–66; Utkarsh Anand, "India Has 31 Lakh NGOs, More than Double the Number of Schools," *Indian Express,* August 1, 2015, http://indianexpress.com/article/india/india-others/india-has-31-lakh-ngos-twice-the-number-of-schools-almost-twice-number-of-policemen/.

14 Amnesty International USA, Columbia University Archive, Box II.1 4, Folder 7. On the reporting role of victims' family members, see Gina Lei Miller, "Filling the Information Gap: How Emigrant Networks Mitigate Problems in Human Rights Abuse Reporting," Paper presented at the Southern Political Science Association annual conference, Orlando, Florida, January 2–5, 2013.

15 AI USA, Columbia University Archive, Box II.1 4, Folder 19.

16 AI USA, Columbia University Archive, Box II.1 4, Folder 7 (Jay C. Carlisle, "Preliminary Report of the Emergency Lawyers Mission to Mexico," March 30, 1975).

17 AI USA, Columbia University Archive, Box II.5 3, Folder 12.

18 "'All You Can Do is Pray': Crimes Against Humanity and Ethnic Cleansing of Rohingya Muslims in Burma's Arakan State," Human Rights Watch, April 22, 2013.

19 Diane F. Orentlicher, "Bearing Witness: The Art and Science of Human Rights Fact-Finding," *Harvard Human Rights Journal* 3 (1990): 83–135; Ann Harrison. "Counting the Unknown Victims of Political Violence: The Work of the Human Rights Data Analysis Group," In *Human Rights and Information Communication Technologies: Trends and Consequences of Use* (IGI Global, 2013), 139–56; Mertus, "Considerations."

20 "Venezuela: Human Rights Watch Delegation Expelled," Human Rights Watch, September 19, 2008, https://www.hrw.org/news/2008/09/19/venezuela-human-rights-watch-delegation-expelled; Simon Romero, "Venezuela Expels 2 After Report on Rights," *The New York Times,* September 19, 2008, A8.

21 Margaret Keck and Kathryn Sikkink, *Activists beyond Borders: Advocacy Networks in International Politics* (Ithaca, New York: Cornell University Press, 1998).

22 While Amnesty International and Human Rights Watch have opened some of their archives, they have restricted documents that offer many of the details that would allow us to construct detailed network maps that would show the finer points of how they extract information. AI USA's archive, housed at Columbia University Libraries, contains hundreds of folders restricted until the mid- to late twenty-first century. While some of the secrecy might be excessive, it makes sense when we consider ongoing risks faced by the victims, witnesses, and facilitators named in the files, who will live well into the twenty-first century.

Chapter 6

WikiLeaks's Rise, Relevance, and Power

It did not take long after the World Wide Web went live in August 1991 for users to recognize its unique secret-spilling opportunities. Would-be whistleblowers no longer had to impress media organization gatekeepers to reach sizable audiences, given the near-zero costs of creating web platforms. Transaction costs also plummeted, given how easy and cheap it was to transfer data from one machine to another.

Organizations' valued secrets began to appear online years before software developers built the first specialized leak platforms. Bulletin boards, usenets, listservs, and similar forums became testing grounds in the early to mid-1990s. Debates raged about whether secret-spilling contributors should be allowed to stay anonymous. High-quality encryption tools, such as PGP ("Pretty Good Privacy"), were available as early as 1991, but they were not widely used and appeared to require sophisticated technical knowledge. Those wanting anonymity had other options, such as the Penet remailer, but their protections proved weak. After a Penet user in California pseudonymously uploaded Scientology documents to the alt.religion.scientology newsgroup, lawyers for the aggressive and deep-pocketed organization forced Penet founder Johan "Julf" Helsingius to identify the leaker.[1]

In 1996, the first site specializing in leaks appeared on the web. John Young and Deborah Natsios's Cryptome quickly developed a reputation for spilling state secrets without regard for the consequences. Nothing was out of bounds, including the names of CIA and MI6 agents, sensitive details of covert operations, and maps of nuclear storage sites and urban natural gas pipelines. "There are no secrets that shouldn't be published," Young said. Plus, Cryptome does not promise protections to its sources. "Don't send us stuff and think that we'll protect you," he once warned. "Cryptome is not trustworthy, and lies."[2]

Perhaps he dialed up the paranoia to make a point about the folly of trusting anyone online. Perhaps it was crypto-anarchist posturing, or just a joke. Whatever the reason, would-be whistleblowers wanting anonymity and a protective, risk-sensitive recipient, had reasons to stay away.

In Cryptome's wake came WikiLeaks, a site touting its anti-secrecy radicalism along with a strong commitment to source protections. It emerged at a time when programmers had developed anonymizing tools to the point where easy, risk-free online leaking seemed like it might actually work.[3] At the very least, governments, corporations, or other entities trying to identify anonymous online leakers would have faced formidable technical challenges.

WikiLeaks came online in 2006 and came of age in 2010, when it published a quartet of major disclosures it received from U.S. Army Specialist Chelsea (née Bradley) Manning.[4] The first featured a classified U.S. Army video showing a July 2007 air attack against suspected anti-government insurgents in Baghdad, Iraq. It immediately made WikiLeaks famous and controversial, with loyal defenders and many enemies.

"Collateral Murder"

WikiLeaks titled its decrypted and edited version of the original July 2007 Army video "Collateral Murder," evoking the convoluted phrase, collateral damage, used by militaries to describe unintentional battlefield killings. It is a wry twist of phrase, but it is nonsensical. The use of collateral—meaning indirect, unintentional, or secondary—clashes with WikiLeaks's accusation that the killings were intentional (i.e., "murder"). Nevertheless, WikiLeaks put the phrase to good effect, and in one version of the video, it was paired with a sharp George Orwell quote: "Political language . . . is designed to make lies sound truthful and murder respectable, and to give an appearance of solidity to pure wind."[5]

After Orwell's quote, WikiLeaks presents humanizing details about the airstrike victims. Then the video cuts to an Apache helicopter camera, which shows it moving over a Baghdad neighborhood where other forces had spotted suspected insurgents earlier that day. The two Army Apaches then hover over the target area, a dusty urban courtyard, where a group of men mill about, some of them carrying black objects. The soldiers identify the objects as small arms, AK-47s, and a rocket-propelled grenade (RPG) launcher. "He's got a weapon too," one says. "He's got an RPG!" WikiLeaks inserted fact-checking text to challenge the soldiers' observations. The black objects that look like weapons, the edited video explains, are actually journalists' cameras and tripods.[6]

After the pilots obtain approval to fire on the suspected insurgents (heard through the audio), we hear the rat-a-tat-tat of Apache gunfire, and, after a short delay, we see the men on the ground quickly scatter, looking for cover. Video reconnaissance of the scene right after that shows bodies strewn about, to the satisfaction of the Army shooters, who celebrate their accomplishment with cheers. When they see a survivor run across the screen, they shoot him too. When a van comes to rescue a crawling survivor, the soldiers eagerly request permission to fire again, to finish the mission. After gaining approval from a commander, they blast through the van, presumably not first noticing the two children inside. WikiLeaks suggests that it is highly unlikely that the pilots missed seeing the kids. Nothing in the video or transcript supports that claim. Still, investigations of the incident confirmed that children and two Reuters employees were among those hit.

WikiLeaks makes other unsubstantiated claims and insinuations in the edited video, such as the suggestion that the soldiers *wanted* to kill innocent noncombatants, including children and journalists, and that their commanders approved. The video purportedly shows "murder," after all, not battlefield killings. It also discounts the pilots' clear statements of their perceptions about the journalists' equipment. WikiLeaks backers have also discounted the government's claim that the Army shooters made a mistake.

While the pilots misperceived the camera equipment as weapons, the reporters carrying it were very likely embedded with armed insurgents. The Army's investigators found a rifle, RPGs, and RPG launchers at the site of the attack, including an RPG under one of the corpses.[7] And the same neighborhood had seen intense combat earlier that day—which likely informed the commanders' choice to attack—as a *Washington Post* reporter documented in a 2009 book:

> All morning long, this part of Al-Amin had been the most hostile . . . . East Al-Amin had been filled with gunfire and some explosions. There had been reports of sniper fire, rooftop chases, and rocket-propelled grenades being fired at Bravo Company, and as the fighting continued, it attracted the attention of Namir Noor-Eldeen, a twenty-two year-old photographer for the Reuters news agency who lived in Baghdad, and Saeed Chmagh, forty, his driver and assistant.[8]

Despite evidence that the Army pilots had engaged armed insurgents in a war zone, along with their documented and understandable misperceptions, WikiLeaks has depicted the episode as clear evidence of America's cruel criminality. Spokesman Kristinn Hrafnsson claimed that the video showed "an obvious war crime." Assange was cagier: "I wouldn't want to prejudge the issue and say for sure that a war crime has committed—been committed. But some are deeply suspicious."[9]

The War Logs

On July 25, 2010, WikiLeaks, in conjunction with *The New York Times*, *The Guardian* (U.K.), and *Der Spiegel* (Germany), released the second batch of disclosures from the Manning files: more than 75,000 of about 91,000 secret U.S.

military documents from the war in Afghanistan, circa 2004–2010. The Afghan War Diary (also sometimes "Afghan war logs") consisted of "significant activity" (SIGACT) reports that detailed a range of military actions, including information about targets sought, detained, or killed; the locations of those actions; and the number of civilians killed and injured. WikiLeaks boasted that the release was "the most significant archive about the reality of war to have ever been released during the course of a war."[10] While the files did provide glimpses into the reality of war, WikiLeaks released thousands of secrets at once. Its media partners were more prudent, publishing relatively fewer documents with more in-depth analysis.

The organizations also disagreed about how to handle names that appeared in the documents, especially Afghanis who had worked with NATO forces. Whereas the media companies asked WikiLeaks to publish them with identity-protecting redactions that would have kept Afghanis safe from Talibani retaliation, WikiLeaks wanted to release them in raw form. Eventually, Assange relented, agreeing to review about 15,000 of the files thought to have especially sensitive identifying information. His motives for what seemed like carelessness were unclear. However, according to *Guardian* reporter Nick Davies, Assange had told him that "if an Afghan civilian helps coalition forces, he deserves to die," which if quoted accurately, shows deliberate negligence and the discounting of Afghani lives.[11] Such indifference to potential retaliation against thousands of Afghani civilians would have been hypocritical for an organization with a strong commitment to source protections. In the other major leaks of 2010, WikiLeaks exhibited greater care with sensitive personal information. But in subsequent years, it backtracked and again published unredacted documents, which shows the organization's disregard for the negative consequences of disclosures.[12] Because Manning gave WikiLeaks the raw, unredacted data in the first place, she should share the blame.

On October 22, 2010, WikiLeaks again drew from the Manning files to release 391,832 secret documents from the Iraq War from 2004 to 2009, "the largest classified military leak in history." The SIGACT reports detailed targets, kill numbers, and other historical operation details. Continuing its media partnership strategy, it teamed up with major news and reporting organizations to coordinate disclosures. *The New York Times*, *The Guardian*, *Der Spiegel*, *Le Monde* (France), *Al Jazeera* (Qatar), the Iraq Body Count project, and the Bureau of Investigative Journalism (U.K.) all joined WikiLeaks in publishing selections from the Iraq War Logs.[13]

Were the War Log Disclosures Justified?

Should the Iraq and Afghan war log disclosures be seen, by chapter 2's standards, as whistleblowing? Clearly the primary source documents, which the U.S. government did not challenge the authenticity of, qualify as clear and convincing pieces of evidence. The disclosures were made publicly; they were not covertly passed to foreign governments who would privately benefit. And there is no clear evidence that the disclosures directly harmed public safety—in this case, Afghani and Iraqi citizens, as well as Americans—although they certainly could have. Assange's decision not to redact the names of NATO collaborators in Afghanistan risked their lives. Pressure from its media partners forced WikiLeaks to spend extra time reviewing and redacting a portion of the documents, but it left hundreds of individuals exposed in the other releases. The U.S. government's Information Review Task Force led by Brigadier General Robert Carr found no clear evidence of such reprisals, in part due to the exhaustive work by a Defense Department-led interagency taskforce of at least a hundred, who scoured the published files for endangered Afghanis, and then coordinated with military units in Afghanistan to help locate them, sometimes deep into Taliban territory. Not all of them were found.[14]

There are many other ways the megaleak could have caused direct or indirect harms to U.S. national security. For instance, Big Data analysts in governments and terrorist groups enjoyed an unexpected windfall of U.S. military information that they could have used to detect strategic or tactical patterns that would have put them at an advantage, without the United States's knowledge. For that and other reasons, the U.S. military was adamant that "this security breach could very well get our troops and those they are fighting with killed. Our enemies will mine this information looking for insights into how we operate, cultivate sources and react in combat situations, even the capability of our equipment."[15] Even so, for scholars without the appropriate security clearance, it is difficult to impossible to measure the amount of damage the leaks may have caused, which gives WikiLeaks supporters the advantage of accurately claiming that no clear evidence of harm exists, even if harm might have occurred.[16]

The war log leaks clearly fail the "was it whistleblowing" test when we consider the other standards developed in chapter 2. The disclosures were certainly not "limited in scope and scale as far as is possible," given the hundreds of thousands of documents dumped online. Neither Manning nor WikiLeaks carefully estimated the risks and benefits of releasing each document or data point. Manning leaked them all at once, and WikiLeaks released them in large batches, often without making case-by-case determinations of whether information specifically showed abuses of public authority.

Critics of excessive government secrecy might argue that agencies routinely overclassify information. Thus, if government officials do not fairly evaluate the costs and benefits of releasing documents, then why should leakers? But excessive government secrecy, typically borne out of risk minimization, is no excuse for a leaker's lack of judiciousness. Let us fairly criticize overclassification as well as reckless disclosure.

One might argue that the public benefit of the disclosures came as least as much from what they said in the aggregate than from what any individual report documented. That is, the public benefited from the war log leaks by learning about the scale and scope of U.S. military violence. Thus, the argument goes, even if there was no clear need to disclose a specific document, its value came in relation to other releases.

While the megaleaks did provide uniquely valuable information, there was likely a better way of accomplishing the public awareness goal that did not involve flagrantly violating the limiting principle—or really, any commitment to cautiousness. A whistleblowing network that was sensitive to the potential negative consequences of disclosures could release *some* of the information to make a point about U.S. military violence, while simultaneously claiming, credibly, that "we have thousands more documents just like that in our possession."

Cablegate

A month after the Iraq War Logs, WikiLeaks released another tranche from the Manning cache: hundreds of thousands of U.S. Department of State (DOS) files. The first batch appeared on WikiLeaks's website on November 28, 2010, along with features in *The Guardian, Der Spiegel, Le Monde,* and *El País* (Spain). *The New York Times* also reported from DOS documents provided by *The Guardian,* without WikiLeaks's permission. None of the outlets, including WikiLeaks, published all 251,287 "Cablegate" files in bulk, at once. The newspapers released DOS cables in dribbles and drabs, while WikiLeaks periodically uploaded larger batches after reviewing documents, probably because of pressure from its media partners, not from the implementation of a harm reduction standard and a new belief in the negative consequences of leaks. And even though WikiLeaks did not release all 250K files at once, we would still need to stretch "limited in scale and scope" too far to justify its release of hundreds at a time, even if the files spilled out over several months, and even if only about half were officially classified (others were sensitive but unclassified).[17]

The cables contain the official communications between U.S. embassies and DOS headquarters in Washington. They cover everything from routine impressions of mundane, low-level meetings with diplomats and civic leaders, to ambassadors' real, unvarnished opinions about foreign heads of state. Some reveal the once protected identities of U.S. informants. Others document the government's strategies of dealing with adversaries, and the ways diplomats work on behalf of citizens and corporations. Many show the more cunning and indelicate parts of statecraft.

Of all of WikiLeaks's four major releases in 2010, "Cablegate" caused the U.S. government and its partners the most grief, judging by their intense reaction. Officials gave dire warnings about irreparable harms. American

diplomacy would never recover from the broken trust of allies and collaborators, they insisted. Several years later, the more grandiose claims seemed less
credible. The international system soon reached a familiar sort of equilibrium,
and DOS found ways to repair relationships, even if some international distrust
lingered. The amount of direct or indirect harms to United States and others'
national interests is probably indeterminate.

Were the Cablegate Disclosures Justified?

Manning's Cablegate megaleak does not qualify as whistleblowing. Many,
perhaps most, of the hundreds of thousands of cables contained the details of
mundane diplomatic communications, with not an abuse of public or private
authority in sight. Some were saucier, containing diplomats' private views of
leaders and conflicts, but still did not document abuses. To be sure, some cables
did discuss abuses, like the famed 2008 cable from the U.S. Embassy in Tunisia,
"Corruption in Tunisia: What's Yours Is Mine," which expressed the ambas-
sador's candid view that then President Zine El Abidine Ben Ali's government
was deeply corrupt. The revelation surprised no one, but it validated suspicions
about Ben Ali with the credibility of a senior U.S. official's unguarded perspective. Its publication did not directly endanger innocent Tunisians, although it
did help to spark the pro-democracy uprising that provoked a violent state
response, causing 240 deaths and 1,464 injuries, before the movement forced
Ben Ali to flee.[18]

The vast majority of the disclosed cables did not contain anything even
coming close to evidence of abuses. Take, for example, the set of cables
from June 23, 2008, the day that the US Embassy in Tunis circulated
"Corruption in Tunisia." The vast majority of them are mundane reports,
with titles like "EMBASSY'S FIRST EVER SHOWING AT MONGOLIAN
TRADE FAIR A MODEST SUCCESS" and "TOKYO MEDIA REACTION—
IRISH REJECTION OF EU TREATY."[19] We might reasonably question why
such missives were secrets in the first place, although full transparency by
default in diplomatic communications would probably render ineffective a
state's diplomacy, which requires confidentiality.[20]

How WikiLeaks Did, and Did Not, Change the History of Leaking and Whistleblowing in 2010

WikiLeaks's breakthrough year had pundits and scholars ruminating about the
ways Assange et al. had changed the "future of whistleblowing." While there
was strong disagreement about whether the megaleaks counted as justified
whistleblowing, many observers insisted that WikiLeaks had forever changed
the way people would spill secrets.[21] Assange's vision of WikiLeaks's impact

was even more grandiose: "I believe geopolitics will be separated into pre- and post-Cablegate phases."[22] While we can put aside the maximalist claims, there is no question that the 2010 disclosures—like the leaked Democratic Party emails during the 2016 U.S. presidential election—showcased WikiLeaks's global powers and demonstrated important new features of computer-enabled leaking.[23]

Technology and Anonymity

While proud of his innovative site, Assange has never claimed that WikiLeaks was a wholly original creation. His hailing of Cryptome's John Young as the "spiritual godfather of online leaking" shows his recognition of WikiLeaks's place in the species's evolutionary history.[24] Still, the key technological innovation, WikiLeaks's strong source protections, did change the game by credibly promising truly anonymous leaking. The feature has been front and center in WikiLeaks's identity and promotions. "Unlike other outlets," WikiLeaks told visitors in 2011, "we provide a high security anonymous drop box fortified by cutting-edge cryptographic information technologies." When Assange explained WikiLeaks to the world in the midst of turbulent 2010, he trumpeted the organization's "unbroken record" of protecting anonymity.[25]

Here is how it worked when Manning uploaded DOS and Department of Defense (DOD) files onto WikiLeaks.org: Before moving them to WikiLeaks's server, the secure uploading platform rerouted the files through a deliberately convoluted network of computers and servers around the world, which masked Manning's identity (IP address and location) and added and removed layers of encryption as it bounced the digital bits around. Once the bits returned to WikiLeaks's protected central server, the system removed all of the encryption layers, like the peeling of an onion. The circumvention technology was not Assange's creation but the free and open source software program called Tor (The Onion Router), which Manning had earlier used for army work monitoring Iraqi militia groups' online activities. On top of Tor, Assange's team claimed to have created a second layer of security to prevent hackers from trying to intercept the uploaded documents once they reached WikiLeaks's server, described as a mass distraction algorithm that launched "hundreds of thousands of fake submissions through these tunnels, obscuring the real documents." On top of the "bank grade encrypted submission" WikiLeaks promised, plus the other tricks, leakers were assured that the site did not keep access logs and that its Swedish- and Belgian-based servers were "protected under Swedish and Belgium press secrecy laws." Altogether, WikiLeaks offered anonymous leakers a level of protection that no other online platforms had been able or willing to offer.[26]

Perhaps WikiLeaks's greatest influence was providing a model of secure online leaking and whistleblowing that others could duplicate. Indeed, WikiLeaks inspired legions of imitators. Dozens of similar sites popped up after 2010, the earliest ones including Associated Whistleblowing Press (AWP), BalkanLeaks, BaltiLeaks, BrasilLeaks, BritiLeaks, BrusselsLeaks, Cop Recorder, CorporateLeaks, CrowdLeaks, EnviroLeaks, FrenchLeaks, GlobaLeaks, GreenLeaks, Indoleaks, IrishLeaks, JumboLeaks, KHLeaks, LeakyMails, Ljost [a AWP product in Iceland], Localleaks, MapleLeaks, MurdochLeaks, Nawaatleaks, Office Leaks, OpenLeaks, OpenWatch Recorder, PinoyLeaks, PirateLeaks, QuebecLeaks, RuLeaks, ScienceLeaks, StateLeaks, TradeLeaks, Tunileaks, and UniLeaks. Secure leak-submission portals soon began to appear on the websites of mainstream publications with large audiences. Many of them picked up SecureDrop, an open source application originally developed by Aaron Swartz and former *Wired* magazine editor Kevin Poulsen, and then completed by the Freedom of the Press Foundation (whose board of directors includes Daniel Ellsberg, Edward Snowden, Glenn Greenwald, and Laura Poitras). Early SecureDrop adopters included *The New Yorker* (as StrongBox), *The Guardian*, *The Washington Post*, *Forbes* (as SafeSource), *The Intercept*, *ProPublica*, Canadian Broadcasting Corporation, The Project on Government Oversight, ExposeFacts.org (Institute for Public Accuracy), the *San Francisco Bay Guardian* (as Bayleaks), TCF MailVault, and Radio24syv (Denmark). Other organizations developed their own submission systems, including *The Wall Street Journal* (SafeHouse), *Al Jazeera* (Transparency Unit), and *El Diario* (Filtrala, an AWP product). Overall, the rapid proliferation of sites and submissions tools reflected WikiLeaks's influence, along with a great deal of technological and journalistic experimentation.[27]

The anonymity guarantees offered by WikiLeaks and its followers remains a disputed feature of whistleblowing. Theorists tend to be critical, believing that credible and justified whistleblowing usually requires identification, to make motives clearer and to ensure all participants have skin in the game (chapter 2). As C. Fred Alford noted, the WikiLeaks model "challenges a long held belief by many of us who study whistle-blowing—that it is important that the whistle-blower have a name and face so that the disclosures are not considered just anonymous griping, or possibly unethical activity. The public needs to see the human face of someone who stands up and does the right thing when none of his or her colleagues dare."[28] Yet, as argued in chapter 2, and as shown in chapters 4 and 5, a general argument against anonymity neglects the nature and severity of retaliation that some whistleblowers face, especially in authoritarian and/or illiberal countries.

Building a Brand

A second innovative and influential feature of WikiLeaks's rise to prominence was its mastery of branding and publicity. Some of the 2010 disclosures probably would have attracted attention with or without a good marketing strategy. But Assange's media savvy and strange charisma, along with the organization's overall plucky character, probably helped to keep the disclosure stories alive longer than they otherwise would have.

WikiLeaks developed its anti-secrecy, anti-establishmentarian, populist identity on its website and in Assange's speeches, books, and media interviews. Once in the news, the organization and its supporters sold a bounty of branded merchandise—posters, backpacks, duffel bags, coffee mugs, shot glasses, shower curtains, smart phone cases, water bottles, umbrellas ("Not So Leaky"), dog bandanas, jewelry, baseball hats, winter caps, kitchen aprons, kids T-shirts, baby onesies ("I Love Leakers"), polos, and hoodies emblazoned with slogans like "Courage Is Contagious. WikiLeaks: Catch the Bug; Blow the Whistle," "WikiLeaks: Encrypt Like It's Nineteen Eighty Four," and "The Truth Is Not Treason," featuring Assange with a U.S. flag taped over his mouth. A Christmas shopper could quickly fill all her family's stockings by visiting "The Official WikiLeaks Shop" on spreadshirt.com. Those looking for more options could find products sold by supporters on e-commerce sites. CafePress alone listed 277 "WikiLeaks Home Accessories designs" in 2016.[29] While amusing, the commercial marketing was a sideshow to its growing public role, which seemed a blend of sincere political action and self-promotion. Even sharply critical books and films, such as the Hollywood thriller *The Fifth Estate* and Alex Gibney's documentary *We Steal Secrets*, added to WikiLeaks's prominence and allure. No other online leaking platform has achieved anything like it.

A New Era of Retaliation Politics?

The Case against Manning (and Others):
The Espionage Act and Aiding the Enemy

Chelsea Manning—the first and so far only WikiLeaks leaker to get caught—chose anonymity when she uploaded hundreds of thousands of classified documents. She took full advantage of WikiLeaks's source protections, described above. On top of that, she used Tor and disk encryption during the file transfer, and regularly used encryption tools for web communications.[30] It is possible that she wanted to be caught, given some puzzling, risk-accepting behaviors in the summer of 2010, but the more likely explanation centers on sloppy operational security and careless, even naïve, online social interactions.

In May 2010, Manning chose to befriend and confide in a well-known hacker and avowed WikiLeaks supporter, Adrian Lamo, who responded to her unsolicited chat invitation. The chat logs, which Lamo provided to *Wired* magazine, portray Manning as an indiscreet confessor of crimes and as someone who clearly needed a friend. They show someone eager to claim credit for clearly criminal acts, while also strangely willing to provide anonymity-breaking clues to a stranger, including her name, army work, gender identity problems she struggled with, and sad childhood memories, all of which could have helped investigators who were trying to track her down.

Early in their first chat on May 21, 2010, "bradass87" gave details about her intelligence analysis work in Iraq and hinted unsubtly about what she had done: "(1:58:31 p.m.) bradass87: if you had unprecedented access to classified networks 14 hours a day 7 days a week for 8+ months, what would you do?" A day later, Manning offered to show Lamo classified government files she had found that referenced him. She also bragged about her leaks to WikiLeaks: "(10:33:28 a.m.) bradass87: this is what i do for friends: http://bit.ly/aLoqUi." (The shortened bit.ly link led to WikiLeaks's Wikipedia page.) She did express concerns about the risks she took (e.g. "(1:39:03 PM) Manning: i cant believe what im confessing to you"), but proceeded nonetheless, basing her trust in Lamo on his reputation as a WikiLeaks supporter, even going as far as giving him her Army Knowledge Online password, which also unlocked the encrypted disk. In their chats, Lamo expressed concern about being "false flagged"—that is, he seemed to worry, or at least joke about, being entrapped by an undercover agent masquerading as a defiant leaker of government secrets: "(10:28:29 a.m.) info@adrianlamo.com: Of course, you could be false flagging me. I say 'Can I see it?' and bam, I'm a criminal." Lamo also tried to solicit more details, while teasing that he might not be who Manning thought he was:

(10:23:34 a.m.) info@adrianlamo.com: I'm a journalist and a minister. You can pick either, and treat this as a confession or an interview (never to be published) & enjoy a modicum of legal protection.
(10:24:07 a.m.) bradass87: assange level?
(10:25:12 a.m.) bradass87: or are you socially engineering;P
(10:25:51 a.m.) info@adrianlamo.com: You must not have done your research ☺
(10:25:57 a.m.) info@adrianlamo.com: I could have flipped for the FBI.
(10:26:05 a.m.) info@adrianlamo.com: Gotten a sweeter deal.

When Lamo teased Manning about working with the FBI, he hinted at a close truth. Lamo at the time worked for a private group called Project Vigilant, which collaborated with the FBI and other government agencies. When Project Vigilant's director Chet Uber heard that Lamo had identified his chat partner "bradass87" with a few minutes of open source research, using clues Manning provided in their chats, Uber urged Lamo to contact Army Counterintelligence, which he did with some reluctance. The army arrested Manning in June 2010.[31]

As soon as the government publicly identified her as the likely leaker, Manning became a hero to WikiLeaks supporters, many of whom did all they could to track and publicize the conditions of her detention, which were often quite harsh. Her supporters succeeded in bringing the global human rights movement to their side, although many organizations had already lined up behind WikiLeaks. Amnesty International, the United Nations Special Rapporteur on Torture, and hundreds of prominent academics implored the United States to soften its approach, which it ultimately did by moving Manning out of solitary confinement at the Marine Corps Brig, Quantico, to a less isolating setting at the prison at Fort Leavenworth. The furor over Manning's detention even drew in DOS's top spokesman, Phillip Crowley, who publicly criticized the Obama administration on this issue, and then resigned.[32]

Beyond the nature of her confinement, Manning's supporters were outraged at the government's charges against her, which included military code violations involving computer and information security, and criminal code violations involving theft, computer access, aiding the enemy, and espionage, as defined by the Espionage Act of 1917. After a court-martial—an adversarial trial run by the military's justice system—Chief Judge Col. Denise R. Lind convicted Manning of almost all of the charges, except aiding the enemy, and sentenced her to thirty-five years in prison, the longest for a leaker in U.S. history. President Obama commuted her sentence in 2017, three days before his second term in office expired.[33]

It was not surprising that Judge Lind dropped the aiding-the-enemy charge, given how historically unusual it was for a leak case. Manning's prosecutors supported their contention by citing the Uniform Code of Military Justice (USMJ) (§904, Article 104), arguing that she fell under the law's description of a "person who . . . without proper authority, knowingly harbors or protects or gives intelligence to or communicates or corresponds with or holds any intercourse with the enemy, either directly or indirectly." They argued Manning must have known the disclosures would aid Al Qaeda, among other enemy organizations. Thus, she must have had "evil intent." The aiding-the-enemy charge against a leaker was so uncommon that prosecutors had to reach back to a Civil War case against U.S. solider Henry Vanderwater, who passed a union military command roster to a newspaper in Confederate Virginia. (President Lincoln's administration won an aiding the enemy court-martial conviction against Vanderwater, who received three months of hard labor and a dishonorable discharge.) The prosecutors' failure to convince Judge Lind, along with the charge's high threshold for proof and limited reach, given its place in military law (i.e., governing military personnel, like Manning, but not civilian leakers), suggests that aiding the enemy is unlikely to surface in many leak cases going forward. Still, USMJ §904's reference to indirect communication with enemies is powerfully vague and thus useful for prosecutors. Furthermore, recent government interpretations of the law suggest the possibility of it being used against *civilians*. In 2006, the military decided that individuals "accompanying" the military or coast guard "in the field in times of declared war or a contingency operation" were subject to the UCMJ, including §904, Article 104. The reinterpretation probably was meant to include private sector contractors who operate with military units. But if the legal interpretation remains authoritative, a civilian leaker accompanying the military could be charged under Article 104.[34]

Whereas the government had to dig up a nearly 150-year-old case to support its aiding-the-enemy charge, it has had an easier time using the Espionage Act against Manning and other leakers. The Nixon administration set the precedent in 1971 against Daniel Ellsberg, the Pentagon Papers whistleblower. Unlike Manning, Ellsberg and his primary collaborator, Anthony Russo, were not convicted of espionage, but that was primarily because of the administration's misconduct, for which District Court Judge William Matthew Byrne Jr. dismissed the case.[35]

Overall, U.S. government prosecutors have used the Espionage Act against eleven defendants in public leak cases from 1971 to 2016 (table 6.1). The uptick in indictments under President Obama resulted in part because of its increased capacity to identify leakers using new technologies, along with the administration's policy of strong deterrence against "insider threats." While leaking to publications for a mass audience is qualitatively different than giving secrets to foreign spy services (i.e., espionage), the interpretation is not unreasonable. Section 793 targets individuals who (1) collect or possess national defense information, (2) transfer it to any unauthorized individuals, and (3) know it could be used to harm the United States and/or benefit "any foreign nation." Section 798, which covers the disclosure of classified information, states that "whoever knowingly and willfully communicates, furnishes, transmits, or otherwise makes available to an unauthorized person, or publishes, or uses in any manner prejudicial to the safety or interest of the United States or for the benefit of any foreign government to the detriment of the United States."

The Saga Starring Assange

The intense government response to Manning and Assange's megaleaks was not unprecedented. The Nixon administration aggressively went after Ellsberg as he and his collaborators worked on publishing the DOD's "Report of the Office of the Secretary of Defense Vietnam Task Force" (the Pentagon Papers), a multivolume secret history of the Vietnam War filled with evidence showing that multiple presidents had lied to the public. The cat-and-mouse game became

TABLE 6.1 U.S. Espionage Act Charges against Leakers, 1971–2016

Leaker	Year	Leak	Sections*	Outcome**
Daniel Ellsberg	1971	Pentagon Papers	793 (c, d, e)	Dismissed
Anthony Russo	1971	Pentagon Papers	793 (c, d, e)	Dismissed
Samuel Morrison	1984	Satellite photos of Soviet ships	793 (d, e)	Convicted, pardoned
Thomas Drake	2010	NSA waste, fraud, abuse allegations	793 (c, e)	Dropped
Shamai Leibowitz	2010	Transcripts of wiretapped Israeli diplomat conversations	798 (a)	Convicted
Chelsea (Bradley) Manning	2010	Military and State Department documents to WikiLeaks	793 (e)	Convicted
Stephen Jin-Woo Kim	2010	North Korean nuclear test documents	793 (d)	Convicted
Jeffrey Sterling	2010	Covert action to sabotage Iran nuclear program	793 (d, e)	Convicted
John Kiriakou	2012	Enhanced interrogation program	793 (d)	Dropped
James Hitselberger	2012	U.S. military and intelligence in Bahrain	793 (e)	Dropped
Edward Snowden	2013	NSA and Five Eyes surveillance programs	793 (d), 798 (a)(3)	Ongoing (Snowden in Russia)

Sources: Jason Ross Arnold, *Secrecy in the Sunshine Era: The Promise and Failures of U.S. Open Government Laws* (Lawrence: University Press of Kansas, 2014); Elizabeth Shell and Vanessa Dennis, "11 'Leakers' Charged with Espionage," *PBS Newshour*, August 21, 2013, http://www.pbs.org/newshour/spc/multimedia/espionage/.
*18 U.S. Code Chapter 37.
**Dropped charges involved plea deals, where defendants pled guilty to other charges in part to avoid the Espionage Act.

front page news, with parallels to the U.S. government's search for Edward Snowden before he fled to Russia.[36]

Still, the level of vitriol against Assange, not a leaker but a publisher, was extraordinary. A bipartisan group of politicians stood squarely in line with the Obama administration to attack him. Vice President Joe Biden argued that Assange was "more like a high tech [*sic*] terrorist" than someone involved with whistleblowing. U.S. Senate Minority Leader Mitch McConnell (R-KY) agreed: "I think the man is a high-tech terrorist." Rep. Candice Miller (R-MI), in a speech on the House floor, called on Attorney General Eric Holder to formally label WikiLeaks a terrorist organization. Rep. Peter King (R-NY) likewise asked Secretary of State Hillary Clinton to add WikiLeaks to the U.S. government's list of foreign terrorist organizations, arguing that "WikiLeaks presents a clear and present danger to the national security of the United States." Clinton only went so far as to say the Cablegate release was "not just an attack on America's foreign-policy interests, but an attack on the international community." Whereas many seemed to favor criminal prosecution, some wanted more aggressive action. Former Alaska Governor and 2008 Republican vice presidential candidate Sarah Palin demanded that the U.S. government assassinate him like it did Al Qaeda leaders (or she at least suggested the possibility as a reasonable one):

> Assange is not a "journalist," any more than the "editor" of al Qaeda's new English-language magazine Inspire is a "journalist." He is an anti-American operative with blood on his hands. His past posting of classified documents revealed the identity of more than 100 Afghan sources to the Taliban. *Why was he not pursued with the same urgency we pursue al Qaeda and Taliban leaders?*

Former House Speaker Newt Gingrich agreed: "Information warfare is warfare, and Julian Assange is engaged in warfare. Information terrorism, which leads to people getting killed, is terrorism, and Julian Assange is engaged in terrorism. He should be treated as an enemy combatant." William Kristol, the influential Washington insider and *Weekly Standard* editor, called for the government to "Whack WikiLeaks," imploring politicians from both parties to let "intelligence agencies, the military . . . do what they need to do to . . . degrade, defeat, and destroy WikiLeaks" not just online, but "in both cyberspace and physical space." Popular radio host Rush Limbaugh was characteristically more direct: "How is it that the WikiLeaks guy remains free? Y'know, back in the old days, when men were men and countries were countries, this guy would die of lead poisoning from a bullet in the brain! And nobody would know who put it there!" That kind of message was echoed by others, including retired Lt. Col. Ralph Peters ("Julian Assange is a cyber-terrorist in wartime. He's guilty of sabotage, espionage, crimes against humanity. He should be killed."), *Fox News* commentator Bob Beckel ("The way to deal with this is pretty simple. We've got special ops forces. A dead man can't leak stuff . . . . The guy ought to be . . . . And I'm not for the death penalty . . . there's only one way to do it: illegally shoot the son of a bitch."), and political scientist Tom Flanagan, a former advisor to and coauthor with Canadian Prime Minister Stephen Harper ("Well, I think Assange should be assassinated, actually. I think Obama should put out a contract and maybe use a drone or something").[37]

Beyond the rhetoric, it was difficult to determine what the U.S. government, and any other aggrieved parties, were actually doing behind the scenes against

Assange and WikiLeaks. Much of that history remains shrouded in secrecy. We do know that WikiLeaks started losing control of its website in late 2010, at the same time as the first Cablegate leaks. Unknown hackers launched denial-of-service attacks, making the site unmanageable and largely inaccessible, although at least one of those attacks appears to have been fabricated by WikiLeaks to buy time while completing a project. Under assault, WikiLeaks.org moved to Amazon Web Services in the hopes of a more secure platform, but Amazon terminated the contract a week later, citing violations of the terms and conditions agreement. WikiLeaks's supporters blamed the U.S. government, insisting it had pressured Amazon to remove the website, which the company denied. The site then reemerged and disappeared repeatedly. Bank of America, MasterCard, VISA, PayPal, and Western Union withdrew their services from the WikiLeaks's donation page, causing the site to lose 95 percent of its revenue-generating infrastructure. WikiLeaks called it a "banking blockade." EveryDNS, the firm which converted WikiLeaks's numerical IP address to WikiLeaks.org, seemed to deliver the fatal blow when it dropped its controversial client. WikiLeaks.org vanished from the web.[38]

But WikiLeaks and its large social network had a plan for emergencies like that. It was hatched in 2008, after U.S. Federal District (California Northern District) Judge Jeffrey S. White blocked WikiLeaks from using its domain name, in a case brought by Bank Julius Baer & Co., after WikiLeaks published confidential and forged corporate files. Those who wanted to visit WikiLeaks could do so, but only by typing 88.80.13.160 into the address bar. Even though Judge White soon reversed his order, following a reconsideration of First Amendment and prior restraint issues, the earlier action underscored a critical vulnerability. To protect court-ordered shutdowns and other attacks, WikiLeaks and its supporters began creating "mirror sites," replicas of the website with different DNS addresses. As companies and governments confronted WikiLeaks in late 2010, its social network was ready. A large army of supporters made and promoted hundreds of mirror sites available. Including the one Assange et al. managed, WikiLeaks.ch, there were 507 of them on December 8, 2010. On that site, WikiLeaks reported that it "is currently under heavy attack. In order to make it impossible to ever fully remove WikiLeaks from the Internet, you will find below a list of mirrors," which included wikileaks.as50620.net, wikileaks.enzym.su, freeus.jsdev.org, and wl.gernox.de. Internet users could also trawl through the WikiLeaks archive on the Pirate Bay, the popular BitTorrent site, among other repositories.[39] Cyberwarriors who wanted WikiLeaks off the Internet had their work cut out for them.

WikiLeaks's defensive strategy was multifaceted. In addition to ensuring the archive would remain available during attacks, it had developed a defensive information weapon with an obscured trigger. In July 2010, WikiLeaks posted a 1.4 gigabyte, heavily encrypted file named "Insurance" (insurance.aes256) on the Afghan War logs page. Insurance soon appeared on torrent sites, including Pirate Bay, and had spread to at least sixty-one torrent seeders. WikiLeaks did not describe Insurance's content, but rumors spread that it contained Manning's entire cache. It was an implied threat: If you cross [some unspecified] line, we'll release the encryption key.[40]

Thus, when WikiLeaks came under attack, the large network surrounding it promoted the mirror sites, developed alternative funding mechanisms, and waited for the key that would unlock Insurance, which they warned was a "poison pill," the "Doomsday Files," or, as Assange's lawyer put it, a "thermonuclear device." Even Grateful Dead lyricist John Perry Barlow, hippie extraordinaire and Electronic Frontier Foundation cofounder, pounded the war drums, sounding like a military commander mobilizing an infantry division: "The first serious infowar is now engaged. The field of battle is WikiLeaks. You are the troops. #WikiLeaks."[41]

In the midst of that conflict, another one arose that deepened the intrigue. Ten days before Cablegate triggered WikiLeaks's "infowar," Interpol issued a Red Notice, which asked all 188 member countries to arrest Assange. The alleged offense had nothing to do with classified leaks. Two anonymous Swedish women in August 2010 had filed rape and molestation complaints against Assange, leading the Prosecutor's Office there to issue an arrest warrant. Assange denied the allegations, and the government withdrew the warrant but asked Assange to travel to Sweden for questioning. Many noted the peculiar timing—the warrant and request came in the midst of the war log leaks—and hypothesized about a CIA "honey trap" covert operation. At the very least, his supporters argued, Assange could never go to Sweden, because the government there would quickly extradite him to the United States. Over the next three months, Assange refused to go, but offered to answer questions elsewhere. On November 18, ten days before Cablegate, a Swedish judge ordered Assange "detained in absentia," leading Interpol to issue the Red Notice. British authorities detained Assange on December 7, refusing bail. Assange spent over a week in jail, before agreeing to house arrest at a friend's country estate in Norfolk, where he remained for 550 days.[42] Saturday Night Live lampooned him as a cackling, brandy sipping villain, hiding out in his luxurious lair.[43]

What would happen to this strangely charismatic leader of the infowar's rebel army, now trapped in a charming English mansion due to Swedish sex assault allegations, which his supporters said were phony constructs of a CIA honey trap operation? First, he continued to run WikiLeaks, although it published nothing as impactful as the 2010's disclosures. Second, the Russian government offered him a television show on its global propaganda network,

RT (Russia Today). The first of twelve episodes of *World Tomorrow*, recorded in April 2012 at the Norfolk estate, featured Hassan Nasrallah, the leader of the terrorist group Hezbollah. Third, he lost an appeal that asked Britain to reject Sweden's extradition request. On May 30, the U.K. Supreme Court voted 5–2 against him. Finally, on June 19, Assange appeared at the door of the Ecuadorian Embassy in London, where he requested political asylum, which Ecuador's left-wing President Rafael Correa granted.[44] Leaving the building, which he was free to do, likely would have meant extradition to Sweden, and then, he suspected, the United States.

Assange spent seven years in the Ecuadorian Embassy before British authorities arrested him on April 11, 2019 (the day before this book went to press), in cooperation with a U.S. extradition warrant, for working with Manning in a "conspiracy to commit computer intrusion."[45] While living in the embassy, he ran WikiLeaks, waged infowar (e.g., uploading ever larger insurance files), wrote books and thousands of Tweets, welcomed visitors, sold WikiLeaks gear ("Free Assange" and "First They Came for Assange" t-shirts); and made occasional speeches from a balcony like some populist South American president from the 1930s.[46] Conflicts with the Ecuadorians sometimes resulted in his Internet access being cut off. In October 2018, he threatened to sue Ecuador. After his arrest and removal from the embassy, Ecuadorian officials told shocking stories about Assange's alleged behavior, from his overall "rudeness" to more specific allegations about "walking around in his underwear," "going weeks without a shower," and smearing feces on the walls "on at least one occasion in an act of open defiance showing how little he thought of his hosts."[47]

While Assange and WikiLeaks still had millions of backers in 2019, the organization lost a significant but unknown amount of its global support network starting in 2016 after it published private emails that "Guccifer 2.0," a front for Russia's Main Intelligence Directorate of the General Staff (GRU), stole from Democratic National Committee servers and leading Democrats' private accounts. The GRU/WikiLeaks hack and leak operation was a part of Russia's broader intervention into the U.S. presidential election that aimed to exacerbate political conflicts and harm Hillary Clinton's campaign and (as it seemed then) ensuing presidency.[48] While the Russian connection and seeming preference for then candidate Donald Trump cost Assange and WikiLeaks many supporters, they picked up new ones, including once sworn enemies. Palin, the former governor and vice presidential candidate who once implied that Assange should be assassinated, published an apology in early 2017:

To Julian Assange: I apologize. . .
Exposing the truth re: the Left having been oh-so-guilty of atrocious actions and attitudes of which they've falsely accused others. The media collusion that hid what many on the Left have been supporting is shocking. This important

information that finally opened people's eyes to democrat candidates and opera-
tives would not have been exposed were it not for Julian Assange.
. . .
Julian, I apologize.
—Sarah Palin[49]

From 2010 until 2018, there were rumors that a U.S. grand jury had indicted
Assange under the Espionage Act, but the government was concealing it while
waiting for him to leave the embassy. More information emerged about a grand
jury investigation related to WikiLeaks, but Assange appeared to have been spared
Espionage Act charges, in part because of the lack of an important legal distinction
between WikiLeaks and other organizations that had published Manning's leaked
files. (That is, the grand jury questioned the basis from which prosecutors could
charge Assange but not *Times* publisher Arthur Ochs Sulzberger Jr., who also
published Manning's leaked files.) In 2018, a federal court accidentally disclosed,
in an apparently unrelated case, that officials had been trying "to keep confidential
the fact that Assange has been charged," and that a court order needed to "remain
sealed until Assange is arrested in connection with the charges in the criminal complaint." The specific nature of those charges, which could have been linked with
the 2010 or 2016 leaks, remained unknown.[50] Finally, as indicated earlier, British
authorities, cooperating with a U.S. extradition warrant, arrested Assange in April
2019 for his and Manning's "conspiracy to commit computer intrusion" in 2010.
The saga that started in 2010 will continue into the 2020s.[51]

The intense retaliation Assange and WikiLeaks experienced as a result
of the 2010 leaks was undeniably extraordinary. No other leak publisher
had experienced anything quite like it. Massive cyberattacks. Sealed grand
jury indictments for conspiracy. Sexual assault charges that, even if credible,
emerged with peculiar timing and a puzzling insistence that Assange answer
questions in Sweden. Nevertheless, much of what makes the case distinctive
resulted from Assange's idiosyncratic decisions and eccentric personality.
He evaded the British, American, and Swedish justice systems by barricading
himself in the Ecuadorian embassy. He threatened major world governments
and their citizens, by circulating the encrypted raw data files Assange's lawyer
called "thermonuclear devices," which could be detonated by releasing a key.
He hosted a TV show on a Russian government channel. For those and other
reasons, the case is not likely to be reflective of how retaliation politics will
play out in other Digital Age cases, even if other megaleaks prompt aggressive
responses.

In some ways, the dramatic experience was not unprecedented. The Nixon
administration tried hard to block *The New York Times* from publishing Ellsberg's Pentagon Papers, claiming the stories would cause "grave and irreparable" danger to the country's security. President Nixon battled the *Times* all

the way up to the Supreme Court, relenting only after the justices ruled 6–3 against the administration.[52]

That is not to say that WikiLeaks and media organizations like the *Times* are qualitatively identical. Clearly they are not. But there is no reason why a leak recipient has to be just like a major newspaper. As the next chapter demonstrates, sites built for leaking and whistleblowing without direct links to the mainstream media are becoming increasingly common and inventive.

Conclusion

WikiLeaks did not invent online anonymous leaking, but it refined the model to near-perfection, and brought it to the attention of billions. It set the table for a new era in the history of leaking and whistleblowing, with its strong source protections, and its ability to draw attention to its "brand" in a crowded, transnational media environment. WikiLeaks's actions have rarely conformed to the whistleblowing conceptualization developed in chapter 2. However, its many followers, with secret-spilling sites of their own, just might. Future researchers might systematically score the various sites for their adherence to that conceptualization.

There are many reasons to doubt that WikiLeaks will become an exemplary whistleblowing organization. The primary reason is that Assange is unlikely to change, given his avowed beliefs, his cypherpunk ethos, his deep hacker roots (as "Mendax" and as a member of the group the International Subversives), his dogmatic personality, as well as his unusual biography, including the conflicts he has had with major world governments and corporations. As long as an unchanging Assange can credibly claim, "I am WikiLeaks," the organization will not likely become a model whistleblowing enterprise.[53]

Notes

[1]   Andy Greenberg, *This Machine Kills Secrets: How WikiLeakers, Cypherpunks, and Hacktivists Aim to Free the World's Information* (New York: Plume, 2012); Hugh B. Urban, "Fair Game: Secrecy, Security, and the Church of Scientology in Cold War America," *Journal of the American Academy of Religion* 74, no. 2 (June 2006): 356–89, at 381. Penet was designed by Johan "Julf" Helsingius. The Scientology conflict was part of a larger conflict involving secret-spilling and accusations of copyright infringement, libel, and slander. Notable cases include *Religious Technology Center v. NetcomOn-line Comm.*, 907 F. Supp. 1361 (N. D. Cal. 1995).

[2]   Greenberg, *This Machine*; "Ask Cryptome's John Young Whatever You'd Like," *Slashdot*, October 31, 2001, http://slashdot.org/story/01/10/29/2330241/ask-cryptomes-john-young-whatever-youd-like; Ian Urbina, "Mapping Natural Gas Lines: Advise the Public, Tip Off the Terrorists," *The New York Times*, August 29, 2004, http://www.nytimes.com/2004/08/29/nyregion/mapping-natural-gas-lines-advise-the-public-tip-off-the-terrorists.html; Thomas Golianopoulos, "The Original WikiLeaker," *Observer*, December 8, 2010, http://observer.com/2010/12/the-original-wikileaker.

[3]   Assange had registered the domain name "leaks.org" in 1999, indicating that he had planned something like WikiLeaks for at least seven years. See Stuart Rintoul and Sean Parnell, "Julian

Assange, Wild Child of Free Speech," *The Australian*, December 11, 2010, http://www.
theaustralian.com.au/in-depth/wikileaks/julian-assange-wild-child-of-free-speech/news-story/
af356d93b25b28527eb106c255c942db.

4   The April 2019 arrest of Julian Assange was linked to a U.S. grand jury indictment that alleges
that WikiLeaks did not merely receive Manning's documents, but conspired with him to break
into Defense Department servers to steal classified information. The trial had not begun by
the time this book went to press on April 12, 2019. *US v. Julian Assange* [grand jury indictment, published in April 2019], March 6, 2018, U.S. District Court for the Eastern District of
Virginia. As noted in chapter 1, Manning dropped Bradley for Chelsea in 2013. Bradley, and
the male pronoun, are used here because they were the terms that Manning used then, and
during the subsequent legal process. I refer to Chelsea and the female pronouns in many other
sections of the book.

5   George Orwell, "Politics and the English Language," *Horizon* 13, no. 76 (April 1946):
252–65.

6   "Collateral Murder" transcript, WikiLeaks, accessed December 22, 2016, https://collateralmu
rder.wikileaks.org/en/transcript.html.

7   Robert Farley, "Gates Said Leaked Military Video of Shooting in Iraq Doesn't Show the
Broader Picture of Americans Being Fired Upon," *PolitiFact*, April 12, 2010, http://www.
politifact.com/truth-o-meter/statements/2010/apr/12/robert-gates/gates-said-leaked-military-
video-shooting-iraq-doe.

8   David Finkel, *The Good Soldiers* (New York: Sarah Crichton Books, 2009), 95.

9   Kristinn Hrafnsson, interview with Amy Goodman, "'An Attack on Journalism': WikiLeaks
on Bradley Manning Trial, FBI Move to Infiltrate Organization," *Democracy Now!* July
2, 2013, http://www.democracynow.org/2013/7/2/an_attack_on_journalism_wikileaks_on_b
radley_manning_trial_fbi_move_to_infiltrate_organization; Julian Assange, interview with
Amy Goodman, "Julian Assange on WikiLeaks, War and Resisting Government Crack-
down," *Democracy Now!*, December 31, 2010, http://www.democracynow.org/2010/12/31/
julian_assange_on_wikileaks_war_and; Greg Mitchell, "Bradley Manning: From 'Collateral
Murder' to Court-Martial," *The Nation*, March 24, 2012, http://www.thenation.com/article/
bradley-manning-collateral-murder-court-martial.

10   "Afghan War Diary," accessed January 10, 2019, https://www.wikileaks.org/afg.

11   "Afghan War Diary." The encoded webpage title (i.e., what appears in the browser tab
label) still reads "Kabul War Diary"—probably an earlier, working title. Alex Gibney, "Can
We Trust WikiLeaks?" *The New York Times*, August 8, 2016, A23; Raffi Khatchadourian,
"Julian Assange, a Man Without a Country," *New Yorker*, August 21, 2017.

12   For example, see WikiLeaks's 2016 AKP emails release at https://wikileaks.org/akp-emails/.
It contained emails from members of Turkey's governing party, the Justice and Development
Party (AKP), over a six-year period. The 2016 release of Democratic National Committee
emails also came without identity-protecting redactions. WikiLeaks's indifference to privacy
is also evident in releases that have nothing to do with "war, spying and corruption," which
the organization claims to be its focus. For example, it published the names of rape victims
and persecuted gay men in Saudi Arabia. See Raphael Satter and Maggie Michael, "Private
Lives Are Exposed as WikiLeaks Spills Its Secrets," *AP*, August 23, 2016, https://apnews.com/
b70da83fd111496dbdf015acbb7987fb.

13   "Iraq War Logs," *WikiLeaks*, accessed January 16, 2019, https://www.wikileaks.org/irq/. Like
the earlier release, the webpage tab title ("Baghdad War Diary") was similarly inconsistent
with the release title.

14   Khatchadourian, "Julian Assange"; Ed Pilkington, "Bradley Manning Leak Did Not Result in
Deaths by Enemy Forces, Court Hears," *The Guardian*, July 31, 2013, http://www.theguardian.
com/world/2013/jul/31/bradley-manning-sentencing-hearing-pentagon; Nick Davies, Jonathan
Steele, and David Leigh, "Iraq War Logs: Secret Files Show How US Ignored Torture," *The
Guardian*, October 22, 2010, https://www.theguardian.com/world/2010/oct/22/iraq-war-logs-
military-leaks.

15   "The Defense Department's Response," *The New York Times*, October 23, 2010, A9.

16 A leaked 2011 Defense Intelligence Agency classified report, touted by its publisher BuzzFeed News as being largely exculpatory, actually reflects a mixed assessment by the task force. Plus, the report is heavily redacted, which should constrain any strong conclusions about its findings. "(U) Final Report of the Department of Defense Information Review Task Force," Defense Intelligence Agency Information Review Task Force, June 15, 2011, https://assets. documentcloud.org/documents/3868778/Wikileaks-Manning-Defense-Department-Damage. pdf;Jason Leopold, "Secret Report Contradicts US Position On Chelsea Manning Leaks," *BuzzFeed News*, June 20, 2017, https://www.buzzfeednews.com/article/jasonleopold/secret-government-report-chelsea-manning-leaks-caused-no#.oeRzaQW8w3.

17 "Cablegate," *WikiLeaks*, accessed July 28, 2014, https://wikileaks.org/cablegate.html; Scott Shane and Andrew W. Lehren, "STATE'S SECRETS; Leaked Cables Offer a Raw Look Inside U.S. Diplomacy," *The New York Times,* November 29, 2010, A1. Less than half (46.7 percent) of the cables were officially classified, although all were written under the assumption they would remain secret until about mid-century, if that. None were marked "top secret," the highest official level. About 6 percent (15,652) of the total had a "secret" stamp, while about over 40 percent (101,748) were classified as "confidential," the lowest level. The rest (133,887) were sensitive but unclassified; according to long-standing executive branch standards, their disclosure would not drastically harm security, but would likely compromise policy implementation and official relationships (domestic and international), and possibly reveal technical information, innocuous in isolation, but harmful when connected to other available information. See Jason Ross Arnold, *Secrecy in the Sunshine Era: The Promise and Limits of U.S. Open Government Laws* (Lawrence: University Press of Kansas, 2014).

18 "Corruption in Tunisia: What's Yours Is Mine," U.S. State Department cable, Tunis, Tunisia Embassy, June 23, 2008, https://wikileaks.org/plusd/cables/08TUNIS679_a.html; "World Report 2012: Tunisia," Human Rights Watch, https://www.hrw.org/world-report/2012/country-chapters/tunisia.

19 This link executes the search on WikiLeaks's Public Library of US Diplomacy (accessed January 9, 2019): https://search.wikileaks.org/plusd/?qproject[]=cg&q=&qtfrom=2008-06-23 &qtto=2008-06-23#result.

20 L. N. Rangarajan, "Diplomacy, States and Secrecy in Communications," *Diplomacy and Statecraft 9*, no. 3 (1998): 18–49; Louise Fréchette, "Foreword: Diplomacy: Old Trade, New Challenges," *The Oxford Handbook of Modern Diplomacy*, edited by Andrew F. Cooper, Jorge Heine, Ramesh Thakur (Oxford University Press, 2013), xxx–xxxv.

21 Kaj Larsen, How WikiLeaks Has Changed Today's Media, *CNN*, June 10, 2011, http://www .cnn.com/2011/WORLD/europe/06/10/wikileaks.journalism/; Emily Badger, "WikiLeaks and the Future of Whistle-blowing," *Pacific Standard*, May 2, 2011, https://psmag.com/wikilea ks-and-the-future-of-whistle-blowing-45be0f534eef#.3rrd46cdx; Tom Cheshire, "What Did Julian Assange's WikiLeaks Achieve?" *Sky News*, August 18, 2014, http://news.sky.com/story /what-did-julian-assanges-wikileaks-achieve-10392713; NWLDEF [National Whistleblower Legal Defense and Education Fund], "Whistleblowers: From the American Revolution to WikiLeaks," July 12, 2011, http://www.whistleblowersblog.org/2011/07/articles/news/events/ whistleblowers-from-the-american-revolution-to-wikileaks/; RT America, "WikiLeaks: How It's Changed the Face of Whistleblowing," September 19, 2012, https://www.youtube.com/ watch?v=Uwi_l-61ubk. Ads for the WikiLeaks thriller film *The Fifth Estate* argued the organization was game-changing: "Triggering our age of high-stakes secrecy, explosive news leaks and the trafficking of classified information, WikiLeaks forever changed the game. Now, in a dramatic thriller based on real events, *The Fifth Estate* reveals the quest to expose the deceptions and corruptions of power that turned an Internet upstart into the 21st century's most fiercely debated organization."

22 Doug Sanders, "WikiLeaks Founder Threatens to Release Entire Cache of Unfiltered Files," *The Globe and Mail,* December 5, 2010, http://www.theglobeandmail.com/news/world/ wikileaks-founder-threatens-to-release-entire-cache-of-unfiltered-files/article1318545.

23 Manning also leaked approximately 800 Guantanamo Bay detainee assessment briefs. *The New York Times* first reported from "The Guantánamo Files" in April 2011. Charlie Savage,

William Glaberson, and Andrew W. Lehren, "Details of Lives in an American Limbo," *The New York Times,* April 24, 2011, A1.

24 Greenberg, *This Machine,* 105.

25 "About," WikiLeaks, accessed January 16, 2019, https://wikileaks.org/About.html; Julian Assange, "Why the World Needs WikiLeaks," TED Talks, July 2010, http://www.ted.com/talks/julian_assange_why_the_world_needs_wikileaks. Assange is labeled a whistleblower on the TED webpage.

26 Charlie Savage, "Soldier Admits Providing Files to WikiLeaks," *The New York Times*, March 1, 2013, A1; Civilian Defense Counsel [redacted] and Military Defense Counsel [redacted] to Military Judge [redacted], Trial Counsel, Joint Force Headquarters, January 29, 2013, Re: Statement in Support of Providence Inquiry—*U.S. v. Private First Class* (PFC) Bradley E. Manning, https://fas.org/sgp/jud/manning/022813-statement.pdf; Cryptome, "WikiLeaks Security Measures," May 21, 2010, https://cryptome.org/isp-spy/wikileaks-spy.pdf; Greenberg, *This Machine*; Kim Zetter, "WikiLeaks Was Launched With Documents Intercepted From Tor," *Wired*, June 1, 2010, http://www.wired.com/2010/06/wikileaks-documents/; Raffi Khatchadourian, "No Secrets," *The New Yorker,* June 7, 2010.

27 Greenberg, *This Machine*; Juan Luis Sánchez, "Medio Colaborador de la Nueva Herramienta de Filtraciones Anónimas: Filtrala," *Eldiario.es*, April 23, 2014, http://www.eldiario.es/redaccion/eldiarioes-colaborador-herramienta-filtraciones-Filtrala_6_252034807.html; "Tunisian Blog Launches Whistleblowing Platform," April 15, 2014, *Global Voices Online*, http://advocacy.globalvoicesonline.org/2014/04/16/tunisian-blog-launches-whistleblowing-platform/; Doug Saunders, "Catch Me and I'll Drop a Bomb of Data, Assange Warns," *The Globe and Mail*, December 6, 2010, A1; Ron Deibert, "After WikiLeaks, a New Era," *Room for Debate, The New York Times*, December 9, 2010, http://www.nytimes.com/roomfordebate/2010/12/09/what-has-wikileaks-started/after-wikileaks-a-new-era. SecureDrop, Freedom of the Press Foundation, accessed July 29, 2014, https://pressfreedomfoundation.org/securedrop/directory. *Wall Street Journal* launched SafeHouse in May 2011 but closed it, in part due to strong criticism from Internet security experts. The link to the SafeHouse page (accessed July 30, 2014) brings readers to a "news tips" page that says "The Wall Street Journal's SafeHouse has been closed. Send traditional news tips, ideas and contact details to newseditors@wsj.com. This is a standard email address." See also Alexis C. Madrigal, "The *Wall Street Journal* Launches a WikiLeaks Competitor, SafeHouse," *The Atlantic*, May 5, 2011, http://www.theatlantic.com/technology/archive/2011/05/the-wall-street-journal-launches-a-wikileaks-competitor-safehouse/238421/. Al Jazeera also launched (in January 2011) and then quickly shut down a leaks platform alternative. See also Rainey Reitman, "Will the Rise of Wikileaks Competitors Make Whistleblowing Resistant to Censorship?" DeepLinks, Electronic Frontier Foundation, February 16, 2011 https://www.eff.org/deeplinks/2011/02/will-rise-wikileaks-competitors-make.

28 Sagar, *Secrets and Leaks;* C. Fred Alford, "WikiLeaks Is No Whistle-Blower," *The New York Times (Room for Debate),* December 9, 2010, http://www.nytimes.com/roomfordebate/2010/12/09/what-has-wikileaks-started/wikileaks-is-no-whistle-blower.

29 Assorted WikiLeaks merchandise viewed on https://shop.spreadshirt.com/wikileaks/ and http://www.cafepress.com/+wikileaks+gifts on July 27, 2016; Rob Walker, "Branding Transparency," *The New York Times Magazine,* January 16, 2011, MM22; Caroline Shin, "Check out All This Weird Julian Assange Merchandise Sold at the WikiLeaks Shop," *Business Insider,* February 24, 2011, http://www.businessinsider.com/julian-assange-wikileaks-merchandise-2011-2?op=1; Vanessa Friedman, "The Branding of Julian Assange," *The New York Times*, October 23, 2014, E6; Lauren Walker, "Assange to Bring WikiLeaks-Branded Clothing to India," October 14, 2014, *Newsweek*, http://www.newsweek.com/assange-bring-wikileaks-branded-clothing-india-277339.

30 Adrian Lamo, Answer to question "What Precautions Did Bradley Manning Take for His Own Safety While Working with Wikileaks?" Quora, June 11, 2015, https://www.quora.com/What-precautions-did-Bradley-Manning-take-for-his-own-safety-while-working-with-Wikileaks-Did-the-government-surpass-his-preparations-or-did-he-want-to-get-caught.

31 Kim Zetter and Kevin Poulsen, "'I Can't Believe What I'm Confessing to You': The WikiLeaks Chats," *Wired*, June 10, 2010, https://www.wired.com/2010/06/wikileaks-chat/; Evan Hansen,

"Manning-Lamo Chat Logs Revealed," *Wired,* July 13, 2011, https://www.wired.com/201 1/07/manning-lamo-logs/; Lamo, "What Precautions Did Bradley Manning Take?"; Ed Pilkington, "Adrian Lamo Tells Manning Trial about Six Days of Chats with Accused Leaker," *The Guardian,* June 4, 2013, https://www.theguardian.com/world/2013/jun/04/adrian-la mo-testifies-bradley-manning; Andy Greenberg, "Stealthy Government Contractor Monitors U.S. Internet Providers, Worked with WikiLeaks Informant," *Forbes,* August 1, 2010, http: //www.forbes.com/sites/firewall/2010/08/01/stealthy-government-contractor-monitors-u-s-internet-providers-says-it-employed-wikileaks-informant/. Lamo seemed to Manning like a trustworthy confidant because he appeared on a leaked list of WikiLeaks's donors. In 2009, WikiLeaks Donor Relations erred in sending an email fundraising pitch to donors in 2009, using the "cc" field instead of "bcc." Everyone on who received the email saw all of the email addresses. Lamo mocked WikiLeaks's capacity to protect identities in a Tweet, which linked to a text file of the email recipients: "Thanks WikiLeaks, for leaking your donor list, including yours truly, by not BCC'ing—http://adrianlamo.com/don.txt—that's dedication." WikiLeaks wound up publishing the list, while snidely referring to Lamo as a "prankster": "A prankster, apparently connected to one of the donors, then submitted this list to Wikileaks [*sic*], possibly to test the project's principles of complete impartiality when dealing with whistleblowers." The episode is important not only because it shaped Manning's decision-making during the chat sessions, but it also reveals an earlier conflict between Lamo and Assange/WikiLeaks. See Ryan Singel, "WikiLeaks Forced to Leak Its Own Secret Info," *Wired*, February 18, 2009, https://www.wired.com/2009/02/wikileaks-force/; Adrian Lamo (@6), Twitter, February 14, 2009, https://twitter.com/6/status/1209430201; "Wikileaks Partial Donors List, 14 Feb 2009," WikiLeaks, https://wikileaks.org/wiki/Wikileaks_partial_donors_list,_14_Feb_2009.

32 Bruce Ackerman and Yochai Benkler, "Private Manning's Humiliation," *New York Review of Books* 58, no. 8 (2011): 62; Ed Pilkington, "PJ Crowley Resigns over Bradley Manning Remarks," *The Guardian,* March 13, 2011, https://www.theguardian.com/world/2011/ mar/13/pj-crowley-resigns-bradley-manning-remarks.

33 Manning's sentence could have been much longer—90 or 136 years, according to different estimates. Charlie Savage and Emmarie Huetteman, "Manning Sentenced to 35 Years for a Pivotal Leak of U.S. Files," *The New York Times,* August 22, 2013, A1; Charlie Savage, "Manning Is Acquitted of Aiding the Enemy," *The New York Times,* July 30, 2013, A1.

34 U.S. Military Code of Justice, Section 904, Article 104, "Aiding the Enemy," http://www.au. af.mil/au/awc/awcgate/ucmj2.htm#904.%20ART.%20104.%20AIDING%20THE%20ENE MY, accessed July 29, 2016; Scott Bomboy, Why Manning's Aiding the Enemy Charge Was so Important," *Constitution Daily,* National Constitution Center, July 30, 2013, http://blog. constitutioncenter.org/2013/07/why-mannings-aiding-the-enemy-charge-was-so-important/; U.S. Secretary of Defense, "UCMJ Jurisdiction Over [sic] DoD Civilian Employees, DoD Contractor Personnel, and Other Persons Serving With [sic] or Accompanying the Armed Forces Overseas During [sic] Declared War and in Contingency Operations," Department of Defense OSD 02927-08, Memorandum for Secretaries of the Military Departments, Chairman of the Joint Chiefs of Staff, Under Secretaries of Defense, Commanders of the Combatant Commands, March 10, 2008, https://www.justice.gov/sites/default/files/criminal-hrsp/legacy/2011/ 02/04/03-10-08dod-ucmj.pdf; General Counsel of the U.S. Department of Defense, "Policy and Procedures Applicable to Dod and United States Coast Guard (USCG) Civilian Personnel Subject to Uniform Code of Military Justice (UCMJ) Jurisdiction in Time of Declared War or a Contingency Operation," Department of Defense Memorandum for Secretaries of the Military Departments et al. [long list on p. 6 of document], January 20, 2012, http://www.dod.gov/ dodgc/images/ucmj_art2_jurisdiction.pdf; Katie Wall and Courtney Kube, "Accused Leaker Bradley Manning Had 'Evil Intent,' Prosecutors Say in Closing Arguments," *NBC News,* July 25, 2013, http://www.nbcnews.com/news/other/accused-leaker-bradley-manning-had-evil-intent-prosecutors-say-closing-f6C10741414; David Leigh and Luke Harding, *WikiLeaks: Inside Julian Assange's War on Secrecy* (New York: Public Affairs, 2011), 25; David Dishneau and Pauline Jelinek, "WikiLeaks Trial Verdict: Bradley Manning Ruling Could Test Notion of Aiding Enemy," *The Associated Press,* July 30, 2013, http://www.huffingtonpost.com/2013/ 07/30/wikileaks-trial-verdict_n_3675635.html.

35 Daniel Ellsberg, *Secrets: A Memoir of Vietnam and the Pentagon Papers* (New York: Penguin, 2003); Martin Arnold, "Pentagon Papers Charges Are Dismissed; Judge Byrne Frees Ellsberg and Russo, Assails 'Improper Government Conduct,'" *The New York Times*, May 12, 1973, A1. Ellsberg and Russo were also charged with theft and conspiracy.

36 Ellsberg's role in American history goes beyond the leak of the Pentagon Papers. It was the illegal break-in of Ellsberg's psychiatrist's office, and then Nixon's obsession with stopping leaks, that set the Watergate scandal into motion.

37 Many other prominent voices, including elected officials Sen. Joe Lieberman (I-CT) and Rep. Mike Rogers (R-MI), called for treason charges and a subsequent execution. Note that Flanagan later indicated he was glibly joking, and clarified: "I never seriously intended to advocate or propose the assassination of Mr. Assange . . . . But I do think that what he's doing is very malicious and harmful to diplomacy and endangering people's lives, and I think it should be stopped." "WikiLeaks Founder Calls for Flanagan Charge," *CBC News*, December 3, 2010, http://www.cbc.ca/news/politics/wikileaks-founder-calls-for-flanagan-charge-1.87 7546; "Meet the Press Transcript for Dec. 19, 2010," *Meet the Press*, NBC News, http:// www.nbcnews.com/id/40720643/ns/meet_the_press-transcripts/t/meet-press-transcript-dec/#. V5u8x6LLJoo [Readers should be aware that NBC's site's transcription service made systemic errors in the transcript, mixing up Biden's remarks with David Gregory's.]; "McConnell: Assange is a 'High-tech Terrorist,'" *Meet the Press*, NBC News, December 05, 2010, http:// www.nbcnews.com/video/meet-the-press/40516927; Sarah Palin, "Serious Questions about the Obama Administration's Incompetence in the Wikileaks Fiasco," *Facebook,* November 29, 2010, emphasis added, https://www.facebook.com/note.php?note_id=465212788434; Greenberg, *This Machine*; William Kristol, "Whack WikiLeaks," *The Weekly Standard,* November 30, 2010, http://www.weeklystandard.com/whack-wikileaks/article/520462;Declan McCullagh, "Congressman Wants WikiLeaks Listed as Terrorist Group," CNET, November 28, 2010, http://www.cnet.com/news/congressman-wants-wikileaks-listed-as-terrorist-group/; "Clinton: WikiLeaks' Release Attacks International Community," *Armed Forces News Service,* November 29, 2010, http://archive.defense.gov/news/newsarticle.aspx?id=61876; Nate Anderson, "Meet the People Who Want Julian Assange 'Whacked,'" *ArsTechnica,* December 3, 2010, http://arstechnica.com/tech-policy/2010/12/meet-the-people-who-want-julian-assan ge-whacked/; WikiLeaks, "U.S. Demands to Assassinate Assange," TheWikiLeaksChannel, November 27, 2012, https://www.youtube.com/watch?v=ZuQW0US2sJw; "Interview with Speaker Gingrich," *Fox News Sunday*, December 5, 2010; Benkler, "A Free Irresponsible Press: WikiLeaks and the Battle over the Soul of the Networked Fourth Estate," *Harvard Civil Rights-Civil Liberties Law Review* 46 (2011): 311–97, at 345.

38 Doug Gross, "WikiLeaks Cut off from Amazon Servers," *CNN*, December 2, 2010, http:// edition.cnn.com/2010/US/12/01/wikileaks.amazon/index.html; "WikiLeaks," *Amazon Web Services,* accessed December 22, 2016, https://aws.amazon.com/message/65348/; Dan Nystedt, "Amazon Says Government Pressure Didn't Lead to Wikileaks Ban," *Computer World,* December 2010, http://www.computerworld.com/article/2514705/technology-law-regul ation/amazon-says-government-pressure-didn-t-lead-to-wikileaks-ban.html; Jane Wakefield, "Wikileaks' Struggle to Stay Online," *BBC News*, December 7, 2010, http://www.bbc.com/ news/technology-11928899; "Banking Blockade," WikiLeaks, June 28, 2011, https://wikilea ks.org/Banking-Blockade.html. On the fabricated attack claim, see the testimony of former WikiLeaks insider James Ball, "Inside the Strange, Paranoid World of Julian Assange," *BuzzFeed,* October 23, 2016, https://www.buzzfeed.com/jamesball/heres-what-i-learned-abou t-julian-assange; Charles Arthur, "WikiLeaks under Attack: The Definitive Timeline," *The Guardian,* December 7, 2010, https://www.theguardian.com/media/2010/dec/07/wikileaks -under-attack-definitive-timeline.

39 Judge Jeffrey White was hearing a case brought by Julius Baer Bank and Trust. *Bank Julius Baer v Wikileaks,* 535 F.Supp.2d 980 (2008) United States District Court, N.D. California; Kevin Poulsen, "Cyberwar against Wikileaks? Good Luck with That," *Wired,* August 13, 2010, https://www.wired.com/2010/08/cyberwar-wikileaks/; "Free Speech Has a Number: 88.80.13.160," *CBS News*, February 20, 2008, http://www.cbsnews.com/news/free-speech-has-a-number-888013160/; Daniel Domscheit-Berg, *Inside WikiLeaks: My Time with Julian*

Assange at the World's Most Dangerous Website (New York: Random House, 2011); "Mirrors," *WikiLeaks,* accessed July 29, 2016, https://web.archive.org/web/20101207060201/http://www.wikileaks.ch/mirrors.html.

40 Insurance was encrypted with an Advanced Encryption Standard (AES) 256-bit key, which is reportedly strong enough for NSA top secret classified documents. Kim Zetter, "WikiLeaks Posts Mysterious 'Insurance' File," *Wired,* July 30, 2010, https://www.wired.com/2010/07/wikileaks-insurance-file/; Dan Nosowitz, "How Secure Is Julian Assange's 'Thermonuclear' Insurance File?" *Popular Science,* December 7, 2010, http://www.popsci.com/technolo gy/article/2010-12/how-secure-julian-assanges-thermonuclear-insurance-file; Ashley Fantz, "Assange's 'Poison Pill' File Impossible to Stop, Expert Says," *CNN,* December 8, 2010, http://edition.cnn.com/2010/US/12/08/wikileaks.poison.pill/index.html; Bruce Schneier, "WikiLeaks Insurance File," *Schneier on Security,* August 4, 2010, https://www.schneier.com/blog/archi ves/2010/08/wikileaks_insur.html; "Ongoing Non-Secret Discussion of Information Security, A/K/A Information Secrecy, A/K/A Information Perfidy," *Cryptome,* August 7, 2010, https://cryptome.org/0002/wl-diary-mirror.htm.

41 Nosowitz, "How Secure"; Fantz, "Assange's 'Poison Pill' File"; Stephen Kurczy, "Will WikiLeaks' Julian Assange, Now Arrested, Take the 'Nuclear' Option," *Christian Science Monitor,* December 7, 2010 http://www.csmonitor.com/World/Europe/2010/1207/Will-WikiLeaks-Julian-Assange-now-arrested-take-the-nuclear-option.

42 Greenberg, *This Machine*; Benkler, "A Free Irresponsible Press"; Kevin Poulsen, "Interpol Issues 'Red Notice' for Arrest of WikiLeaks' Julian Assange," *Wired,* November 30, 2010, https://www.wired.com/2010/11/assange-interpol/; "Julian Assange Sex Assault Allegations: Timeline," *BBC News,* February 5, 2016, http://www.bbc.com/news/world-europe-11949341; Sari Horwitz, "Julian Assange Unlikely to Face U.S. Charges over Publishing Classified Documents," *Washington Post,* November 25, 2013; Hillary Hurd, "If Assange Leaves the Ecuadorian Embassy, What Next?" *Lawfare,* August 3, 2018, https://www.lawfareblog.com/if-assa nge-leaves-ecuadorian-embassy-what-next.

43 "A Message from Mark Zuckerberg," *Saturday Night Live,* accessed December 23, 2016, http://www.nbc.com/saturday-night-live/video/a-message-from-mark-zuckerberg/n12987; "WikiLeaks: TMZ Edition, *Saturday Night Live,* accessed December 23, 2016, http://www .nbc.com/saturday-night-live/video/wikileaks-cold-open/n12957.

44 "The World Tomorrow with Julian Assange," accessed January 16, 2019, https://worldtomor row.wikileaks.org/; Hurd, "If Assange Leaves"; "Julian Assange Loses Extradition Appeal at Supreme Court," *BBC News,* May 30, 2012. https://www.bbc.com/news/uk-18260914.

45 *US v. Julian Assange* [grand jury indictment], March 6, 2018, U.S. District Court for the Eastern District of Virginia. The publication of the indictment and the arrest occurred on the same day, April 11, 2019. (Coincidentally, this book went to press the following day.) In March 2019, a federal judge jailed Manning for refusing to testify before Assange's grand jury. Charlie Savage, "Manning Is Sent to Jail over a Refusal to Testify," *The New York Times,* March 8, 2019, A13.

46 WikiLeaks released three insurance files—different from 2010's "Insurance"—in August 2013 (3.6 GB, 49 GB and 349 GB torrents). A WikiLeaks book written by two *Guardian* reporters disclosed the password. However, there was intense disagreement about whether the password worked when the book was published, or if it was temporary. WikiLeaks also released an encrypted 88-GB insurance file in June 2016. Mark Stockley, "What's Wikileaks Hiding in its 400GB of 'Insurance' Files?" *Naked Security, Sophos,* August 20, 2013, https://nakedsecurity. sophos.com/2013/08/20/whats-wikileaks-hiding-in-its-400gb-of-insurance-files/; James Ball, "Unredacted US Embassy Cables Available Online after WikiLeaks Breach," *The Guardian,* August 31, 2011, https://www.theguardian.com/world/2011/sep/01/unredacted-us-embassy-cables-online; Bruce Schneier, "Unredacted U.S. Diplomatic WikiLeaks Cables Published," *Schneier on Security,* September 1, 2011, https://www.schneier.com/blog/archives/2011/09/unr edacted_us_d.html; Zach Whittaker, "Wikileaks 'Insurance' File Decrypted: Names of Informants Exposed," *ZDNet,* http://www.zdnet.com/article/wikileaks-insurance-file-decrypted-names-of-informants-exposed/.

47 Sewell Chan, "Ecuador Ends Web Access for Assange, Prompting Ire," *The New York Times*, March 29, 2018, A4; Karen Zraick, "Assange Says He Is Suing Ecuador for Violating Rights," *The New York Times*, October 19, 2018, A7; Associated Press, "Why Ecuador Ended Asylum for 'Spoiled Brat' Julian Assange," *NBC News*, April 12, 2019, https://www.nbcnews.com/news/world/why-ecuador-ended-asylum-spoiled-brat-julian-assange-n993711.

48 DNC email database, accessed January 14, 2019, https://wikileaks.org/dnc-emails/; *US v. Viktor Borisovich Netyksho et al.*, 1:18-cr-00215-ABJ, Document 1, U.S. District Court for the District of Columbia, July 13, 2018; Office of the Director of National Intelligence, "Assessing Russian Activities and Intentions in Recent US Elections," U.S. Intelligence Community Assessment, ICA 2017-01D, January 6, 2017.

49 Sarah Palin, Facebook, January 3, 2017, https://www.facebook.com/sarahpalin/posts/to-julian-assange-i-apologize-please-watch-sean-hannitys-interview-with-julian-a/10154916952353588/. After WikiLeaks published the Democrats' emails during the 2016 campaign, Trump proclaimed "WikiLeaks, I love WikiLeaks" at a Pennsylvania rally. On the day President Trump's administration ordered Assange arrested on conspiracy charges in 2019, he changed his tune, saying "I know nothing about WikiLeaks." "Accountability for Assange" (editorial), *The Wall Street Journal*, April 12, 2019, A16.

50 Josh Gerstein, "Report: WikiLeaks' Founder Julian Assange Indicted in U.S.," *Politico*, February 28, 2012, http://www.politico.com/blogs/under-the-radar/2012/02/report-wikileaks-founder-julian-assange-indicted-in-us-115779; Sari Horowitz, "Assange Not under Sealed Indictment, U.S. Officials Say," *The Washington Post*, November 18, 2013, https://www.washingtonpost.com/world/national-security/assange-not-under-sealed-indictment-us-officials-say/2013/11/18/8a3cb2da-506c-11e3-a7f0-b790929232e1_story.html. The court error was discovered by Seamus Hughes, https://twitter.com/SeamusHughes/status/1063232297674162176. *US v. Seitu Sulayman Kokayi*, Case 1:18-cr-00410-LMB, Document 5, U.S. District Court for the Eastern District of Virginia, August 22, 2018.

51 In 2017, because Assange had been out of reach in the embassy for so long, Sweden reversed course and stopped pursuing Assange for the sexual assault allegations. Steven Erlanger and Christina Anderson, "Assange Rape Inquiry Is Dropped, but His Legal Troubles Remain Daunting," May 19, 2017, *The New York Times*, A7. Once Assange was arrested in April 2019, one of the Swedish women who accused him of assault asked her government to open a new case against him. "Accountability for Assange" (editorial).

52 Ellsberg, *Secrecy*; *New York Times Company v. United States* 403 U.S. 713; "Supreme Court, 6–3, Upholds Newspapers on Publication of Pentagon Report," *The New York Times*, July 1, 1971.

53 Julian Assange, "Conspiracy as Governance," December 3, 2006, available at http://cryptome.org/0002/ja-conspiracies.pdf; Julian Assange, "State and Terrorist Conspiracies," November 10, 2006, http://cryptome.org/0002/ja-conspiracies.pdf; WikiLeaks, Twitter, October 24, 2016, https://twitter.com/wikileaks/status/790620754614378496; zunguzungu [*sic*], Julian Assange and the Computer Conspiracy; "To Destroy This Invisible Government," *ZUNGU-ZUNGU*, November 29, 2010, https://zunguzungu.wordpress.com/2010/11/29/julian-assange-and-the-computer-conspiracy-%E2%80%9Cto-destroy-this-invisible-government%E2%80%9D/; L. Gordon Crovitz, "Julian Assange, Information Anarchist," *The Wall Street Journal*, December 6, 2010; Julian Assange, Jacob Appelbaum, Andy Müller-Maguhn, and Jérémie Zimmermann, *Cypherpunks: Freedom and the Future of the Internet* (New York: OR books, 2012); Ball, "Inside The Strange, Paranoid World"; Khatchadourian, "No Secrets"; Gibney, "Can We Trust"; Jonathan Fildes, "Wikileaks Defectors to Launch Openleaks Alternative," *BBC News*, http://www.bbc.com/news/technology-11981301.

Chapter 7

The Wide World of Whistleblowing on the Web

From Rodney King's Witness to WITNESS

As technologists experimented with online leaking platforms in the 1990s and early 2000s (chapter 6), a separate group, with fewer tech credentials, independently developed a new form of whistleblowing for the Information Age. The pioneer of this second set of innovators was never a computer programmer, and probably not a hacker. Neither was his whistleblowing platform a website; it had little to do with the Internet until well into the 2000s. Peter Gabriel was a rock star who had a good, pre-Internet idea that seeded in 1988, flowered in 1992, expanded through the 1990s, and finally went online in the mid-2000s. What became known as WITNESS empowered human rights defenders with handheld video cameras and a global network that specialized in publicizing their documented evidence of abuses. Already well developed before the ideas behind Google or WikiLeaks even occurred to their creators, WITNESS eventually recognized the power of the Web as a force multiplier and continued to grow into the 2010s.

While touring the world in 1988 with Amnesty International (AI) for the "Human Rights Now!" tour, Gabriel had many occasions to speak with human rights victims and witnesses. Their stories of torture and repression gripped his imagination and conscience. They resonated not only because of how disturbing they were but also because the incidents were ones that anyone could empathize with, given the universality of struggles against injustices. Gabriel recounted his response to a story a Chilean torture survivor shared with him in 1985: "From my very privileged position, the only reference point" for her treatment under the military dictatorship was a childhood experience getting beaten by kids outside school. "I was stripped; I was attacked; I was abused" for no reason at all. While the wounds of a schoolyard attack by bullies paled in comparison with the injuries, pain, and humiliation inflicted by well-trained torturers, Gabriel always remembered how powerless he felt, both during and after the assault. "You could suffer in [that] way and then have your whole experience, your story, denied, buried and forgotten." It amounted to "double victimization."[1]

While on tour with AI, Gabriel began recording victims' stories with a handheld video camera. Some of those stories had already moved through AI's network. But Gabriel spotted a niche. He realized victims' voices and stories, captured on video, had a power that contemporaneous text and photo-based human rights reporting did not. The vivid testimonies would give abusers no quarter and might even have a deterrent effect. "It seemed that whenever there was a camera around . . . it was a great deal harder . . . for those in power to bury the story."[2] In a world where just about anyone could capture sound and images with a handheld camera, the powerless had a way of turning the tables against the powerful, it seemed, by gathering credible evidence to hold them accountable.

Gabriel's idea was to start an organization that would support human rights defenders who wanted to use video cameras to capture abuses as they occurred, or to record victim and witness testimonies. The cameras were relatively expensive then, especially for people in developing countries, so the organization would supply handhelds and technical training to local human rights defenders, who would work with local populations. The organization would then broadcast the videos as widely as possible. After the project idea simmered for a couple of years, Gabriel pitched it to the new human rights–focused Reebok Foundation, whose leaders did not immediately grasp the power of live action video and taped testimonies. Until the Rodney King beating incident.[3]

Like practically everyone alive and conscious in 1991, Reebok Foundation officials watched the grainy videotape shot by a witness, George Holliday, who captured Los Angeles police officers severely beating King after a car chase. The viral video (although no one called it that then) frequently played on network and cable television. Police brutality and urban racial politics quickly reemerged as major national political issues in the United States, after a twenty-some year lull. When the officers were acquitted, LA convulsed into riots. The ensuing street conflicts, which included more police abuse, killed fifty-three and injured more than 2,000.[4]

No one could deny the power of that video. King's injuries were severe enough that, absent the tape, he might still have received media attention. Yet the apartment balcony-shot video offered direct, though limited, evidence of the altercation, and immediately put to rest much of the skepticism that might have greeted King's accusation, all else equal. It reached tens of millions of viewers and instantly raised awareness about the case and the broader issues. With changed minds, Gabriel's patrons reconsidered his project idea. In 1992,

Gabriel launched WITNESS with the support of the Reebok Foundation and Human Rights First.[5]

By November 1999, WITNESS had provided cameras and training to individuals in forty-seven countries, and had established links with 125 human rights organizations. About six and a half years later, it had reached human rights defenders in over sixty countries. By November 2006, it had collected "almost 3,000 hours of footage of human rights abuses from people in more than 75 countries," with the continuing growth facilitated by rapidly increasing access to the Internet and decreasing costs of video cameras. By August 2014, it had worked with 300 organizations in 80 countries, trained 5,000 people, and curated 2,000 videos. A late October 2016 tally on WITNESS's website showed that it had partnered with 360 organizations in 97 countries, trained 6,000 individuals, and reached 260 million viewers. WITNESS's growth is also evident when comparing its financial reports. In 2002, it brought in nearly $1.31 million in revenues and spent just over $1.15 million. Ten years later it reported over $4.7 million in revenues, and the same amount in expenditures—a growth of over 300 percent for the organization. Although revenues and expenditures ebbed and flowed in the 2000s and 2010s, WITNESS continued on a growth trajectory.[6]

Part of WITNESS's success came from its early decision to develop its network with relatively autonomous partner organizations. While all worked in support of a common human rights–based mission, and while all used WITNESS-provided training, capital, and network access, WITNESS avoided the costs of managing hundreds of organizations spread around the world. After initial investments, the organizations had discretion and WITNESS fielded an influx of videos. The network continued to grow as its partners created their own links with other organizations and individuals. The strategy probably contributed to WITNESS's enduring role as the most central node within the increasingly competitive "video for change" network. Outside of the large global human rights organizations like AI, it was *the* place for human rights defenders to send videos.

WITNESS Online

WITNESS has maintained a website since at least December 1996, and it began offering visitors access to a limited video archive by the late 1990s. By the mid-2000s, when web technology decreased the costs of video streaming, WITNESS expanded its web offerings and its online presence more broadly. In 2006, it partnered with Global Voices Online (GVO), a citizen journalism portal, to create the Human Rights Video Hub Pilot website ("The Hub")—an online, open access platform for videos that documented human rights violations. The first Hub video post on September 7, 2006, presented "police excesses" in Malaysia.

Later Hub videos showed police violence against nonviolent protesters in Zimbabwe, forced home evictions of Mayan Q'eqchi' people in Guatemala, and soldiers shooting citizens protesting authoritarianism in Guinea, among others. Human rights activists, witnesses, and victims had posted videos on YouTube and Google Video before The Hub's launch, but never before had a site focused exclusively on broadcasting street-level evidence of rights violations. The Hub became known as the "YouTube for Human Rights."[7]

Despite its successes, The Hub had a relatively short shelf life. After fifteen months as a pilot program at GVO, and over two and a half years on WITNESS's own servers, the organization closed The Hub to new videos in August 2010. According to WITNESS Director Yvette Alberdingk Thijm, the closure resulted in part from unspecified "technical difficulties," as well as competition from newer sites, such as Small World News and Organization for Visual Progression, that worked to raise awareness of human rights cases and issues but did not publish videos from whistleblowers. Two months before WITNESS shuttered The Hub, it began a new partnership with the biggest video site of all, YouTube.[8]

YouTube first featured WITNESS-curated videos and then developed a separate YouTube Human Rights Channel in May 2012, with content by WITNESS as well as Storyful. The channel has had modest success in reaching viewers. YouTube counted 6,545 subscribers to the channel by August 2016, and its videos drew 444,909 views overall (in January 2019, there were 7,121 subscribers and 584,510 views). By the same time, WITNESS's separate YouTube channel had 7,899 subscribers, and its videos drew 3,949,851 views overall (in January 2019, 9,578 and 4,675,386, respectively). By contrast, AI's channel in August 2016 had 40,402 subscribers, and its videos drew 12,303,340 views overall (in January 2019, 60,101 and 15,540,272, respectively).[9]

Activity on the channel slowed in 2014 and 2015. WITNESS uploaded only five videos between January 2014 and April 2015: "GRAPHIC Berkut, riot police beat, undress and humiliate man" (January 2014); "Police Strike and Deport Migrants Crossing into Melilla" (October 2014); "Year in Review" (December 2014); "El Centro Community Job Center gather held a vigil for a day labor killed in Staten Island" (January 2015); and "CUBA: Intimidation and Harassment of Activists" (April 2015). The channel's final video, uploaded on September 2015, promoted a new project called WITNESS Media Lab, headquartered back at Witness.org.

WITNESS's Influence

Assessing the precise impact of a single WITNESS video would require an intensive case study. Thus, we should refrain from making claims about the overall impact of WITNESS's videos. Clearly WITNESS has raised awareness about human rights problems in general and has exposed many once hidden violations. The videos have also held perpetrators accountable by documenting their actions, although they are not always "named and shamed" directly (e.g., viewers might see abuses by functionaries of some agency or another, as with a police officer beating a protester). But the videos have occasionally had more tangible influence.

For example, prosecutors at the International Criminal Court used video evidence captured by a WITNESS partner, Ajedi-Ka (Association des Jeunes pour le Developpement Integre-Kalundu), to help convict Congolese warlord Thomas Lubanga Dyilo on child soldiering charges. Additionally, a Kosovar Albanian WITNESS partner furnished "eight hours of videotaped interviews with survivors of village massacres" to the International War Crimes Tribunal in Yugoslavia. Gathering evidence for trials is a central function of WITNESS's mission: "WITNESS identifies ways for citizens to capture and preserve footage to improve its chances of it being used in the courtroom. Through tools, training, and advocacy efforts, we aim to help activists capture and use video as evidentiary material."[10]

WITNESS videos have had other measurable effects. For instance, they gave indigenous tribes in Kenya leverage in their conflict with the government over land reform implementation. They helped Brazilian antihuman trafficking activists force the government to more aggressively and effectively use the federal Mobile Inspection Squads to help girls and women who had escaped from criminals' networks. They empowered citizen lobbyists in the United States in their efforts to persuade Congress to pass the Elder Justice Act of 2010, which targeted elder care abuse. The videos did not always have tangible results, but WITNESS and its partners can claim some important wins, on top of the substantial power of shaping perceptions and public opinion—including in mainstream media reporting based on their work (e.g., in 2001, on BBC, CNN, and CBS Evening News).[11]

What WITNESS and WikiLeaks Have in Common, and Not

WITNESS became a web-centric enterprise years after its launch. In that way, it differs from WikiLeaks, Cryptome, and other platforms which have worked exclusively in the online space. Still, it embraced the new information environment as soon as video streaming became feasible in the late 1990s. About a half decade later, starting with The Hub in 2006, and then the YouTube channels, WITNESS transformed again, by soliciting video contributions from individuals more directly, along with its growing corps of global partners. A half decade after that, it launched video-capturing Android apps (ObscuraCam and

CameraV: Secure Visual Proof) that it created in partnership with the Knight News Foundation and the Guardian Project.[12]

Other differences between the cases are obvious. WikiLeaks's core mission and modus operandi—publishing state secrets, often in bulk, without regard for the negative consequences of disclosure—conflicts with WITNESS's more measured case-by-case approach. WITNESS specializes in audiovisual information, whereas WikiLeaks publishes text documents, with the exception of the "Collateral Murder" video. On the one hand, that difference matters little here, as both media types transmit legible information. The two sites publish different media types largely because of what they feature: state secrets, in WikiLeaks's case, and evidence of human rights violations, in WITNESS's case. On the other hand, WITNESS and others (e.g., Holliday) have shown the unique power of video. The difference matters not only in characterizing the distinctive natures of the organizations but also in crediting WITNESS for its pioneering influence in weaponizing videos for human rights whistleblowing.

Another difference involves source protection. WikiLeaks has guaranteed anonymity as a matter of course from its founding. Its iron-clad protection of sources' identities was one of its main innovations. WITNESS, by contrast, has historically placed less of an emphasis on source protection. That does not mean it neglected or showed indifference to contributors' privacy interests. Once it launched The Hub, with its open, direct submissions system, it seemed to make source protection a higher priority. It has also provided detailed instructions to contributors to help protect their identities (e.g., "How You Can Protect Your Safety & Security Online"). As far back as April 11, 2008, it promoted Tor, the anonymizing circumvention technology used by WikiLeaks and others focused on online privacy. Earlier (pre-Hub) versions of Witness.org contained less detailed information about protecting contributors' anonymity, in part due to the relatively limited options available then. But WITNESS did clearly recognize its importance. For instance, a January 2003 "Tips and Techniques" document for people who were recently given video cameras ("Congratulations on receiving your video camera!") instructed interviewers how to silhouette an interviewee:

> If you are filming an interview in a room and there is plenty of sunlight coming through the window, sit with your back facing the window and sit your interveiwee [sic] facing the light source so that the sunshine will light their face. If you sit them with their back to the window shooting into the light source, the camcorder will take its reading from the brightest image in the frame and close down its iris so as not to over-expose the shot. This will result in your interviewee becoming silhouetted in the picture, a good technique if you want your interviewee's identity to remain a secret but not if you want them to be seen.

Five years later, when WITNESS directly solicited videos from Hub website visitors, it highlighted the "5 things you should know about us and your safety and security," including that the organization used secure servers and that they would "never share, sell or trade your personal information. Ever."[13] WITNESS clearly recognized that its expanded model of video solicitation and publishing required a different security protocol, which it continued to adapt and strengthen over time, along with technological change.

Both WITNESS and WikiLeaks are outside recipients in chapter 2's basic typology, and both actively solicit secrets from would-be whistleblowers. Yet WITNESS has never had to tread as carefully as WikiLeaks, mostly because it does not brazenly solicit and publish classified national security secrets from the world's most powerful governments, who have strong laws to deter and punish solicitation. WikiLeaks solicits secrets with much greater caution, as evident in its firm denials that it even does so. Its treatment of solicitation on its website suggests Assange's nervous awareness of the laws' power: "like other media outlets conducting investigative journalism, we accept (but do not solicit) anonymous sources of information."[14]

To what extent does WikiLeaks's claim that it "does not solicit" hold up to scrutiny? Some, including Bradley Manning's prosecutors, have argued that a WikiLeaks page headlined "Draft: The Most Wanted Leaks of 2009" shows the organization's solicitation of classified information. It identifies a wish list of secrets, including "A mirror of the complete Intellipedia site," which the CIA called "the Intelligence Community's version of Wikipedia." In addition to other U.S. secrets (e.g., "Cheney and Rumsfeld Archives"), WikiLeaks asked readers to send documents from governments, businesses, and other organizations (e.g., the Bilderberg Group) from around the world, including "documents showing that the United Nations Security Council ignored requests to investigate potential genocide in Darfur"; "The complete details of Goldman, Sachs & Co.'s counterparty exposure to AIG prior to the Federal bailout of AIG in September, 2008"; and "internal Kremlin, FSB and SVRR documents and emails into the series of Moscow [apartment] building bombings shortly before Putin's Presidential election." WikiLeaks has denied that it wrote the list, claiming that it was crowdsourced, which is at least partly true, as users could have edited the entries like they would on a Wikipedia page. However, it is possible, indeed likely, that WikiLeaks staffers also contributed to the list. If a leaker supplied the WikiLeaks-entered information request, then a solicitation charge becomes more plausible. WikiLeaks no longer can claim that it just passively received information; it asked for it. That difference is important in U.S. law, since persuading someone to commit a crime (e.g., stealing and transferring classified information) is generally prohibited. But the public, impersonal nature of the list suggests the weakness of that charge. There is an important difference between Assange asking all website visitors for Intellipedia and requesting it from a CIA official directly. The former is protected First Amendment speech.

WikiLeaks's claim that it is a media organization not unlike the *Times* makes First Amendment considerations even more salient.[15]

The issue is further complicated by WikiLeaks's offer of a "cash prize up to 1000 EUR [€]," presumably for the most popular entry, according to rules not clearly specified. What was once a request for information becomes more like a financial inducement. WikiLeaks has also offered "bounties"—large rewards for specific secrets, with the requests clearly initiated by WikiLeaks. On June 2, 2015, WikiLeaks announced a "$100,000 REWARD" for "the missing [classified draft] chapters of the Trans-Pacific Partnership 'TPP'" treaty, of which the United States was one of the many negotiating parties.[16] It announced another bounty for information related to the October 3, 2015, U.S. bombing of a Doctors Without Borders (Médecins Sans Frontières) hospital in Kunduz, Afghanistan, which killed twenty-two staff members and patients. The United States accepted blame for the airstrike, which occurred in a war zone, but claimed it was a mistake (commanding officer Gen. John F. Campbell testified, "We would never intentionally target a protected medical facility.").[17] Despite the added complexities of the bounties, the same legal protections are relevant. As long as WikiLeaks keeps its requests and inducements impersonal, it can credibly cite First Amendment protections and deny that it illegally solicited information because it did not ask any specific individuals. While WikiLeaks is likely safe under the law, its requests and inducements sure do resemble solicitations.

Conclusion

While WikiLeaks and WITNESS both publish secrets, they have quite different origins, missions, priorities (i.e., content, source protections), and legal concerns related to solicitation. Both have been influential, but they represent only two of countless other secret-spilling sites that have exploded onto the scene during the Digital Age. The next section examines some of those, with a focus on the historical turn toward crowdsourcing.

Crowdsourcing Secret-Spilling

When WITNESS expanded in 2006 to include web uploads on The Hub, it joined a young but growing "video for change" online community, which overlapped with a broader group of citizen journalists. Prominent sites included the Independent Media network (launched in 1999), Video Volunteers (launched in 2003), and Global Voices Online (2004). Like WikiLeaks and WITNESS, they maintained open submission platforms, welcoming contributions from anyone, although some remained centrally managed (also like WikiLeaks and WITNESS) in that editors decided what would be published. But unlike WikiLeaks and WITNESS, the sites were not built primarily for publishing secrets. Contributors tended to report under-covered stories, often with the goal of elevating cases and issues on activist and policy agendas.

Crowdsourcing hit its stride in the mid-2000s, with the launch and near-instant success of YouTube (February 2005), which quickly demonstrated the potential of a decentralized, user-driven model. YouTube's (generally) open submissions platform, however, did not attract much leaking and whistleblowing. The vast majority of uploads were about as far from whistleblowing as you can get—cat videos, not corporate fraud. The founders of LiveLeak (October 2006) presumably hoped to fill that niche, given the name. But that site evolved into a more general-purpose uploading site like YouTube, albeit with looser rules.[18]

IPaidABribe.com: Reporting the Baksheesh of Daily Life

A small but important segment of open access, crowdsourced, decentralized sites have more narrowly focused on whistleblowing. IPaidABribe ["I paid a bribe"] was one of the first. Swati Ramanathan, Ramesh Ramanathan, and Sridar Iyengar (all of the non-profit Janaagraha) launched IPaidABribe in August 2010 with a singular and ambitious purpose: to significantly reduce corruption in India. Transparency International's (TI) leading comparative corruption index had pegged India at 3.3 out of 10 in 2010. If TI gave out grades, India would have earned an "F" (33 percent) for its failure to control corruption. To fight that menace, IPaidABribe's founders opted for a microlevel solution: they asked Indians to report their personal experiences with petty, street-level corruption (rather than grand political corruption), which pervades Indian society, especially in the public sector. Indeed, TI's 3.3 score might underestimate the amount of corruption ordinary Indians face, given that the index is constructed in large part with "expert" rather than mass surveys.[19]

IPaidABribe instructed its prospective contributors to report bribes (*baksheesh*) that they had to pay to obtain basic goods and services from the government, including "ration cards, passports, driving licences . . . *khatas* [property transfers], house building . . . [and] trade licences." A randomly chosen, anonymous post, detailed a probably typical Bangalorean shakedown:

> I had applied for a new passport and after about 20 days, I got a call on 15 August 2014 from Bhrasht Nagar police station for verification of my identity. He asked me to come on 16th August and meet him to complete the process.
>   I went to the police station at 4 pm on 16th August 2014, with all my identification documents and met sub-inspector Bhoop Singh. After looking at my documents he asked me to pay him Rs [Rupees] 1000. I asked him why was he asking me for money and told him that I had all the required documents in place for him to complete the process. His tone suddenly changed and he said 'if I don't sign, then you won't get your passport.'

I told him that I didn't have Rs 500 to pay him. In a very angry tone he asked me to show my wallet and how much money I had. I was scared and wanted to get the passport process done, since my company was planning to send me abroad in a week's time. I told him I had only Rs 350 with me. He asked me to give that to him, which I did. He signed some papers and asked me to leave. I got my passport but the process left a bad taste for me. I was taken aback by the policeman's attitude and I request action to be taken against him.

The post, from August 2014, was one of tens of thousands of others that had accumulated on IPaidABribe during the four years since its launch.[20]

IPaidABribe grew very quickly. Within two and a half months, it had attracted 120,000 hits; by the end of 2011, 820,000. Users by then had shared 16,725 baksheesh encounters with officials. The vast majority (86.3 percent) reported that they paid up, while 10.4 percent said they had resisted a bribe demand—they clicked on "I didn't pay a bribe [after being asked]." Only 3.3 percent of those who chose to share their experiences reported that they "didn't have to pay a bribe," which could mean a demand was rescinded or that they weren't asked to pay in the first place.[21]

IPaidABribe's growth continued even after its novelty wore off. By early 2014, users had reported more than 25,000 incidents, totaling nearly $11.8 million (71 crore rupees). By September 2015, IPaidABribe had catalogued 48,379 incidents in 639 cities, totaling more than $42.5 million (282 crore rupees). In January 2019, the number had risen to 171,346 reports in 1072 cities, with a cost of more than $407 million (2869.58 crore rupees).[22] That large dead-weight loss in the Indian economy is only a small fraction of the total amount, given the incomplete reporting. Not all Indians who paid bribes reported them for a variety of reasons, including fear of retaliation, lack of Internet access, and unawareness of IPaidABribe. Still, India had nothing like it before. IPaidABribe's founders hoped that with thousands of detailed, albeit unverifiable reports, the site would begin to haunt the minds of clerks and cops. Maybe it would deter them; they would think twice about demanding their baksheesh, for fear of being identified and reported on by journalists and reprimanded by similarly risk-averse government officials. Maybe it would even change the culture of corruption in India.[23]

IPaidABribe contributors have the option of posting anonymously, and there is no evidence that the site has failed to protect its sources. However, a highly motivated official seeking to retaliate would not need to search long to find his adversary. The IPaidABribe reporter from Bangalore who sought a passport (introduced earlier) revealed the dates and specific circumstances of his interaction. With a little paperwork and memory jogging, Bangalore sub-inspector Bhoop Singh probably could identify the individual who posted the story of their interaction. Passport offices tend to keep good records.

Although many of the bribe reports detail small-level abuses of power, Indian contributors to the website, and others like it, have reason to worry about retaliation. Threats against whistleblowers and "right to information" activists—who file Right to Information requests under the 2005 law, and then scour government documents for corruption—are especially severe in India. A culture of retribution and intimidation has grown up alongside a transparency and anti-corruption movement, of which IPaidABribe is a part. Beyond the typical—the ended careers, the false rumors, and the routine harassment—whistleblowing Indians who report on corruption have too often become the recipients of credible death threats. We know they were credible because many offenders have followed through. Dozens of whistleblower and RTI activists have been assassinated, tortured, and/or assaulted, with some estimates going up to thirty killed and fifty-five assaulted since 2008. The hand of government officials was sometimes clearly seen: witnesses to Shashidhar Mishra's murder alleged that street lights above him shut off just before two motorcyclists shot him with silenced guns. Then the lights returned. If IPaidABribe has put fear into the hearts of crooked cops and clerks, the murders and the widespread harassment have had a chilling effect at least as strong. After the prominent murder of Amit Jethwa, one RTI activist was despondent: "Our hearts are broken after his death . . . . You cannot fix the system. Everybody is getting money. If I give my life, what is the point?" The chilling effect was strong enough that for at least its first year, IPaidABribe did not identify individual offenders by name, only their offices and locations. In response to strong feedback from users and supporters, Ramanathan et al. changed the policy, and let website posters identify the bribers by name.[24]

The Globalization of IPaidABribe and Its Spinoffs

The scale and scope of IPaidABribe's influence on Indian corruption and politics remains unclear. A modest increase in India's TI rating after 2010 (e.g., to 4.0 in 2017) was caused by many factors.[25] Senior officials have insisted that they use it to crack down on corruption. For instance, a commissioner of the State Transport Department in Karnataka said he "use[d] that website to cleanse my department." Even if we assume their sincerity, we have no evidence about how much cleansing has actually occurred.[26] Moreover, the site's deterrent effect is unmeasurable.

Yet as a model for fighting petty corruption with street-level whistleblowers, the site has had global influence. The *idea* of IPaidABribe, along with the replicable technology, circled the globe quickly after its release. By March 2012—about a year and a half after its launch—activists in more than seventeen countries had proposed bringing and adapting IPaidABribe to their societies.

Not all of those partnerships worked out. In September 2015, fifteen countries, including India, had IPaidABribe sites up and running, in Africa, Asia, Europe, and South America. Fourteen others reportedly had sites under development. By January 2019, the number of online sites remained at fifteen, with the same fourteen under development (Table 7.1). IPaidABribe labeled those fourteen "coming soon" in September 2015 as well as January 2019.[27]

The market for anti-corruption sites also became competitive. Although IPaidABribe failed in China, ill-treated Chinese could choose from twenty-five other sites already online in 2012, including woxinghuile.com. Greek activists launched teleiakaipavla.gr, "Stop it. Period," also unaffiliated with Janaagraha, in 2012. It appeared moribund in late 2014. An Englishwoman in the Malaysian state of Sarawak created the Sarawak Report in February 2010, which tracked corruption and illegal deforestation. Moroccans unveiled Mamdawrinch ("We will not bribe.") in February 2012, with help from the local Transparency International (TI) office. Another TI-linked organization, Corruption Watch, launched its site in South Africa in January 2012 and grew quickly after that. Like several others, Corruption Watch let victims and witnesses use a variety of methods—with a variety of languages, and varying degrees of potential anonymity—to report incidents, including texts, emails, postal mail, phone calls, faxes, website submissions, Facebook posts, and walk-ins.[28]

TABLE 7.1 Countries with IPaidABribe Websites

Online	Under Development
Azerbaijan	Afghanistan
Colombia	Argentina
Greece	Armenia
Guyana	Brazil
Hungary	Cameroon
India	Ethiopia
Kenya	Mali
Liberia	Mexico
Morocco	Moldova
Pakistan	Nepal
Serbia	Philippines
Sri Lanka	Senegal
Syria	Sierra Leone
Ukraine	Tunisia
Zimbabwe	

In Russia, where corruption is as monumental as the country's size—embezzlement in the state procurement system alone reached as least 1 trillion rubles ($24 billion) in 2010, sapping Russia's economic growth rate by half—a group of entrepreneur activists in October 2012 introduced Bribr, a free Android and iOS app. Within a week, Bribr's contributors had reported "1.55 million rubles (almost US$50,000) in bribes," all of the petty corruption variety. By December 2012, reports totaled over US$8 million. However, by September 2015, Bribr seemed to have disappeared altogether, not unlike other anti-corruption forces in Russia. One of Bribr's developers, Eugenia Kuyda, was still alive in June 2015, but she had moved on to a restaurant take-out app, first in Moscow and then in San Francisco.[29]

If Russian officials disliked Bribr, they detested RosPil (launched January 2011), because it tackled higher level political corruption. Instead of soliciting citizens' everyday experiences with petty corruption, RosPil ("to saw off") asked its thousands of users to scour long, technical government procurement contracts with an eye for irregularities. In just three months, they identified enough problems to force the government to cancel contracts worth almost US$7 million. RosPil's founder, Alexei Navalny, became one of Russia's leading opposition figures. It was probably a combination of his uncompromising anti-corruption work and his audacious criticisms of Vladimir Putin and his party, United Russia, which led Putin's government to repeatedly charge Navalny with corruption.[30]

Other Corruption-Reporting Apps

IPaidABribe, RosPil, and the aforementioned sites kept their focus on corrupt officials in individual countries. IPaidABribe did go global, but its franchise model perpetuated its individual country focus. There was IPaidABribe in Kenya, IPaidABribe in Ukraine, and so on, each one with the Janaagraha organization's signature platform, all under the IPaidABribe logo. By contrast, a second group of corruption-reporting sites were distinctly transnational.

Bribecaster, for instance, allowed individuals from any country to report the details of a bribe experience on its website or Android app. After staying active for over three years, it went defunct by August 2016. Bribespot, which launched in 2011, worked in an almost identical way, and on more devices, given its iOS and Android versions. Its creators also appeared more willing to invest in marketing, which attracted mainstream press attention (*New York Times, BBC, Fast Company, Voice of America*). Its web and app interfaces were also noticeably more cared for than Bribecaster's, which had broken and empty "About" and "Contact" links that lingered for months. It seemed poised to become *the* go-to corruption-reporting app. While Bribespot still had a public presence in January 2019, its status was uncertain. Its marketing arm had withered. Its last tweet and Facebook post appeared in September 2014. More important, its developers appeared to have dropped the ball. The Android version was last updated on May 28, 2014. Privacy-conscious whistleblowers would have reason to think twice about using such an outdated platform. While Bribespot, like Bribecaster, encrypted contributors' submissions, the nearly long delay in a security update would rightly be viewed with suspicion. Would-be whistleblowers would have legitimate concerns about being identified.[31]

Governments too have gotten into the corruption-reporting game, with predictably mixed results. The president of Kenya, for instance, was lauded for launching a much-publicized reporting website in 2013—only for it to disappear soon after, then reappear on a different address, then disappear once again. (Meanwhile, Kenya's version of IPaidABribe continued without interruption.) In mid-2015, the Kenyan government had made a public commitment—to Kenyans and to U.S. president Barack Obama—to relaunch a secure, lasting platform. Nothing had emerged by August 2016.[32] Finally, the Ethics and Anti-Corruption Commission launched a corruption-reporting initiative, with multiple reporting channels, including anonymous website posting (other options included email, phone, and office visits). It was still functional in January 2019.[33]

Government-run corruption-reporting platforms have problems beyond their technical shortcomings. A more serious problem involves the reasonable lack of trust citizens would have in using government sites, especially in nondemocracies. After all, those reporting on corruption are implicating government officials. Individuals considering reporting their personal corruption experiences could reasonably wonder whether anything stops government officials from accessing the reporting website for malicious or self-serving ends, including extracting personal identifying data for retaliation purposes.

China's government, for instance, unveiled its own corruption-reporting site in 2009. Chinese citizens did not take to it like the authorities had hoped. A spokesman for China's Central Commission for Discipline Inspection (CCDI), which ran the state-run corruption-reporting platforms (first the website, and later some apps), tried to reassure potential posters: "Many Internet users have said 'If I report a case then how will I be protected?' They fear that if they do report then they will be subject to revenge attacks. I can tell everyone in a responsible way, all reports logged on the CCDI's website will receive legal protection, and we will severely deal with revenge attacks." He promised to protect website posters, especially if they provided their full contact details.[34]

Election Monitoring Apps

Another crowdsourcing tool that lets individuals report abuses of public authority focuses on election irregularities. There were more than a dozen election monitoring smartphone apps in 2016, each one inviting citizens to report local-level polling place incidents. Certainly not all such incidents would be classified as whistleblowing-worthy secrets. When a local official shuts down a polling place hours earlier than election rules require, he does so publicly, as the citizens standing in line outside would attest. But the apps' reporting frameworks have made other kinds of secret-spilling possible. Citizens can flag a wide variety of suspicious behaviors, including payoffs, threats, access restrictions, document destruction, and ballot box stuffing. The apps and web platforms differ in idiosyncratic ways and not all operate in what we would consider well-functioning democracies, including 14! (Hungary); Election Watch Reporter (India); LEVRA: Lebanese Election Violence Risk Assessment (Lebanon); Map an Election Bribe (Malaysia); Txeka-la (Mozambique); Election Monitor (Nigeria); EVC (Nigeria); IWITNESS (Nigeria); Revoda (Nigeria); VoteMonitor (Nigeria); and Вибори 2014 [Election 2014] (Ukraine). As far as we can tell, all of those were independent, private-sector apps. Others under development in late 2015 included apps in Burundi, South Africa, and Uganda; many more had appeared by early 2019.[35]

Government agencies have released their own election monitoring apps to empower citizens and to crowdsource their monitoring work (or at least to complement it). Some originated from agencies with positive, trustworthy reputations, such as Mexico's Instituto Nacional Electoral's (INE) app. Others have emerged from governments hostile to democracy and political competition, such as Belarus's Vochy (Вочы) app. The English translation of *Vochy*, "Eyes," fittingly describes the likely government surveillance function of the app. Russia also released an app for the 2012 election—probably also a tool, at least in part, for the government's domestic intelligence service (FSB).

The genre of election monitoring apps is still a relatively small and new one. None have so far caught on widely, or "scaled up," in Silicon Valley-speak. And none have so far created a replicable template for source protection, an especially important feature for apps in democratizing countries.

The Power of Maps: Maptivism, Crisis Mapping, and Beyond

Another turn in the history of crowdsourced platforms came about when Google Maps enabled users to customize maps for their own purposes. Developers around the world immediately began to experiment with the new geospatial tools. Retailers put "pins" on maps to mark their stores. Taxi companies and riders estimated cab fare prices with point to point directions. Geographic information system (GIS) developers linked government census data with map sections, so that users could click on the map to retrieve the information about the people who live there. Politicos played with political geography tools, such as making parts of the United States blue or red depending on how citizens there voted in the last election. Those and other uses of historical data created immeasurable value for Google Map users, as did real-time applications, like Ubilabs's Tour de France "live tracker" of cyclists moving through the French countryside.[36]

For people caught in a natural or political crises, the real-time applications soon proved potentially life-saving. Take, for example, the explosion of inter-ethnic violence in Kenya after the disputed presidential election of December 27, 2007. Both of the main competitors—incumbent president Mwai Kibaki and opposition leader Raila Odinga—had subordinates who engaged in elec-toral fraud. But Kibaki claimed an official victory, which enraged Odinga sup-porters, some of whom probably did not know of their side's fraud. After the official announcement, groups of marauding Odinga supporters attacked sus-pected Kibaki supporters, based in part on ethnic/tribal markers. Government troops struck back, as did masses of Kibaki supporters, and the ensuing crisis spiraled into an all-out deadly ethnic conflict, in which about 1,200 Kenyans died, many of them innocent people who had little to no involvement with the election. In the midst of the violence, a small group of Kenyan technologists quickly developed a Google Maps-powered application that drew from on-the-ground observers' reports via texts or website submissions. Ushahidi—Swahili for evidence or witness—mapped ethnic violence as fast as users sent data. The accumulated data helped analysts inside and outside of Kenya estimate the scale and scope of the attacks. The crisis ended in April 2008 with a coali-tion government, but the lingering ethnic resentments and damage to Kenyan democracy lasted longer.[37]

After the crisis, Ushahidi's founders recognized the wider uses of their plat-form—what they started calling the "Ushahidi engine"—for crisis mapping and quickly adapted it to other contexts. They brought a version to South Africa in May 2008, renamed it United for Africa, and encouraged South Africans to help track and map anti-immigrant attacks, which appeared to be on the rise. Later that year the Kenyans hurriedly adapted the Ushahidi engine to the Democratic Republic of the Congo, to track everything from riots and property theft to sexual assaults and killings, much of it related to the Congo's seemingly endless wars. All of Ushahidi's experiments demonstrated the existing and potential power of the technology. Not only could victims and witnesses report incidents that would otherwise go unreported, but they could feed crucial data to domes-tic and international journalists and human rights advocates, who could draw from the evidence in their own reporting on the larger context. Plus, the very presence of crowdsourced crisis-mapping tools might deter violent men from acting out, at least the more or less rational ones who have some concern the evidence might come back to haunt them in courts or elsewhere.[38]

As with the election monitoring apps, not all crowdsourced reports will disclose whistleblowing-worthy *secrets*. But the apps' potential for whistleblowing is large, as are their other possible uses. Individuals and organizations have already used crisis reporting and recovery apps in Africa and the Caribbean in the wake of natural disasters, such as in Haiti after the terrible earthquake of 2010. These mapping tools will increasingly become central to how people respond to crises, natural and political, in the years ahead.[39]

Conclusion

A key challenge of writing a chapter like this one is about selection, specifically what *not* to include. Technologists and software developers continuously experiment, throwing up new and updated secret-spilling platforms. Many attract attention due to their novelty but then fade into obscurity, or just disappear from app stores. American Civil Liberties Union (ACLU) of Arizona, for instance, released "ACLU-AZ Stop SB1070," an app that encouraged Arizonans to report alleged racial profiling incidents as a result of the state law that had empowered law enforcement officials to check the immigration status of individuals stopped for other infractions. Yet the reported incidents would not have qualified as whistleblowing, at least according to chapter 2's standards, because police officers enforcing the law would not officially have abused their public authority, even if citizens who were forced to prove their citizenship status largely because of their race or ethnicity might contest the law's legitimacy. Just as a recreational drug user might believe U.S. marijuana laws lack legitimacy, but still be liable under those laws, a person stopped in Arizona had to abide by SB1070, even if she disagreed with it. People tend to disagree about what constitutes justly used government authorities. Indeed, those disagreements are what make politics so contentious, whether about immigration, abortion, war, surveillance, or many others.[40]

Chapter 2 introduced a related selection problem: that it is difficult to determine *a priori* the precise characteristics of what counts as a whistleblowing-worthy secret. The ACLU app (ACLU-AZ Stop SB1070) did not last long, but others with broader police monitoring purposes have proliferated, from early models like Cop Recorder and OpenWatch to the ACLU's Mobile Justice apps for seventeen states and the District of Columbia, along with ACLU-NY's Stop and Frisk Watch. We would need another chapter or more to analyze this trend toward street-level transparency and secret-spilling, along with the increasingly common police cameras mounted on officers' cars and uniforms, which would need to be placed in the history of what became known as "cop watching," such as the Black Panthers' "policing the police" operations in the 1960s and 1970s.[41]

The continuing proliferation of secret-spilling sites, along with the increasingly common use of encryption, will force scholars of whistleblowing to reconsider the value of anonymity. I have defended anonymous whistleblowing in this book in stronger terms than other scholars have elsewhere. But anonymity can certainly be abused in this domain. The rise and fall of the PostSecret app is a case in point. The popular website PostSecret, which let users share deep, personal secrets, spun off an app of the same name. It launched in September 2011 but shut down less than four months later. Its administrators could not respond quickly enough to the volley of posts that were "pornographic . . . gruesome and . . . threatening." On the one hand, Oscar Wilde had a point with his insight (a favorite of Julian Assange's), "Give a man a mask and he'll tell you the truth." On the other hand, men hiding behind masks can more easily spread lies (and filth).[42]

Overall, there are benefits and costs to online anonymous secret-spilling. Without anonymity, we would probably have less whistleblowing. With it, we suffer a glut of spilled secrets, as well as lies, filth, and trivialities. Compared to the centralized media model of the past, which empowered a small number of journalists and editors to separate the wheat from the chaff, the filtration method going forward in the new media age will be more decentralized and democratic, with crowdsourced verification and a broader-based deliberation about whether the leak was justified and the leaker warranted in remaining anonymous (or not).

* * *

A still under-examined question, relevant to the new media environment as well as the old, concerns *how* leakers and whistleblowers obtain their secrets. In some cases, the decision to leak comes after they have the information. The secrets are already in hand. But in many other cases, leakers and whistleblowers seek out the information, sometimes going to great lengths to get it, including breaking and entering. The next chapter focuses on this latter group.

Notes

1   David Kushner, "Peter Gabriel's YouTube for Human Rights: The Hub," *Fast Company*, November 1, 2008, http://www.fastcompany.com/1042498/peter-gabriel%E2%80%99s-youtube-human-rights-hub; "Our Story," Witness, accessed July 30, 2014, http://witness.org/about/our-story; Peter Gabriel, "Fight Injustice with Raw Video," TED Talks, February 2006, http://www.ted.com/talks/peter_gabriel_fights_injustice_with_video; Christopher John Farley, "Peter Gabriel on Witness, Human Rights and WikiLeaks," *Speakeasy (The Wall Street Journal)*, December 2, 2010, http://blogs.wsj.com/speakeasy/2010/12/02/peter-gabriel-on-witness-human-rights-and-wikileaks.

2   Kushner, "Peter Gabriel's"; "Our Story," Witness.org, Gabriel, "Fight Injustice"; Farley, "Peter Gabriel."

3 Kushner, "Peter Gabriel's"; "Our Story," Witness.org, Gabriel, "Fight Injustice"; Farley, "Peter Gabriel."

4 On the prevalence of and lack of accountability for "police brutality" during the 1990s in the United States, as well as the major analytical problems in documenting incidents systematically, see Allyson Collins, *Shielded from Justice: Police Brutality and Accountability in the United States* (New York: Human Rights Watch, 1998).

5 Gabriel, "Fight Injustice"; Farley, "Peter Gabriel"; Witness, "Our Story."

6 WITNESS, "2002 Annual Report," https://witness.org/about/annual-report/; WITNESS, "Financial Statements and Supplementary Information" (Fiscal Year 2012, June 30, 2012), https://www.guidestar.org/ViewEdoc.aspx?eDocId=2024587&approved=True; Mary Jordan, "Amateur Videos Are Putting Official Abuse in New Light," *Washington Post*, November 15, 2006.

7 The Internet Archive's first record of a WITNESS website is dated December 22, 1996 (accessed August 10, 2016) https://web.archive.org/web/20010401000000*/http://witness.o rg. See also Yvette Alberdingk Thijm, "Update on the Hub and WITNESS' New Online Strategy," August 18, 2010, *WITNESS Blog*, http://blog.witness.org/2010/08/update-on-the-hub-and-witness-new-online-strategy/; Mark Glaser, "Can Witness, Global Voices Make Human Rights Video Go Viral?" PBS Mediashift, September 20, 2006, http://www.pbs.org/mediashift/2006/09/can-witness-global-voices-make-human-rights-video-go-viral263/; Kushner, "Peter Gabriel's YouTube"; Sameer Padania, "Malaysia: Cellphone video captures police excess," *Global Voices Online*, September 7, 2006, http://globalvoicesonline.org/2006/09/07/malaysia-cellphone-video-captures-police-excess/; Gavin Simpson, "Forced Evictions in Guatemala: Whose Land Is It Anyway? *Global Voices Online*, March 4, 2007, http://globalvoicesonline .org/2007/03/04/forced-evictions-in-guatemala-whose-land-is-it-anyway/; Gavin Simpson, "Guinea-Conakry: Standing up to a power-hungry President," *Global Voices Online*, March 13, 2007, http://globalvoicesonline.org/2007/03/13/guinea-conakry-standing-up-to-a-power-hungry-president.

8 The Human Rights Channel on YouTube lists its launch date as November 19, 2005, which means the company created it about seven years before WITNESS got involved. "About," The Human Rights Channel on YouTube, accessed January 16, 2019, https://www.youtube.com/user/humanrights/about. WITNESS did not to respond to my inquiry about The Hub's technical difficulties. Thijm in 2010 had criticized "arbitrary take-down[s]" of flagged videos by major sites like YouTube. Alberdingk Thijm, "Update." Presumably Google had changed its policies and actions by 2012 to mollify WITNESS's concerns. Email from Georgia Popplewell [Managing Director of Global Voices Online], October 15, 2014. For some background about YouTube's video removal practices, see Electronic Frontier Foundation, "A Guide to YouTube Removals," accessed October 16, 2014, https://www.eff.org/issues/intellectual-property/guide-to-youtube-removals. By October 2014, the main video for change association included fourteen members, not all of them structured like WITNESS, and the group not encompassing of the diverse array of analogous platforms on the web. The fourteen members included B'tselem, Digital Democracy, EngageMedia, FLOSS Manuals, InsightShare, Kampung Halaman, MIT Center for Civic Media, Organisation for Visual Progression, Pusat KOMAS, Small World News, SocialTIC, Tactical Technology Collective, Video Volunteers, and WITNESS. See Video for Change Community, accessed October 15, 2014, https://www.v4c.org/en.

9 "About," WITNESS, accessed August 11, 2016, https://www.youtube.com/user/Witness/about; "About," Amnesty International, accessed August 11, 2016, https://www.youtube.com/user/AmnestyInternational/about. Steve Grove and Sameer Padania, "Neda Soltan and the Power of Human Rights Video," June 12, 2010, *YouTube Official Blog*, http://youtube-global.blogspot.com/2010/06/neda-soltan-and-power-of-human-rights.html; Sameer Padania, "New Collaboration with YouTube on The Power of Human Rights Video," *WITNESS*, June 12, 2010, https://blog.witness.org/2010/06/new-collaboration-with-youtube-on-the-power-of-human-rights-video.

10 Gabriel, "Fight Injustice"; Michael Pollak, "Screen Grab; Vivid Documents of Human Atrocities," *The New York Times*, November 11, 1999, G6. Witness became independent in 2001. See Witness, "Our Story." The Human Rights Channel Slogan Is "Filmed by Citizens...

Verified by Storyful… Curated by Witness." See "Human Rights Channel: 2013 Year in Review," Human Rights Channel, December 23, 2013, https://www.youtube.com/watch?v=Mil3zPB_S-4&feature=youtu.be. See also David Smith, "Congo Warlord Thomas Lubanga Convicted of Using Child Soldiers," *The Guardian,* March 14, 2012, http://www.theguardian.com/world/2012/mar/14/congo-thomas-lubanga-child-soldiers; "Peter Gabriel: A WITNESS for Human Rights," *NBC News,* February 9, 2012, http://www.nbcnews.com/id/46332591/ns/us_news-giving/t/peter-gabriel-witness-human-rights/;Ajedi-Ka, "Challenging the Use of Child Soldiers in the Democratic Republic of Congo," WITNESS, accessed May 18, 2014, http://www2.witness.org/index.php?option=content&task=view&id=31, archived version at http://web.archive.org/web/20071212064223/http://www.witness.org//index.php?option=content&task=view&id=31; "Our Work," WITNESS, accessed August 2, 2014, http://witness.org/our-work/; "Legal Protection for Elderly Americans," Witness, accessed August 1, 2014, http://witness.org/legal-protection-elderly-americans; "Some of Witness's Success Stories," WITNESS, accessed August 1, 2014, http://www2.witness.org/index.php?option=com_content&task=view&id=1011&Itemid=70.

[11] Gabriel, "Fight Injustice"; Pollak, "Screen Grab"; WITNESS, "Our Work"; WITNESS, "Some of Witness's Success Stories"; WITNESS, "An Age for Justice: Confronting Elder Abuse in America," accessed December 27, 2016, https://witness.org/portfolio_page/pursuit-justice-americas-elders/; "2001 Annual Report," Witness, https://witness.org/about/annual-report.

[12] "ObscuraCam: Secure Smart Camera," Guardian Project, accessed December 27, 2016, https://guardianproject.info/apps/obscuracam/; "CameraV: Secure Verifiable Photo & Video Camera," Guardian Project, accessed December 27, 2016, https://guardianproject.info/apps/camerav.

[13] "Training: Tips and Techniques," WITNESS, January 1, 2003, https://web.archive.org/web/20021213121824/http://www.witness.org/int.html?training/index.html; "How to Upload Your Video," WITNESS, accessed December 27, 2016, https://web.archive.org/web/2008041122145 2/http://hub.witness.org/en/node/6; "How You Can Protect Your Safety & Security Online," WITNESS, accessed December 27, 2016, https://web.archive.org/web/20080112073534/http://hub.witness.org/en/protect. On the April 2008 security page, it featured the "5 things you should know about us and your safety and security: 1. We use dedicated servers that are hosted on secure machines. 2. We will never share, sell or trade your personal information. Ever. 3. We are working with the foremost specialists in digital security and are committed to utilizing the latest technology to optimize your safety and security on the Hub. 4. You have control as to how you communicate to us and how we communicate with you. 5. We will never spam you. Ever."

[14] "About: What Is WikiLeaks?" WikiLeaks, accessed January 12, 2019, https://wikileaks.org/About.html. WikiLeaks has used the same solicitation language for many years (e.g., on May 5, 2011, archived at http://webcache.googleusercontent.com/search?q=cache:NfKfP6Vlou8J:https://wikileaks.org/About.html+&cd=1&hl=en&ct=clnk&gl=us). The solicitation question is relevant to the discussion in chapter 6 about how U.S. law interprets "aiding the enemy." The Defense Department has said that it does "not regard Mr. Assange as a member of the 'enemy,' a military objective, or someone who should be dealt with by the US military." However, it "has warned Mr. Assange and WikiLeaks against soliciting service members to break the law by providing classified information to them, and that it is our view that continued possession by WikiLeaks of classified information belonging to the United States government represents a continuing violation of law." See "INTERPOL Red Notice for Julian Assange remains in force," August 16, 2012, http://www.interpol.int/en/News-and-media/News/2012/PR065/; Philip Dorling, "US Calls Assange 'Enemy of State,'" *The Sydney Morning-Herald,* September 27, 2012, http://www.smh.com.au/federal-politics/political-news/us-calls-assange-enemy-of-state-20120926-26m7s; Jake Tapper, "Are Troops Talking to Assange 'Communicating With the Enemy'?" *ABC News,* September 28, 2012, http://abcnews.go.com/blogs/politics/2012/09/are-troops-talking-to-assange-communicating-with-the-enemy/; "US Military Refers to Julian Assange and WikiLeaks as the 'Enemy' with the 'Victims' Being 'Society,'" WikiLeaks, September 26, 2012, https://wikileaks.org/US-Military-Refers-to-Julian.html; Letter to FOIA requestor, FOIA Office, U.S. Air Force, May 31, 2012, https://wikileaks.org/IMG/

pdf/Assange-WikiLeaks-Enemy-USAF-FOI.pdf; Charlie Savage, "U.S. Tries to Build Case for Conspiracy by WikiLeaks," *The New York Times,* December 15, 2010, A1; Trevor Timm, "Virtually Everything the Government Did to WikiLeaks Is Now Being Done to Mainstream US Reporters," *Freedom of the Press Foundation,* May 21, 2013, https://pressfreedomfound ation.org/blog/2013/05/virtually-everything-government-did-wikileaks-now-being-done-m ainstream-us-reporters; David Dishneau and Pauline Jelinek, "Prosecution Wrapping up in WikiLeaks Trial," July 1, 2013, *Associated Press,* http://bigstory.ap.org/article/gis-trial-wiki leaks-case-enters-5th-week.

15 Geoffrey R. Stone, "Government Secrecy vs. Freedom of the Press." *Harvard Law and Policy Review* 1 (2007): 185; Geoffrey R. Stone, "Freedom of the Press and Criminal Solicitation," May 21, 2013, *Huffington Post,* https://www.huffingtonpost.com/geoffrey-r-stone/freedom -of-the-press-and_b_3314833.html. Manning's prosecutors failed to convince Judge Lind that Manning had read the "Most Wanted" article. The presence of the Moscow apartment bombing item on the WikiLeaks wish list complicates the increasingly popular argument that emerged in the United States in 2015–2016 that the organization is a Russian "front organiza- tion." It does not necessarily disqualify that argument, given the possibility of later Russian ties and Russian intelligence's mastery of psychological operations. Another, unrelated point: The standards for solicitation charges are murky. Should the government always charge leak publishers for solicitation when they ask insiders for classified secrets? Already the govern- ment appears to recognize and tacitly endorse the core solicitation role of national security reporters, who cultivate connections with security insiders. Steven Aftergood, "Reporter Deemed 'Co-Conspirator' in Leak Case," *Secrecy News,* May 20, 2013; http://fas.org/blogs/ secrecy/2013/05/kim-rosen-warrant/ ["'soliciting' and 'encouraging' the disclosure of classified information are routine, daily activities in national security reporting"]. See also "Intellipedia Celebrates Third Anniversary with a Successful Challenge," CIA, April 29, 2009, https://ww w.cia.gov/news-information/featured-story-archive/intellipedia-celebrates-third-anniversary. html. WikiLeaks objected to the claim it had authored the most wanted list on its " 'We Steal Secrets: The Story of WikiLeaks': The Annotated Transcript" (of Alex Gibney's film), May 23, 2013, https://wikileaks.org/IMG/html/gibney-transcript.html: "Gibney falsely attributes the 2009 'Most Wanted Leaks' list to Julian Assange. It was compiled by human rights NGOs, activists, lawyers, journalists and historians nominating the censored documents they consid- ered the most important to uncover." See chapters 6 and 8 for more about this case. See also Daniel Ellsberg, "Daniel Ellsberg's WikiLeaks Wish List," July 30, 2010, *Washington Post,* http: //www.washingtonpost.com/wp-dyn/content/article/2010/07/30/AR2010073002673.html. Assange frequently spoke about his evolving "wish list." Another example is from a 2011 inter- view in which he ruminated how leaked NSA intercepts and congressional emails "wouldn't be a bad start" to a "long wish list . . . for the United States" that would "transform the balance of power" in the United States? That too is protected speech. Interview with Julian Assange, *To the Best of Our Knowledge,* November 6, 2011, http://www.ttbook.org/book/transcript/ transcript-wikileaks-founder-julian-assange-0.

16 "WikiLeaks Issues Call for $100,000 Bounty on Monster Trade Treaty," WikiLeaks, June 2, 2015, https://wikileaks.org/WikiLeaks-issues-call-for-100-000.html; Eric Bradner, "How Secretive Is the Trans-Pacific Partnership?" *CNN,* June 12, 2015, http://www.cnn.com/2 015/06/11/politics/trade-deal-secrecy-tpp/. While he may have referred to the bounty, Assange seemed to suggest he had also engaged in more direct solicitations in a different interview. "The TPP is an international treaty that has 29 different chapters. We have released four of them, and we are trying to get the remainder." "Julian Assange on the Trans-Pacific Partner- ship: Secretive Deal Isn't About Trade, But Corporate Control," *Democracy Now!,* May 27, 2015, www.democracynow.org/2015/5/27/julian_assange_on_the_trans_pacific. On some broader questions about what we might recognize as solicitations, see Kelly McBride, "When It's O.K. to Pay for a Story," *The New York Times,* June 9, 2015, A23.

17 "WikiLeaks' Most Wanted," WikiLeaks, accessed January 12, 2019, https://wikileaks.org/ pledge/; Missy Ryan and Tim Craig, "Top U.S. General in Afghanistan: Hospital Was 'Mis- takenly Struck,'" *The Washington Post,* October 6, 2015.

18 That LiveLeak isn't really a leak site is not in dispute. Its homepage clearly reflects its interest in a general audience who probably do not visit the site looking for government and corporate leak videos. For instance, on February 8, 2017, it featured these "must see" videos: "Idiots provoke police by entering station with rifles and facemasks"; "Extremely skilled cat steals a piece of bacon from the bird feeder"; and "Aluminum Bat vs Skull." Also note that YouTube never had an anything goes policy for uploading videos, and since its acquisition by Google the restrictions have grown tighter, especially with content that violates copyrights, depicts pornographic acts, and incites criminal violence.

19 Stephanie Strom, "Web Sites Shine Light on Petty Bribery Worldwide," *The New York Times,* March 7, 2012, B1; "Corruption Perceptions Index 2010," Transparency International, accessed October 24, 2014, http://www.transparency.org/cpi2010/results; "Corruption Perceptions Index: In Detail," Transparency International, accessed December 27, 2016, http://www.transparency.org/cpi2013/in_detail; T. R. Raghunandan, "Tackling Corruption; The Ipaidabribe.com Way," Presentation at the World Bank, nd, http://siteresources.worldbank.org/EASTASIAPACIFICEXT/Resources/WB_I_Paid_a_Bribe_Initiative_-_Raghunandan.pdf. Raghunandan points out that poor Indians have been the worst hit: the added costs prevent poor people from accessing some public services. He also notes that the corruption types have important links. In particular, retail and grand corruption schemes sometimes share a common criminal paymaster. That is, "corruption syndicates" use agents in both channels to forcibly extract rents from citizens.

20 Anonymous, "Paid a Bribe of Rs 350 for Passport Verification at Bhrasht Nagar Police Station," IPaidABribe, August 16, 2014, Report #169357, http://www.ipaidabribe.com/reports/paid/paid-a-bpaid-a-bribe-of-rs-350-for-passport-verification-at-bhrasht-nagar-police-stationribe#gsc.tab=0. Note that the linked page misreports the contributor's post date as September 22, 2017. An earlier draft of this chapter from before that date reported the same 2014 post. Indeed, I recorded it in notes as early as October 24, 2014.

21 Raghunandan, "Tackling Corruption"; Samantha Power, "A US-India Partnership on Open Government," The White House, November 7, 2010, http://www.whitehouse.gov/blog/2010/11/07/a-us-india-partnership-open-government. It is worth noting that reports of this sort are not verifiable, given the secret nature of corruption. Those by anonymous posters are even less provable.

22 IPaidABribe, accessed February 2014, September 2015, and January 2019, http://www.ipaidabribe.com.

23 Strom, "Web Sites Shine Light"; Raghunandan, "Tackling Corruption"; Mike Nguyen, "Open Governments, Open Data: Getting the Technological Toolkits Right," *SAIS Review of International Affairs* 34, no. 1 (Winter–Spring 2014): 83–6, at 84.

24 Raghunandan, "Tackling Corruption"; Lydia Polgreen, "Right-to-Know Law Gives India's Poor a Lever," *The New York Times,* June 29, 2010, A1; Lydia Polgreen, "Indians Use Information Law, at a Deadly Risk," *The New York Times,* January 23, 2011, A1; Akash Kapur, "Prying Open India's Vast Bureaucracy," *The New York Times,* June 17, 2010, http://www.nytimes.com/2010/06/18/world/asia/18iht-letter.html; Jason Burke, "Dying for Data: the Indian Activist Killed for Asking too Many Questions," *The Guardian,* December 27, 2010, https://www.theguardian.com/world/2010/dec/27/india-rti-activists-deaths; Alasdair Roberts, "A Great and Revolutionary Law? Four Years of India's Right to Information Act," *Public Administration Review* 70, no. 6 (2010): 925–33; Mehul Srivastava and Andrew MacAskill, "In India, Whistle-Blowers Pay with Their Lives," *Business Week,* October 20, 2011, http://www.businessweek.com/magazine/in-india-whistleblowers-pay-with-their-lives-10202011.html. The estimates (thirty killed, fifty-five assaulted) are unverified and on Wikipedia, and thus should be used cautiously. "Attacks on RTI Activists in India," Wikipedia, accessed January 12, 2019, https://en.wikipedia.org/wiki/Attacks_on_RTI_activists_in_India.

25 "Corruption Perceptions Index," Transparency International, accessed January 12, 2019, https://www.transparency.org/news/feature/corruption_perceptions_index_2017.

26 Mukti Jain Campion, "Bribery in India: A Website for Whistleblowers," *BBC News,* June 5, 2011, http://www.bbc.com/news/world-south-asia-13616123; Asch Harwood, "IPaidABribe in India and Kenya," *Africa in Transition* [Council on Foreign Relations], March 8, 2012,

http://blogs.cfr.org/campbell/2012/03/08/guest-post-ipaidabribe-in-india-and-kenya/; Raghu-nandan, "Tackling Corruption."

27 Some of the IPaidABribe launch failures included sites in China, Ghana, Kosovo, and South Africa. The table was constructed using Ipaidabribe.org, accessed September 13, 2015 and January 12, 2019. See also Strom, "Web Sites Shine Light." Ghana was listed under "Coming Soon!" on ipaidabribe.org in October 2014; Ang, Yuen. "Authoritarian Restraints on Online Activism Revisited: Why 'I-Paid-A-Bribe' Worked in India but Failed in China." *Comparative Politics* 47, no. 1 (2014): 21–40. IPaidABribe, accessed September 13, 2015 and January 12, 2019, http://www.ipaidabribe.com/.

28 Gerry Mullany, "Malaysia Denies Entry to Journalist," *The New York Times*, July 5, 2013, A6; Anne-Marie Slaughter and Eleanor Meegoda, "Harnessing Connection Technologies for Development," in *Old Problems, New Solutions: Harnessing Technology and Innovation in the Fight Against Global Poverty*, The 2012 Brookings Blum Roundtable Policy Briefs, 2012, 19–31; John Psaropoulos, "Naming and Shaming Hits Greece," *Al Jazeera*, October 10, 2012, http://www.aljazeera.com/indepth/features/2012/10/2012101081514604283.html. Teleiakaipavla's website was down on repeated visits in late 2014. However, someone affili-ated with the organization continued to tweet as of September 2014 (at https://twitter.com/teleiakaipavla). Tarik Nesh-Nash, "How to Fight Corruption with Online Tools: Best Practice from Morocco," *Space for Transparency* (Transparency International), May 8, 2013, http://blog.transparency.org/2013/05/08/how-to-fight-corruption-with-online-tools-best-practice-from-morocco/; Nicky Rehbock, "A Year of Corruption-Busting in South Africa," *Space for Transparency* (Transparency International), February 7, 2013, http://blog.transparency.org/2013/02/07/a-year-of-corruption-busting-in-south-africa.

29 The Russian procurement corruption statistics came from a 2010 study, cited in Nikolay Petrov, "The Navalny Effect: RosPil.net," *Carnegie Endowment for International Peace*, December 8, 2010, http://carnegieendowment.org/2010/12/08/navalny-effect-rospil.net/21ux. Ruble to dollar exchange calculated on October 27, 2014, on xe.com, when 1 USD = 42.2506 RUB. Tom Balmforth, "Smartphone App Lets Russians Call Out Bribes," *Radio Free Europe/Radio Liberty*, October 11, 2012, http://www.rferl.org/content/russia-bribr-smartphone-app-corruption/24736489.html; Alexandra Nikolchev, "Bribr: A New Russian Anti-corrup-tion App," *The Daily Need*, PBS, December 13, 2012, http://www.pbs.org/wnet/need-to-know/the-daily-need/bibr-a-new-russian-anti-corruption-app/15709/; Maeve Shearlaw, "30 under 30: Moscow's Young Power List," *Guardian*, June 8, 2015, http://www.theguardian.com/world/2015/jun/08/30-under-30-moscows-young-power-list; Julia Ioffe, "Net Impact," *New Yorker*, April 4, 2011; Greg Brown, "Crowdsourcing to Fight Corruption: Aleksei Navalny and the RosPil Experiment," *Sunlight Foundation*, August 6, 2013, http://sunlightfoundation.com/blog/2013/08/06/crowdsourcing-to-fight-corruption-aleksei-navalny-and-the-rospil-experiment.

30 The fact that Russian government contracts were accessible and online may be hard to believe. The transparency came courtesy of then president Dmitry Medvedev's anti-corruption initia-tive in 2010. David M. Herszenhorn, "Protests Erupt over Sentence of Putin Critic" *The New York Times*, July 19, 2013, A1; Petrov, "The Navalny Effect"; Ioffe, "Net Impact"; Brown, "Crowdsourcing to Fight."

31 Bribespot's transnational nature emerged after earlier experiments with the country-by-country franchise model. Neither Bribespot nor Bribecaster clearly described the anonymizing source protections very well on their websites, although Bribespot's messaging did improve, and Bribecaster's developer clarified the encryption method in an email. Email from Manas Mittal, September 26, 2015. Bribecaster (http://bribecaster.org) was developed by com-puter science students at University of California at Berkeley's College of Engineering and MIT's Computer Science and Artificial Intelligence Laboratory. Manas Mittal, "Bribecaster: Documenting Bribes Through Community Participation," EECS Department, University of California, Berkeley, Technical Report No. UCB/EECS-2014-85, May 16, 2014; Manas Mit-tal, Wei Wu, Steve Rubin, Sam Madden, and Björn Hartmann, "Bribecaster: Documenting Bribes through Community Participation," In Proceedings of the ACM 2012 Conference on Computer Supported Cooperative Work Companion, https://people.eecs.berkeley.edu/~

bjoern/papers/mittal-bribecaster-cscw2012-poster.pdf; Ann Carrns, "Report Your Bribes Via a Smartphone App," *Bucks (The New York Times)*, May 31, 2011, https://bucks.blogs.nytimes.com/2011/05/31/report-your-bribes-via-a-smartphone-app/.

32 The first website link (http://www.president.go.ke/en/category/corruption.php) led to an error page on July 11, 2014 (and other attempts). The relaunched website (at http://www.president.go.ke/report-corruption/) also disappeared at that address on September 24, 2015. "Kenyan President Kenyatta Sets up Anti-Bribery Website," *BBC News*, October 31, 2013 http://www.bbc.com/news/world-africa-24756493; The White House Office of the Press Secretary, "Government of the Republic of Kenya—Government of the United States of America Joint Commitment to Promote Good Governance and Anti-Corruption Efforts in Kenya," July 25, 2015, https://www.whitehouse.gov/the-press-office/2015/07/25/government-republic-kenya-government-united-states-america-joint.

33 "Report Corruption—EACC," Ethics and Anti-Corruption Commission, Government of Kenya, accessed January 12, 2019, http://www.eacc.go.ke/report-corruption.

34 "China to Protect Online Whistleblowers, But Only via Official Site," *Reuters*, September 12, 2013 http://www.reuters.com/article/2013/09/12/us-china-corruption-idUSBRE98B09B20130912; Ivar Kolstad and Arne Wiig, "Does Democracy Reduce Corruption?" *Democratization* (September 2015): 1–21; Daniel Treisman, "What Have We Learned about the Causes of Corruption from Ten Years of Cross-National Empirical Research," *Annual Review of Political Science* 10 (2007): 211–44; Sean Silbert, "Keeping Tabs on Chinese Corruption: There's an App for That," *Los Angeles Times*, January 8, 2015, http://www.latimes.com/world/asia/la-fg-app-china-corruption-20150108-story.html; Vanessa Piao, "China Lets Citizens' Fingers Do the Talking to Report Graft," *Sinophere, The New York Times*, June 19, 2015, http://sinosphere.blogs.nytimes.com/2015/06/19/china-communist-party-corruption-app; "China 'to Protect Whistle-blowers' Amid Corruption Fight," *BBC News*, October 28, 2014, http://www.bbc.com/news/world-asia-china-29797985. On the Bhutanese case, see http://www.anti-corruption.org.bt/?q=node/102 and Strom, "Web Sites Shine Light."

35 Most of the apps listed were discovered through simple searches in the Google Play Android app store in September 2015, December 2015, June 2016, and January 2019. Others were described in "Uganda's Election Monitoring App," Africa Live, *CCTV Africa*, August 22, 2015, https://www.youtube.com/watch?v=M4CIWoLohnI. See also "Russia's presidential election marked by unequal campaign conditions, active citizens' engagement, international observers say," Office for Democratic Institutions and Human Rights, Organization for Security and Cooperation in Europe (OSCE), March 5, 2012, http://www.osce.org/odihr/elections/88661; Ellen Barry and Michael Schwirtz, "Fraud Allegations Detailed and Protesters Detained after Putin Victory," *The New York Times*, March 6, 2012, A4; "Map an Election Bribe" in Malaysia, accessed May 21, 2013, http://election.sarawakreport.org/#6/3.57921/108.39111.

36 Pamela Fox, "Introducing the Maps API Demo Gallery," Google Maps API Blog, February 28, 2008, http://googlemapsapi.blogspot.com/2008/02/introducing-maps-api-demo-gallery.html; Sterling Quinn, "Using Google Maps to Visualize ArcGIS Data & Services," Google GEO Developers Blog, August 12, 2008, http://googlegeodevelopers.blogspot.com/2008/08/using-google-maps-to-visualize-arcgis.html; Matthias Weber, "Tour de France Live Tracker 2008," PSFK, July 10, 2008, http://www.psfk.com/2008/07/tour-de-france-live-tracker-2008.html.

37 Personal communication with Douglas Kimemia, Virginia Commonwealth University, September 29, 2015; "Five Great Styled Maps Examples," Google GEO Developers Blog, October 1, 2010, http://googlegeodevelopers.blogspot.com/2010/10/five-great-styled-maps-examples.html; Jeffrey Gettleman, "Disputed Vote Plunges Kenya into Bloodshed," *The New York Times,* December 31, 2007, A1; David Adewumi, "Kenyan Tech Bloggers Launch Crisisreport Site," VentureBeat, January 15, 2008, http://venturebeat.com/2008/01/15/kenyan-tech-bloggers-launch-crisis-report-site/; "Deal to End Kenyan Crisis Agreed," *BBC News,* April 12, 2008, http://news.bbc.co.uk/2/hi/africa/7344816.stm; Gabriel Gatehouse, "Kenya Violence: Survivors' Tales," *BBC News,* September 10, 2013, http://www.bbc.com/news/world-africa-24021833.

38   Erik Hersman, "The Ushahidi Engine in South Africa," Ushahidi blog, May 26, 2008, http: //www.ushahidi.com/blog/2008/05/26/the-ushahidi-engine-in-south-africa/; Erik Hersman, "Ushahidi Deploys to the Congo (DRC)," Ushahidi blog, http://www.ushahidi.com/blog/ 2008/11/07/ushahidi-deploys-to-the-congo-drc/; "Web Tool Maps Congo Conflict," *BBC News*, December 10, 2008, http://news.bbc.co.uk/2/hi/technology/7773648.stm.

39   Maja Bott and Gregor Young, "The Role of Crowdsourcing for Better Governance in International Development," *PRAXIS: The Fletcher Journal of Human Security* 27, no. 1 (2012): 47–70; Independent Assessment of South Sudan's Crisis and Recovery Mapping and Analysis (CRMA) project, United Nations Development Program Bureau for Crisis Prevention and Recovery, July 2014, http://erc.undp.org/evaluation/evaluations/detail/7645.

40   All three of the examples in this and the next paragraph (ACLU-AZ Stop SB1070, Cop Recorder, and OpenWatch) were designed by Rich Jones, a developer featured in Greenberg, *This Machine Steals Secrets*. The SB1070 app appeared in June 2013 and lasted at least a year; it was defunct by August 2016. The ACLU-AZ subsequently provided a nonanonymous website platform and a phone number. The original Android app page was at "ACLU-AZ Stop SB1070," accessed July 12, 2014, https://play.google.com/store/apps/details?id=net.openw atch.acluaz. See also Miguel Otarola, "ACLU Unveils App to Document Arizona Racial-profiling Claims," *The Arizona Republic*, June 18, 2013, http://archive.azcentral.com/news/ politics/articles/20130618arizona-app-racial-profiling-aclu-abrk.html; "Help Stop SB 1070 in Arizona!" American Civil Liberties Union, accessed August 12, 2016, https://action.aclu.org/ secure/az/help-stop-sb-1070-arizona; Andy Greenberg, "OpenWatch Turns Your Smartphone into a 'Reverse Surveillance Camera,'" *Forbes,* June 22, 2011, http://www.forbes.com/sit es/andygreenberg/2011/06/22/openwatch-turns-your-smartphone-into-a-reverse-surveillance-camera.

41   Gary T. Marx and Dane Archer, "Citizen Involvement in the Law Enforcement Process: The Case of Community Police Patrols," *American Behavioral Scientist* 15, no. 1 (1971): 52; "'Policing the Police': How the Black Panthers Got Their Start," *Fresh Air*, NPR, September 23, 2015, http://www.npr.org/2015/09/23/442801731/director-chronicles-the-black-panthers-rise-new-tactics-were-needed.

42   Paul Lewis and Dominic Rushe, "Revealed: How Whisper App Tracks 'Anonymous' Users," *The Guardian,* October 16, 2014, http://www.theguardian.com/world/2014/oct/16/-sp-reveal ed-whisper-app-tracking-users; Brian Anthony Hernandez, "PostSecret App Discontinued Because of 'Malicious' Posts," *Mashable*, January 2, 2012, http://mashable.com/2012/01/02 /postsecret-app-discontinued-because-of-malicious-posts/; http://www.cnet.com/news/posts ecret-shuts-down-iphone-app-due-to-abusive-posts/; Greenberg, *This Machine*, 152.

Chapter 8

Exfiltrators

Like almost anything WikiLeaks related in the early 2010s, Alex Gibney's documentary film *We Steal Secrets: The Story of WikiLeaks* caused controversy when it hit theaters in May 2013. The night before its release, WikiLeaks founder Julian Assange characterized the film as an unscrupulous hit job, and posted an annotated transcript which aims to show every falsehood and unfounded accusation. Someone working with the film had fittingly leaked the script.

A central plank of Assange's critique involves the film's name. "The title," he argues, "is false. It directly implies that WikiLeaks steals secrets. In fact, the statement is made by former CIA/NSA director Michael Hayden [in a scene of the film] in relation to the activities of US government spies, not in relation to WikiLeaks. This is an irresponsible libel. Not even critics in the film say that WikiLeaks steals secrets." Assange was correct that the only person in the film who says the phrase is General Hayden, who offers a frank acknowledgment of what spy agencies do:

> Look, everyone has secrets. Some of the activities that nation states conduct in order to keep their people safe and free need to be secret in order to be successful. If they are broadly known, you cannot accomplish your work. Now look, I'm going to be very candid, alright? **We steal secrets.** We steal other nations' secrets. One cannot do that above board and be very successful for a very long period of time.[1]

In a short video response on the film's Facebook page, Gibney concedes Assange's point about Hayden's remark, but offers a flabby defense of his use of the phrase: it "puts the whole context of secrets, and leaking secrets, in a broader perspective."[2]

What Gibney does not say in the video is that his title is not altogether unfair. While stealing secrets is not the primary way WikiLeaks gets its information, the title is accurate, albeit misleading as a general descriptor. On at least one occasion, WikiLeaks stole secrets for a hack and leak operation, and admitted it.

In 2006, its first year of operation, WikiLeaks opportunistically siphoned data flowing from China through a Tor node. Chinese hackers, who probably worked for the government, were transmitting secrets that they had taken from other governments, and WikiLeaks found a way to grab data packets en route. WikiLeaks acknowledged the hack in a May 2010 Twitter post that linked to a Raffi Khatchadourian article that had first reported it ("Some WikiLeaks documents were siphoned off of Chinese hackers' activities. WikiLeaks in The New Yorker."). Like Khatchadourian, who argues that "the initial tranche served as the site's foundation," Kim Zetter in *Wired* makes the hack and subsequent leak central to WikiLeaks's origin story, because it increased WikiLeaks's prominence, which attracted donors. Both writers show that the operation helped set WikiLeaks on a positive trajectory so that, by 2008, Assange could boast that "[w]e have received over one million documents from thirteen countries."[3] There is no evidence that WikiLeaks staffers have snatched secrets from Tor networks, or any other networks, since 2006.

Stealing Secrets without Apology

Given Assange's legal predicament in 2013 (chapter 6), his touchiness about being accused of stealing secrets is understandable. The film's release came amidst rumors of a U.S. grand jury investigating his possible crimes, as well as the ongoing trial of *US v. Manning*, in which prosecutors were arguing that the WikiLeaks founder had solicited classified documents from Chelsea (née Bradley) Manning. Assange's nervousness about his legal fate was evident on Twitter: "'We Steal Secrets': an unethical and biased title in the context of pending criminal trials and investigations. It is the prosecution's claim and it is false."[4]

But is secret-stealing always wrong? Intelligence agencies, as Hayden notes in the film, steal other countries' secrets as a matter of course. Another former CIA director, George Tenet, has described his agency's work similarly, and proudly: "I cannot explain what we do here other than to say we steal secrets for a living and we take those secrets and put them into all-source products that make a difference to somebody. If anybody thinks we are doing anything else here, they can come talk to me. But let's be blunt about we do. There is no dishonor in it. We steal secrets for a living."[5] Tenet's point is that espionage can be honorable when it enhances national security and advances other legitimate national interests. It pursues defensible ends with devious means.

This chapter focuses on another class of secret-stealers who use devious means for defensible ends. Whereas spies typically transfer stolen secrets to governments, who usually keep them concealed, exfiltrator whistleblowers make it a priority to publish the secrets that they steal. Despite not being spies, they act like spies. They plan secret-stealing operations with some of the collection tactics used by intelligence agencies. They use hidden cameras and drones. They use false fronts and identity covers. They run black bag jobs. Their tradecraft may be limited by their resources and training, but that has not stopped some from succeeding.

The Citizens' Commission to Investigate the FBI

On March 8, 1971, eight left-wing political activists burglarized a Federal Bureau of Investigation (FBI) office in Media, Pennsylvania, a Philadelphia suburb. Their core mission was to steal the FBI's secrets. The self-described "Citizens' Commission to Investigate the F.B.I." (CCIF) did not know exactly what they would find in the FBI's file cabinets and desk drawers, but they hoped they would come across documents proving that the Bureau had engaged in illegal spying and worse. Like other activists of the era, CCIF members suspected that the FBI had surveilled, disrupted, and tried to eradicate U.S.-based political groups. But they lacked clear evidence. The CCIF decided that there was only one way to expose the Bureau's abuse of authority: they needed to turn the tables and "pull a black-bag job on the FBI."[6]

It worked. Because of their careful planning and the FBI office's lax security, CCIF members managed to break in and abscond with bags filled with classified documents. They hit one unexpected obstacle—a newly installed lock on the door—but overcame it because one member, Keith Forsyth, had taken a locksmithing class to prepare for the big night. Once inside, the CCIF team found reams of barely secured papers. In their scramble in the dark office, the burglars grabbed whatever their bags could hold, altogether about a thousand documents. They hoped any clanking and stumbling around would be muted by the upstairs residents' radios and TVs blaring the "Fight of the Century" boxing match pitting Muhammad Ali against Joe Frazier.[7]

The CCIF fled to a safe house outside Philadelphia to see what they had taken. They soon realized that they had struck a goldmine. The files matter-of-factly described the FBI's Counterintelligence Program (COINTELPRO) operations against Communist, New Left, Black Nationalist, civil rights, Puerto Rican nationalist, and white power groups, among others. COINTELPRO was one of several FBI programs focusing on groups thought to have links with hostile foreign powers or plans to engage in political violence.[8] Americans had a right to know about what the FBI had been doing, the CCIF decided, and so the group reached out to journalists and members of Congress.

At first, no one wanted to help. Antiwar Senator George McGovern (D-SD) and civil rights advocate Representative Parren Mitchell (D-MD) opted not to partner with people who had burglarized an FBI office. Selected newspaper reporters also rebuffed the CCIF. Wanting to spill the FBI's secrets through any means possible, the CCIF turned to local chapters of the War Resisters League and the Black Panther Party, who eagerly published some of the files. But those organizations had limited reach. Finally, about two weeks after the burglary, the CCIF found a *Washington Post* reporter, Betty Medsger, who recognized the story's importance, and decided that the benefits of disclosing classified information outweighed the risks. Once she brought the story to a national audience, other reporters and analysts rushed in.[9]

The COINTELPRO revelations, along with others in the 1970s, placed the FBI and other U.S. intelligence agencies under an unprecedented amount of public scrutiny. Congressional committees launched high-profile investigations, which revealed additional details about COINTELPRO and other programs. Reporters filed Freedom of Information Act (FOIA) requests for more documents, and sued the government after receiving rejections, sometimes winning their cases.[10] The CCIF's burglary, along with later leaks, FOIA releases, investigative reporting, and congressional investigations, led to a barrage of intelligence reforms that placed constraints on the FBI and other agencies, including the Foreign Surveillance Intelligence Act in 1978 and Attorney General Edward Levi's guidelines for FBI investigations in 1976.[11]

Despite a determined but relatively short-lived investigation (MEDBURG, for Media burglary), the FBI failed to identify any CCIF members. After the statute of limitations had run out, six of them allowed Medsger to reveal their identities in her 2014 book.[12] When asked about the burglary's meaning, some described it as an act of whistleblowing, if not by name. "We thought somebody needed to confront [FBI Director J. Edgar] Hoover and document what many of us knew was happening," Bonnie Raines said. "We did it," John Raines concurred, "because somebody had to do it. . . . [W]e exposed a crime that was going on. When we are denied the information we need to have to act as citizens, then we have a right to do what we did."[13]

Going Undercover: Exfiltrating Infiltrators

Chapter 2's development of the outsider whistleblower concept challenged the notion that whistleblowers must be organizational insiders. Recall the example of a smartphone-wielding activist standing outside a window of a poultry processing plant, recording abuses that occurred inside. She gave the pictures to a local reporter, who showed them on the evening news. The conceptualization of whistleblowing did not disqualify her just because she was not a company employee.

Of course, poultry processing plants tend not to have windows exposing their shop floors. Animal welfare activists who want to expose suspected abusive practices cannot expect to stand outside with cameras, or find incriminating documents in dumpsters outside. To overcome the obstacle, some have ventured inside, deceitfully becoming insiders with no loyalty to or identification with the targeted organization.

PETA and the Silver Spring Monkeys

Alex Pacheco's life as an animal rights activist began in the late 1970s inside a Toronto slaughterhouse, where his senses were assaulted by "the stench of the blood, the excrement everywhere, the screaming of the animals." He was visiting a friend who worked there. According to Pacheco:

> As we walked up to what looked like a warehouse, two men wearing long aprons came out through a garage-type door. They were red head to toe with blood. They were big guys and carried between them a soaking wet, newborn or ready-to-be-born calf, upside down by his ankles. He was three to four feet long and two to three feet high, and he was very much alive and struggling. The top of the dumpster was at least eight feet off the ground. They stood there and swung the thrashing calf like a sack of potatoes, one, two, and then heaved him up. But he didn't go over the top; he hit the side and fell to the pavement. They picked him up and threw him again, and again he didn't go in. The third time, they managed to hurl him over the top and into the dumpster. We then went inside. There before us was all the stark horror of terrified cows, chickens, and pigs undergoing grisly deaths. Pregnant pigs were disemboweled and all the wriggling baby pigs were on the conveyor belt among the animal organs and treated just like the organs.

After that harrowing experience, Pacheco joined the fledgling animal rights movement while continuing his studies at Ohio State University (OSU)—reading Peter Singer, going vegetarian, organizing protests, and denouncing alleged animal abuses in campus media interviews, such as local farmers who routinely castrated unanaesthetized cows. Pacheco's work sometimes drew hostile reactions, like the night when angry OSU agriculture students allegedly threatened to castrate *him* the same way. He soon left Columbus to work with anti-whaling activists aboard the Sea Shepard, a "200 foot ship . . . on a search and destroy mission. The bow of the ship had been reinforced with tons of poured concrete as part of preparations to ram the world's most notorious illegal pirate whaling ship, the Sierra." Pacheco then traveled to the U.K. to work with an anti-fox hunting group, who led hunters' dogs astray with a fake scent of their prey the activists had spread throughout the English woods. Back in the United States in 1980, he cofounded the People for the Ethical Treatment (PETA) with Ingrid Newkirk, a veteran animal welfare campaigner in Washington, DC.[14]

Pacheco and Newkirk wanted PETA to focus on animals used in research and the meat, poultry, and dairy industries. They were not the first to focus on research animals. The anti-vivisection movement emerged in the nineteenth century, and the Humane Society had completed laboratory investigations starting in the 1950s (see below). Newkirk herself had previously done some preliminary investigative work in laboratories. In 1981, Pacheco offered to pick up where she had left off, and secured a volunteer position at a laboratory near his home, the Institute for Behavioral Research (IBR). In 1985, he recounted what he remembered of what he depicted as a rat- and roach-infested lab:

> I saw filth caked on the wires of the cages, [feces] piled in the bottom of the cages, urine and rust encrusting every surface. There, amid this rotting stench, sat sixteen crab-eating macaques and one rhesus monkey, their lives limited to metal boxes just 17¾ inches wide. In their desperation to assuage their hunger, they were picking forlornly at scraps and fragments of broken biscuits that had fallen through the wire into the sodden accumulations in the waste collection trays below. The cages had clearly not been cleaned properly for months. There were no dishes to keep the food away from the faeces, nothing for the animals to sit on but the jagged wires of the old cages, nothing for them to see but the filthy, faeces-splattered walls of that windowless room, only 15 ft. square.

Pacheco also claimed to have witnessed untreated injuries and illnesses, saying monkeys were not given even basic cleanings after severe "lacerations or self-amputation injuries."[15] There are reasons to question the veracity of every detail of his testimony, not least the lab's financial interest in maintaining its investment in the monkeys, and the other employees' supposed toleration of the disturbing conditions.

The lab did a range of experiments on its monkeys. According to Pacheco and PETA, one study involved intentionally damaging neurosurgery. Another tested the monkeys' reactions to near-starvation diets, which also tracked their reactions to being teased about their plight. Pacheco recounted the details:

> Twelve of the seventeen monkeys had disabled limbs as a result of surgical interference (deafferentation) when they were juveniles . . . to monitor the rehabilitation of impaired limbs . . . I was given two monkeys and told to put them in separate cages in a room. The monkeys, Augustus and Hayden, were deprived of food for two to three days, and I was to go alone into their room, set up video equipment to record events and feed them about fifty raisins each. After some weeks I was to withhold their food for three days and then, instead of giving them the raisins, I was just to show them the raisins but not allow them to eat, and then record their frustrated reactions . . . I was to take a monkey from the colony and strap him into a homemade immobilizing chair, where he would be held at the waist, ankles, wrists and neck. The acute noxious stimuli were to be applied with a pair of haemostats (surgical pliers) clamped and fastened on to the animal, and locked to the tightest notch. I was to observe which parts of the monkey's body felt pain. (The noxious stimuli used to be administered by using an "open flame"—a cigarette lighter.) . . . [One monkey] had been in such bad shape that he had begun to mutilate his own chest cavity.

Pacheco and Newkirk's plan was to collect evidence of abuse so they could build an animal cruelty case against the lab and its director, Dr. Edward Taub, based on alleged violations of the Animal Welfare Act of 1966.[16]

Pacheco began photographing as much as he could. The busy lab during daytime hours made undercover work difficult, so he seized an opportunity to work nights and weekends. Being there during unusual hours also allowed him to sneak in scientists who could write affidavits and testify as expert witnesses. He showed his photos to other activists, including the writer Cleveland Armory, who provided cash for cameras and walkie-talkies, which they used for operational security. Pacheco and Newkirk's dark network of exfiltrators quickly grew to include Newkirk, Armory, Dr. Geza Teleki, Dr. Michael Fox, Dr. Ronnie Hawkins, Dr. John McArdle, Donald Barnes, and probably others who chose to remain anonymous. In early September, they decided to contact local law enforcement.[17]

Pacheco and a lawyer (and probably Newkirk) went to the Montgomery County police department, photographs in hand. Evidently they were persuasive enough. The police obtained a warrant, raided Dr. Taub's lab, and rescued the surviving rhesus and crab-eating macaques. After the National Zoo and local animal shelters declined to house them, the macaques found refuge in an activist's basement, where they enjoyed constant care, soap operas, good food, and toys. But as the legal case against Dr. Taub proceeded, they monkeys lost their suburban refuge. They were dragged around, and dropped in and out of government and university labs, at one point winding up under Dr. Taub's care, following an appellate court decision about their custody. Eventually, in the early 1990s, all of the monkeys were euthanized.[18]

By that time that happened, Pacheco and Newkirk had developed PETA into a prominent "direct action"–oriented animal welfare organization. Indeed, infiltration exfiltrations became a PETA specialty, something that distinguished it from most other groups. Since its founding through 2007, PETA ran more than seventy-five "undercover investigations," targeting cosmetic firms, Las Vegas stars, factory farms, ranchers, furriers, clothing designers, and oil companies, among others.[19]

PETA has achieved an impressive record of forcing change. The Silver Spring investigation prompted not only front page news coverage, but also, as Pacheco proudly boasted, the "world's first and only police confiscation of laboratory animals," the closure of a lab because of cruelty charges, and "the first arrest warrant, criminal trial and conviction of a research scientist on cruelty charges." PETA's other investigations have forced large corporations as diverse as McDonalds, Maybelline, and General Motors, to change their purchasing, manufacturing, and quality control/testing policies. The investigations have also paved the way for congressional action, and have helped activists score victories in federal courts.[20] Since 2007, it has managed at least six more investigations, including those of: a commercial research laboratory in North Carolina, which shut down because of the publicity; research laboratories at the University of Utah, a case that led to a change in Utah state law; a reptile and rat breeder in California, whose animals were seized and whose owner faced 223 "felony cruelty-to-animals and related charges"; and angora wool (rabbit fur) businesses, which suffered after the publicity led more than 300 companies to stop buying and selling it (e.g., Calvin Klein, Marks and Spencer, H&M, Tommy Hilfiger).[21]

This Kind of Whistleblowing Has Long Been Central to the Animal Welfare Movement

Animal welfare organizations had deployed infiltration-exfiltration methods decades before PETA was formed. Some, like PETA, have collected evidence of alleged abuses. Others, such as the Animal Liberation Front (ALF), focused on exfiltrating animals—opening the cage door and letting them run into the wild.

The Humane Society of the United States (HSUS) launched its first investigations in the late 1950s, shortly after Fred Myers founded the organization. A HSUS investigator in 1958 infiltrated a Tulane University laboratory by gaining employment there. He found and reported a variety of concerns, including "inadequate caging," "unsupervised and frivolous operations and procedures by undergraduate students," and "denied postoperative care." The HSUS in those early years targeted everything from a dogfighting ring in Mississippi to a medical facility in California.[22]

More recently, Mercy for Animals (MFA) has emerged as a major player in undercover investigations. In many ways MFA is like PETA, minus the latter's repertoire of contentious protest tactics, such as crashing fashion shows and throwing pies and fake blood on fur wearers. Founded in 1999, MFA conducted at least seventy-five undercover investigations from 2001 to 2018, which targeted major corporations (e.g., Butterball LLC, Tyson Pork) as well as smaller players (e.g., Quality Egg of New England).[23]

Animal Enterprises Strike Back

PETA, HSUS, and MFA's investigations have inflicted legal, financial, and reputational costs onto animal-reliant industries. Many businesses have stepped up their defenses in response, for instance by more thoroughly vetting job applicants to keep infiltrators out. Still, the continued success of undercover investigators in securing jobs at targeted businesses shows that employers have yet to solve the adverse selection problem—and they probably never will. Job candidates can misrepresent their biographies, and mask their intentions. Vetting them thoroughly would require more resources than are warranted for generally low-wage jobs.

While many animal-reliant businesses did what they could internally to adapt to the growing threat, some opted for politics. While slaughterhouse owners and hog farmers may have lacked PETA's disruptiveness and pluck, some had other resources for political combat: money and powerful allies. They channeled those resources into policy fights in state legislatures.

The first win came in 1990, when the Kansas state house passed the "Farm Animal and Field Crop and Research Facilities Protection Act." The law enumerated the ways people could be held criminally liable for acts committed on farms and in labs, including undercover investigations by activists posing as employees: "No person shall, without the effective consent of the owner and with the intent to damage the enterprise conducted at the animal facility: Enter an animal facility, not then open to the public," while "remain[ing] concealed," to "take pictures by photograph, video camera or by any other means."[24]

Montana followed suit a year later, passing the Farm Animal and Research Facilities Protection Act of 1991. The title alone ("Farm Animal . . . Protection") must have been deeply frustrating for activists who believed *they* were the ones protecting farm animals. The language of the law closely resembled Kansas's, with explicit references to concealment and taking "pictures by photograph, video camera, or other means with the intent to commit criminal defamation," among other damages. Under the law, damages inflicted upon the animal-reliant business in excess of $500 incurred penalties of $50,000 and/or a prison term of up to ten years. That is ten years in prison for shooting an undercover video on a farm in Montana. North Dakota passed a similar law, also in 1991.[25]

After a twenty-year delay, a new wave of ag-gag laws emerged in state legislatures. Figure 8.1 captures the breadth of the legislative efforts, as well as their mixed record. After failures in Minnesota and New York in 2011, ag-gag bills passed in Iowa and Utah in March 2012, and in Missouri in July 2012. Idaho's agriculture interests scored a victory two years later, after the state house declared animal rights activists' undercover operations a "crime of interference with agricultural production" when one "enters an agricultural production facility that is not open to the public and, without the facility owner's express consent or pursuant to judicial process or statutory authorization, makes audio or video recordings of the conduct of an agricultural production facility's operations."[26] Figure 8.1 provides the state of the political battle as of January 2019.

Some of the laws crack down on infiltrating exfiltrators, but leave alone more conventional whistleblowers.[27] Some also contain quick reporting requirements, forcing individuals who claim to have evidence of animal abuse to immediately share it with local law enforcement officials. At first glance, quick reporting might seem beneficial to the cause of animal welfare. Why wait to report abuses? However, the industry-supported provisions more likely thwart activist or journalistic investigations for two reasons. First, investigators need time to compile evidence to show patterns of abuse. Second, local government officials,

FIGURE 8.1 State-Level Ag-Gag Legislation in the United States. *Source*: Courtesy of the American Society for the Prevention of Cruelty to Animals (ASPCA). Copyright © 2019. The American Society for the Prevention of Cruelty to Animals (ASPCA). All Rights Reserved.

including those in police departments, often have close associations with business owners (e.g., the Amy Meyer case, described in note 26). In those cases, anything animal welfare organizations share with police officers, including the identities of their undercover investigators, will likely be shared with business owners. Undercover investigators who are forced to share their evidence and identities with law enforcement officials who have close animal-reliant business links risk losing their jobs, which would end their investigations.[28]

"Drones on the Farm": Confronting and Circumventing Ag-Gag Laws

The battle between animal welfare activists and industrial livestock producers did not end with the blows delivered by ag-gag laws. A few high-profile media features and legal cases increased public awareness of the conflict, which brought fresh scrutiny of the attempts to legally ban and deter exfiltrating infiltrators. *New York Times* columnist Mark Bittman probably did more than anyone in raising awareness of the laws, most of all by coining the memorable phrase "ag-gag laws."[29] Partly because of that increased awareness, animal welfare groups' lobbying efforts have persuaded more than twenty state legislators to reject ag-gag laws. They have had success in the courts as well. State supreme courts have ruled ag-gag laws unconstitutional in Idaho, Iowa, Utah, and Wyoming (figure 8.1). The Animal Legal Defense Fund won a federal case in 2015 against the Governor of Idaho in the U.S. District Court, in which the plaintiffs argued that Idaho's law violated the First and Fourteenth Amendments to the U.S. Constitution. If other federal lawsuits in Utah, North Carolina, and Wyoming produce conflicting decisions, the conflict could rise to the Supreme Court.[30]

Activists challenging ag-gag laws also took to the skies. In June 2013, authorities in Garden City arrested a paragliding photographer working on a *National Geographic* story about the food production system in Kansas. When George Steinmetz returned to earth after taking aerial photographs of a feedlot, local police charged him with criminal trespassing. Although officials did not charge him under Kansas's ag-gag law, news of the case ricocheted around the activist community.[31]

The Steinmetz episode got independent investigative reporter Will Potter thinking about new ways activists and journalists could turn the tables. Even before Steinmetz's arrest, Potter had thought about how aerial photography might be deployed to circumvent ag-gag laws, and to avoid the hassle and risks

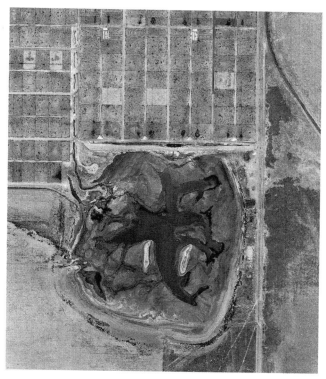

FIGURE 8.2   Satellite Photograph of a Texas Feedlot. *Source*: Mishka Henner.

of infiltrating businesses. He had come across a series of simultaneously beautiful and disgusting photos of feedlots that MishkaHenner created using satellites (see, for example, figure 8.2). "It made me wonder what else we could see from aerial-drone photography," Potter remembered. Using the crowdsourced fundraising website Kickstarter, he proposed a clever new project: *Drone on the Farm: An Aerial Exposé* ("What are factory farms hiding with 'ag-gag' laws? I'll combine drone photography with investigative reporting to find out.") Supporters reached Potter's goal of $30,000 in five days, after the June 9, 2014, launch. Continued expansions of the project's goals netted total contributions north of $75,000 by March 2015. The first photos appeared on Kickstarter in December. By that point, others had tried drone activism as well.[32] A year and a half later, Texas banned drone photography over "concentrated animal feeding operations."[33] The whistleblowing drone wars are just beginning.

A Likely Future: Hacktivist Whistleblowing

The phenomenon of hacking—gaining "unauthorized access to or control over a computer system, network, [or] a person's telephone communications" (Oxford English Dictionary)—is older that most people realize. Some historians trace it as far back as 1878, when mischievous teenage boys hired by the Bell Telephone Company intentionally redirected customers' calls. Histories that rely on narrower definitions of hacking, in which outsiders break into computers or telecommunications systems, often start with exploits from the 1950s and 1960s, such as Josef ("Joybubbles") Carl Engressia, Jr.'s discovery in 1957 that high-pitched whistling (2600 Hz) disrupted AT&T's switching system, which inspired generations of "phreakers." But pioneering credit should go to Nevil Maskelyne, who in 1903 hacked into Guglielmo Marconi's telegraph system. While John Ambrose Fleming was on stage showing the supposedly secure new technology to an audience at London's Royal Institution, Maskelyne replaced the presentation's anodyne messages with embarrassing slurs (e.g., that Marconi was "diddling the public"). Hacking became much more widespread once IBM and Apple expanded the consumer market for personal computers in the early 1980s. It crossed the threshold into popular culture with the commercial success of the 1983 film *War Games*, in which a teenage hacker played by Matthew Broderick seems to inadvertently trigger a potential "global thermonuclear war."[34]

Hackers break into government, corporate, and personal machines for a variety of reasons, from the intellectual challenge and the thrill of trespassing to more serious criminal pursuits, including stealing secret data for personal, organizational, or state interests. Only rarely have hackers stolen and then published whistleblowing-worthy evidence of abuse. Given the amount of secret spilling we have seen in the information age (chapter 7), the lack of exfiltrating whistleblowing via hacking is surprising.

While there is a sizable and growing community of self-identified "hacktivists"—*hack* plus *activists*—the hacktivist and whistleblowing worlds have seldom overlapped. Yet it seems likely that the gap will soon narrow, given the rise of hacktivism and the community's embrace of Digital Age leakers, including Snowden, Manning, and, before the 2016 U.S. election, WikiLeaks. Hacktivism so far has generally followed the *Oxford English Dictionary*'s definition of it: "the practice of gaining unauthorized access to computer files or networks in order to propagate a social or political message."[35] It is a short line from that to taking those files and publishing them. Since there is little difference between breaking into a network and breaking into a physical office in order to exfiltrate information, this new kind of hacktivism is a type of exfiltrating whistleblowing (or leaking, when it fails to meet chapter 2's standards).

Instead of whistleblowing, hacktivists have typically tried to exert influence by vandalizing and taking down networks and websites. When Assange first became famous as the hacker Mendax—which means liar in Latin—he and two other suspects allegedly inserted a worm (a self-replicating malware program) into NASA's computer network, apparently to protest the launch of the nuclear-powered spacecraft Galileo. NASA staffers saw a half-serious, half-cheeky message on their computer screens: "WANK: Worms Against Nuclear Killers; Your System Has Been Officially WANKed; You talk of peace for all, and then prepare for war." More recently, hacktivists have expanded their repertoire, such as waging distributed denial of service (DDoS) attacks on targeted websites, to overwhelm them, and render them inaccessible.[36] Hacktivists and fellow travelers have published stolen secrets before, but they have typically done so more in the spirit of war than of whistleblowing.

Anonymous

Take, for example, "Anonymous," a dark, transnational network of hackers and "mischief-makers," probably best characterized using Howard Reingold's concept of a virtual community.[37] It is an informal, decentralized group of individuals who, for the most part, have never met in person, but who share some of the same sociopolitical values. To be sure, Anonymous has had no fixed set of ideas, and no unchanging mission statement. But its public statements and operational history have shown several core values: free speech and its corollary, anti-censorship; free access to information and its corollaries, anti-secrecy, anti-copyright, and anti-anti-piracy; and radical decentralization, as a general organizing principle, and as an organizational approach for Anonymous in particular. Some of Anonymous's unpredictable operations have shown widespread but not complete agreement among Anons about other values, such as anti-racism and anti-fundamentalism. Perhaps most of all, Anonymous values the pursuit of *lulz*, a kind of *Schadenfreudean* comedic thrill, a "deviant style of humor and a quasi-mystical state of being" that is usually not overtly political. Indeed, *lulz* was probably the group's founding principle; Anonymous emerged spontaneously while a bunch of hackers and computer mischief-makers pursued it.[38]

Because of the group's commitment to radical decentralization, its self-proclaimed members have often insisted that Anonymous does not have any leaders. While that is true in the formal sense, it has appeared at times to have had an "informal leadership class"—comprised of "soft leaders," "self-appointed organizers," or "choreographers"—which members occasionally have tolerated in the hot pursuit of "epic wins," such as crippling a website. But grumbling about annoying, self-appointed "leaderfags" is probably the more common expression of Anonymous culture.[39]

The number of Anons probably reaches from the tens of thousands up into the millions, but Anonymous maintains no membership lists because, as the name suggests, everyone involved hides their identities. But we can get a sense of its size, and global reach, by looking at maps showing Anonymous-organized public demonstrations during "Million Mask Marches," which have involved hundreds of street demonstrations on every continent.[40] While not all who have donned Guy Fawkes masks and marched in Anonymous demonstrations have taken part in its online operations, the network appears to be very large, in part because the organization requires nothing of its members, and does not exclude newcomers. Joining requires little more than self-identification and online participation, however sporadic that is.[41]

Hacktivism has become an increasingly prominent feature of Anonymous's operations, as many Anons developed an almost "accidental taste for justice" during conflicts with the Church of Scientology (in Project Chanology), the Westboro Baptist Church, and the state and corporate enemies of WikiLeaks. The turn toward political operations created internal divisions. One faction expressed concern about preserving Anonymous's *lulz*-ian core, and argued that the group should focus its energies on exploits in that vein. Hacktivism would make it too earnest, they said. Too many Anons would become obnoxiously self-important. There would be an outbreak of "leaderfags."[42]

The intra-Anon political divide caused the creation of subgroups, some of which have engaged in more overtly political operations. But the network has numerous branches that transcend the politics question. Gabriella Coleman, a cultural anthropologist who completed years of participant observation/ethnographic field work with Anonymous, found that it is "not a united front, but a hydra—comprising numerous different networks."[43] Some of those network branches exhibit more of an overt political consciousness, while others more closely resemble "social bandits," Eric Hobsbawm's term for rebels and outlaws who live on the fringes of society.[44]

The secrets Anonymous and its splinter groups have so far exfiltrated and published after their hacktivist exploits have generally not been whistleblowing-worthy, according to chapter 2's standards. Few have revealed abuses of public authority, for instance. The group has more often violated the personal privacy of its targets by publishing ("doxing"; that is, leaking personal documents) their names, passwords, phone numbers, social security numbers, and credit card numbers. One operation, for example, sprung from many Anons' opposition to an Arizona immigration law (SB 1070: Support Our Law Enforcement and Safe Neighborhoods Act). SB 1070 critics argued that it would incentivize racial profiling and civil liberty violations by law enforcement officials. LulzSec—one of Anon's splinter groups—organized an operation it named Operation *Chinga La Migra* (i.e., "Operation Fuck the Border Patrol/Immigration Police"). LulzSec announced the operation with a mostly lulz-free statement:

> We are releasing hundreds of private intelligence bulletins, training manuals, personal email correspondence, names, phone numbers, addresses and passwords belonging to Arizona law enforcement. We are targeting AZDPS specifically because we are against SB1070 and the racial profiling anti-immigrant police state that is Arizona.
>
> The documents classified as "law enforcement sensitive," "not for public distribution," and "for official use only" are primarily related to border patrol and counter-terrorism operations and describe the use of informants to infiltrate various gangs, cartels, motorcycle clubs, Nazi groups, and protest movements.
>
> Every week we plan on releasing more classified documents and embarrassing [sic] personal details of military and law enforcement in an effort not just to reveal their racist and corrupt nature but to purposefully sabotage their efforts to terrorize communities fighting an unjust "war on drugs."
>
> Hackers of the world are uniting and taking direct action against our common oppressors—the government, corporations, police, and militaries of the world. See you again real soon! ;D

The authors of the statement displayed a public spirited and even altruistic motivation for doxing government officials. But the leaking was indiscriminate, and it aimed to reveal secrets about "border patrol and counter-terrorism operations," as well as personal details of public officials in the hopes of shaming them.[45] Whether or not the operation was ethically justified in general, it did not amount to whistleblowing, as conceptualized in this book.

Another LulzSec project, Operation AntiSec (anti-security), launched with an unmistakable whistleblowing charge: "If you're aware of the corruption, expose it now." LulzSec pitched this public interested, secret-spilling mission in revolutionary terms, declaring itself a "popular front" against the "corrupt governments, corporations, militaries and law enforcement of the world." In practice, AntiSec's perspective on what counted as a whistleblowing-worthy secret resembled WikiLeaks's. It explicitly rejected the need for any kind of careful scrutiny in its disclosures, proceeding from the assumption that all classified government and corporate information (especially from banks and security companies) contained evidence of wrongdoing: "[Our] top priority is to steal and leak any classified information, including email spools and documentation." AntiSec was ultimately short-lived and short on disclosures.[46]

On a few occasions, Anonymous has shown how hacktivist whistleblowing might work. One operation targeted an apparent cover-up of a rape investigation in Steubenville, Ohio, which centered on two high school boys who sexually assaulted an intoxicated sixteen-year-old girl at a party. Upon hearing of efforts by police and school officials to protect the two young football stars from a serious investigation, Anonymous hacktivists launched Operation Roll Red Roll, in which Anons found and published documents that identified the teenaged perpetrators, which helped to break bureaucratic logjams and lead to their indictments, as well as felony charges against Steubenville City Schools Superintendent Michael McVey, along with misdemeanor charges against two coaches and a principal from the elementary school. The operation is not above criticism. The disclosures, for instance, revealed two juveniles' personal data, which defied the strong norm in American journalism against revealing the identities of minors. Moreover, the revelations themselves did not undercover evidence of abuse, even if it did force investigators to do their jobs. Still, compared with all Anonymous hacktivist operations that preceded it, Roll Red Roll came closest to approximating the exfiltrating whistleblowing model. It was one of small number of cases in which the hacktivist and whistleblowing worlds collided, even on a conscious level among its protagonists. When the FBI identified Deric Lostutter (aka KYAnonymous) as one of the operation's hackers, he hired Whistleblower Defense League as counsel as the government contemplated charges.[47]

A separate Anonymous operation targeting the security firm HBGary Federal (HBGF) also shows the seeds of a hacktivist whistleblowing future. It was launched after HBGF CEO Aaron Barr publicly boasted in a *Financial Times* article that he had infiltrated Anonymous, and identified its leaders. HBGF had partnered with two other firms, Palantir and Berico (together, "Team Themis"), in investigative and strategic planning work for Bank of America, which had been girding itself for what WikiLeaks had warned would be damning revelations about the bank. Anonymous, which had rallied to WikiLeaks's defense during 2010, became a target of Team Themis, as did WikiLeaks-friendly journalists, especially Glenn Greenwald. Given HBGF's offensive maneuver against Anonymous, the hackers' attack on HBGF's servers was likely driven by self-interest and revenge, along with any public-interested motivations. Nevertheless, along with quite a bit of indiscriminate leaking from the servers, Anonymous released a smaller number of possibly incriminating documents, including a Palantir slide featuring a set of "potential proactive tactics" against

WikiLeaks and its supporters, including cyberattacks and disinformation operations to "sabotage or discredit," including the use of forgeries. Other disclosures showed proposals to pressure Greenwald so that he would stop supporting WikiLeaks. Some of the actions could have crossed legal lines. Many of the eye-raising documents discussed potential actions, which may never have been taken. In any case, Anonymous's HBGF operation shows how a highly motivated group of hacktivists might use their skills to exfiltrate and then publish evidence of abuse.[48]

Anonymous has never promoted itself as a whistleblowing group. Thus, the small amount of whistleblowing-like behavior, relative to much more indiscriminate leaking, vengeful attacking, and goofing off, should not come as a surprise. What makes Anonymous so interesting and important in the context of this book is not only that "it was the largest and most populist disruptive grassroots movement the Internet had . . . fomented" (Coleman), but that it has demonstrated, in its own chaotic and defiant ways, the opportunities for and mechanisms of hacktivist whistleblowing in the Internet era. Anonymous might not ever specialize in that way—but some group or individual will. Perhaps it will be an Anonymous splinter group. Perhaps it will be a copycat group, such as Russia's Anonymous International. In any case, it is only a matter of time.[49]

Conclusion

There is an ethical dilemma at the heart of exfiltration whistleblowing. On the one hand, those who do it commit crimes, act deceptively, or otherwise engage in uncivil, even exploitative behaviors. Other kinds of whistleblowers might sometimes engage in illicit or proscribed behaviors, but exfiltrators do it as a rule. On the other hand, without them, abuses would remain concealed. How we weigh the social benefits against the social costs is an important question for later research, although the roughly consequentialist, case-by-case approach adopted in this book would be a good place to start.

For some, the unsavory, problematic nature of exfiltration whistleblowing only becomes clear when the tides are turned against exfiltrators. For example, in response to PETA's activism against Sea World (the marine animal–based theme park company), the firm sent an employee to infiltrate the group. When PETA detected Sea World's covert operation, the company pointed to PETA's long, proud history of "undercover investigations." *Why shouldn't we*, Sea World implied, *be allowed to do the same*? Other companies, such as Burger King, have spied and infiltrated activist groups who had few qualms about using the same tactics.[50]

Exfiltrators would likely defend their actions by comparing their ends to that of the corporations. *We* are finding and disclosing abuses, they might say, while *they*—the abusers—are trying to undermine *us,* the truth-tellers. There is no basis for equivocation, given the ends, so their argument might go. But this Machiavellian path is littered with its own ethical quandaries, let alone all the bodies placed there by fanatical ends-justify-the-means adherents in history. These are treacherous waters, especially because the subjective element is largely inescapable. What is an abuse? Who are the good guys? Outside of Hollywood blockbusters, these are often questions without clear answers.

Notes

1 "'We Steal Secrets: The Story of WikiLeaks': The Annotated Transcript," WikiLeaks.org, May 23, 2013, https://wikileaks.org/IMG/html/gibney-transcript.html.

2 "Alex Gibney explains the title of WE STEAL SECRETS" [video], We Steal Secrets: The Story of WikiLeaks official Facebook page, Facebook, May 31, 2013, https://www.facebook.com/video.php?v=10201316164571951.

3 Raffi Khatchadourian, "No Secrets: Julian Assange's Mission for Total Transparency," *The New Yorker*, July 6, 2010, http://www.newyorker.com/magazine/2010/06/07/no-secrets; WikiLeaks, May 31, 2010, https://twitter.com/wikileaks/status/15107062068. Kim Zetter, "WikiLeaks Was Launched with Documents Intercepted from Tor," *Wired*, June 1, 2010, http://www.wired.com/2010/06/wikileaks-documents/; Dave Gilson, "WikiLeaks's Sketchy Origins," *Mojo Blog (Mother Jones)*, June 2, 2010, http://www.motherjones.com/mojo/2010/06/wikileaks-assange-tor-new-yorker; Nancy Scola, "WikiLeaks' Profile Sparks Debate over (Mis?)Using Tor," *Tech President*, June 4, 2010, http://techpresident.com/blog-entry/wikileaks-profile-sparks-debate-over-misusing-tor.

4 WikiLeaks, Twitter, January 21, 2013, https://twitter.com/wikileaks/status/293479074964332544. In addition to the legal investigations, Assange and his supporters had other issues to worry about. A leaked, classified Army Counterintelligence Center (ACC) document from 2008 seemed to suggest that ACC considered WikiLeaks to be a threat to national security. Another military document similarly appeared to label WikiLeaks an official enemy. The classified (SECRET/NOFORN) Army document said that WikiLeaks was a

potential force protection, counterintelligence, operational security (OPSEC), and information security (INFOSEC) threat to the US Army. The intentional or unintentional leaking and posting of US Army sensitive or classified information to Wikileaks.org could result in increased threats to DoD personnel, equipment, facilities, or installations. The leakage of sensitive and classified DoD information also calls attention to the insider threat, when a person or persons motivated by a particular cause or issue wittingly provides information to domestic or foreign personnel or organizations to be published by the news media or on the Internet. Such information could be of value to foreign intelligence and security services (FISS), foreign military forces, foreign insurgents, and foreign terrorist groups for collecting information or for planning attacks against US force, both within the United States and abroad.

Manning's federal government prosecutors used the report in its opening arguments in 2013 to demonstrate that Manning, an Army Specialist, knew the government considered leaking to WikiLeaks akin to aiding an enemy. Someone in the government had leaked the report to WikiLeaks before the trial. The Air Force declassified and released its document in September 2012 in response to a Freedom of Information Act request (from an unknown requestor). It cited the Espionage Act section against "communicating with the enemy" in an investigation into an Air Force analyst who expressed support for the organization. She was never charged. Kevin Gosztola, "Army Intelligence Report on WikiLeaks 'Threat' Being Used to Argue Bradley Manning Knew He'd Aid Enemy," *The Dissenter*, June 4, 2013, http://dissenter.firedoglake.com/2013/06/04/army-intelligence-report-on-wikileaks-threat-being-used-to-ar gue-bradley-manning-aided-the-enemy/; "Wikileaks.org—An Online Reference to Foreign Intelligence Services, Insurgents, or Terrorist Groups?" Counterintelligence Analysis Report, NGIC-2381-0617-0, Cyber Counterintelligence Assessments Branch, Army Counterintelligence Center, Department of Defense Intelligence Analysis Program, 2, accessed November 13, 2014, http://file.wikileaks.org/file/us-intel-wikileaks.pdf; Letter to FOIA requestor, FOIA Office, U.S. Air Force, May 31, 2012, https://wikileaks.org/IMG/pdf/Assange-WikiLeaks-Enemy-USAF-FOI.pdf.

5 Brian Latell, "An Interview with Director of Central Intelligence George J. Tenet," *Studies in Intelligence*, Document #0006122146, at 9, http://www.foia.cia.gov/sites/default/files/DOC_0006122146.pdf; Dan Lamothe, "New Trove of CIA Articles on Al-Qaeda, the Cold War and the Beirut Bombing, among Many Subjects," *Washington Post*, September 18, 2014, http://www.washingtonpost.com/news/checkpoint/wp/2014/09/18/new-trove-of-cia-articles-on-al-qaeda-the-cold-war-and-the-beirut-bombing-among-many-subjects/.

6 Tim Weiner, *Enemies: A History of the FBI* (New York: Random House, 2012), 293.

7 Betty Medsger, *The Burglary: The Discovery of J. Edgar Hoover's Secret* (New York: Vintage, 2014); *1971*, film, Directed by Johanna Hamilton, Fork Films, Big Mouth Productions, Motto Pictures, 2014.

8 Whether or not COINTELPRO's *tactics* were justified is a separate question from whether the FBI had reasonable justifications for launching and maintaining counterintelligence investigations. In many cases, the Bureau had reliable intelligence showing worrisome connections with foreign Communist powers, especially at the leadership level of organizations such as Students for a Democratic Society and its offshoots, Weatherman and Venceremos Brigades; and the Black Panther Party. See, for example, Darren E. Tromblay, *Political Influence Operations: How Foreign Actors Seek to Shape U.S. Policy Making* (Lanham, MD: Rowman and Littlefield, 2018). COINTELPRO operations were classified, but FBI agents sometimes signaled their presence to targets, for strategic purposes. One FBI file, which the CCIF burglars had discovered and leaked, described an operation's objective: "To enhance paranoia and make people [i.e. activists] think there are FBI agents behind every mailbox."

9 Medsger, *The Burglary*.

10 Kathryn S. Olmsted, *Challenging the Secret Government: The Post-Watergate Investigations of the CIA and FBI* (Chapen Hill: University of North Carolina Press, 2000). NBC News's Carl Stern won a FOIA lawsuit, which forced the release of more COINTELPRO-New Left documents. Medsger, *The Burglary*. Michael Isikoff, "NBC Reporter Recalls Exposing FBI Spying," *NBC News*, January 8, 2014, https://www.nbcnews.com/news/investigations/nbc-reporter-recalls-exposing-fbi-spying-n5901.

11 William Meyer, *The Changing American Mind* (Ann Arbor: University of Michigan Press), 22; "Americans Still Have Moderately Favorable Opinion of FBI," Gallup, July 18, 2001, http://www.gallup.com/poll/4696/americans-still-moderately-favorable-opinion-fbi.aspx

12 Six of eight CCIF members claimed credit in Betty Medsger's 2014 book. William Davidon was the ringleader, whose day job was Professor of Physics at nearby Haverford College. John Raines, a Freedom Rider and Professor of Religion at Temple University, was joined by his wife Bonnie Raines. Bob Williamson was a social worker in 1971; Keith Forsyth drove cabs and served as the chief lock picker. Both of them had done activist burglaries before as part of the Camden 28, a group that broke into a draft board office to sabotage the Vietnam conscription process. Judi Feingold joined the CCIF as a dedicated antiwar activist. Medsger, *The Burglary*. Athan G. Theoharis, ed., *The FBI: A Comprehensive Reference Guide* (Westport, CT: Greenwood, 1999), 78.

13 Medsger, *The Burglary*; Michael Isikoff, "After 43 Years, Activists Admit Theft at FBI Office that Exposed Domestic Spying," *NBC News*, January 6, 2014, http://investigations.nbcnews.com/_news/2014/01/06/22205443-after-43-years-activists-admit-theft-at-fbi-office-that-exposed-domestic-spying?lite.

14 Alex Pacheco, "The Choice of a Lifetime," *Between the Species* (Winter 1990): 36–9; "Alex," Alex Pacheco, accessed February 7, 2015, http://www.alexpacheco.org/alex/alex; Peter Carlson, "The Great Silver Spring Monkey Debate," *The Washington Post Magazine*, February 24, 1991, 14. The fox hunting group was Hunt Saboteurs Association.

[15] Pacheco, "The Choice"; Alex Pacheco and Anna Francione, "The Silver Spring Monkeys," in Peter Singer, ed., *In Defense of Animals* (New York: Basil Blackwell, 1985), 135–47.

[16] Pacheco and Francione, "The Silver Spring Monkeys"; "I Am an Animal," film, Directed by Matthew Galkin, 2007, HBO Documentary; Carlson, "The Great Silver Spring Money Debate."

[17] Sean F. Everton, *Disrupting Dark Networks* (Cambridge University Press, 2012); Pacheco and Francione, "The Silver Spring Monkeys"; Carlson, "The Great Silver Spring Money Debate."

[18] Pacheco and Francione, "The Silver Spring Monkeys; Carlson, "The Great Silver Spring Money Debate."

[19] "I Am an Animal," HBO; "PETA's Milestones for Animals," PETA, accessed January 14, 2019, http://www.peta.org/about-peta/milestones/;

[20] "I Am an Animal," HBO; "PETA's Milestones"; "Investigations," Alex Pacheco, accessed January 14, 2019, http://www.alexpacheco.org/investigation/investigations.

[21] Associated Press, "Lab Quits Research After Video of Animal Treatment," *The New York Times*, September 16, 2010, A18; "PETA Has Decimated the Angora Industry. Now Let's Win Against Mohair," PETA, accessed January 14, 2019; https://www.peta.org/features/how-peta-beat-the-angora-industry-mohair-next/; "Some of the 300+ Brands That Have Banned Angora Wool," PETA, accessed January 14, 2019, https://www.peta.org/living/personal-care-fashion/more-brands-ban-angora/; "Victory: Utah Ends Mandatory Cat and Dog Pound Seizures," PETA, accessed January 14, 2019, https://www.peta.org/blog/victory-utah-ends-m andatory-cat-dog-pound-seizures/; "PETA's Milestones for Animals," PETA, accessed January 14, 2019, http://www.peta.org/about-peta/milestones/.

[22] Bernard OresteUnti, *Protecting All Animals* (Washington DC: Humane Society of the United States), 162–4; "Seizure Law Beat in Miami But Another Enacted in New Orleans," *HSUS News*, September 1958, 2; "Tulane Lab Study Exposes Cruelty,"*HSUS News*, September 1958, 4.

[23] "Undercover Investigations," Mercy for Animals, accessed January 14, 2019, http://www.mercyforanimals.org/investigations.

[24] Kansas State Legislature, Farm Animal and Field Crop and Research Facilities Protection Act, L. 1990, Ch. 192, § 1 http://www.kslegislature.org/li/b2015_16/statute/047_000_0000_cha pter/047_018_0000_article/047_018_0025_section/047_018_0025_k/; K. S. A. 47-1825 – 1830, Animal Law Legal Center, Michigan State University College of Law, accessed December 28, 2016, https://www.animallaw.info/statute/ks-ecoterrorism-chapter-47-livestock-and -domestic-animals; Ted Genoways, "Gagged by Big Ag," *Mother Jones* (July/August 2013).

[25] "Title 81. Livestock, Chapter 30. Protection of Farm Animals and Research Facilities, Part 1. Farm Animal and Research Facility Protection Act," Montana code, accessed December 28, 2016, http://leg.mt.gov/bills/mca_toc/81_30_1.htm; "Chapter 12.1, 21.1, Animal Research Facility Damage," North Dakota code, accessed December 28, 2016, http://www.legis.nd.gov/cencode/t12-1c21-1.pdf?20150327133603.

[26] "What Is Ag-Gag Legislation?" American Society for the Prevention of Cruelty to Animals (ASPCA), accessed January 14, 2019, http://www.aspca.org/animal-protection/public-policy /ag-gag-legislation-state; "Taking Ag-Gag to Court," Animal Legal Defense Fund (ALDF), accessed December 28, 2016, http://aldf.org/cases-campaigns/features/taking-ag-gag-to-co urt/; Jeff Zalesin, "An Overview of 'Ag-gag' Laws," Reporters' Committee for Freedom of the Press, Summer 2013, http://www.rcfp.org/browse-media-law-resources/news-media-law/news-media-and-law-summer-2013/overview-ag-gag-laws. Wyoming has a broader law from 1977 which, according to the Animal Legal Defense Fund, "imposes penalties for gathering resource data information" with "the practical effect is to criminalize undercover recording operations." W. S. 1977 § 6-3-414, https://www.animallaw.info/statute/wy-ecoterrorism-%C2% A7-6-3-414-trespassing-unlawfully-collect-resource-data. See also Will Potter, "Tennessee Politician: "Eco-terrorists Are, Uh, I Guess Left-wing Eco-greenies," *Green Is the New Red,* July 24, 2008, http://www.greenisthenewred.com/blog/tennessee-politician-definingeco-terro rists/484/. A case from Utah is illustrative. According to her testimony of the conflict, Amy Meyer, an animal rescuer, had frequently driven past the interstate side of Dale Smith Meat-packing Company in Draper City, usually speeding by too fast to see anything interesting. But after hearing that one could "witness the horror of cows struggling for their lives as they

were led to their violent deaths" from the side street off the highway, she decided to see for herself. From the easement outside the fenced off property in April 2013, she saw a range of "horrors," from contentious cows refusing to enter the building of their death to a clearly sick one being hauled around by a tractor. She claimed she instinctively started recording the scene on her smartphone. Not long after she began filming, a company officer sped to the fence and confronted her, citing Utah's ag-gag law, which the governor had recently signed. Local police soon arrived, probably hastened by the fact that the mayor of Draper City owned Dale Smith Meatpacking Company. The police officers did not arrest her, but Draper City officials did file a misdemeanor charge eleven days later, with the chance of six months in prison. National news coverage about Meyer's ordeal pressured prosecutors to dismiss the charge "without prejudice." See Will Potter, "First 'Ag-Gag' Prosecution: Utah Woman Filmed a Slaughterhouse from the Public Street," *Green Is the New Red*, April 29, 2013, http://www.greenisthenewred.com/blog/first-ag-gag-arrest-utah-amy-meyer/6948/; Jim Dalrymple II, "Woman Facing Misdemeanor for Video Recording Utah Slaughterhouse," *The Salt Lake Tribune*, April 30, 2013, http://www.sltrib.com/sltrib/news/56235040-78/meyer-gollan-monday-utah.html.csp; Leighton Akio Woodhouse, "Charged With the Crime of Filming a Slaughterhouse," *The Nation*, July 31, 2013, http://www.thenation.com/article/175506/charged-crime-filming-slaughterhouse; "Stunning Ag-gag Bill News," The Food Revolution Network, August 9, 2013, http://web.archive.org/web/20150618074505/http://foodrevolution.org/blog/tag/amy-meyer/; Ladd Brubaker, "Bill Targets Animal Rights Activists' Videos, Photos On Farms," *Desert News*, February 15, 2012, http://www.deseretnews.com/article/865550197/Bill-targets-animal-rights-activists-videos-photos-on-farms.html?pg=all.

27 Iowa's law, which was later ruled unconstitutional by the state's supreme court, did not prohibit taking pictures or using video cameras inside businesses under some conditions. People who did not apply for the job in order to collect evidence, but who decided later to record audio or video while working (i.e., they decided to do so a result of their work experience), were immune from criminal charges under the law—although state whistleblower protection laws might still fail to shield them from retaliation. The law specifically targeted individuals who gained "access to an agricultural production facility by false pretenses" or make "a false statement or representation as part of an application or agreement to be employed at an agricultural production facility, if the person knows the statement to be false, and makes the statement with an intent to commit an act not authorized by the owner of the agricultural production facility." Iowa 717A.3A, Agricultural Production Facility Fraud, https://www.legis.iowa.gov/docs/code/717A.3A.pdf.

28 Genoways, "Gagged."

29 ALDF, "Taking Ag-gag"; Zalesin, "An Overview"; Editors, "Eating With Our Eyes Closed," *The New York Times*, April 10, 2013, A22; Editors, "Cruelty to Farm Animals Demands Exposure," *Washington Post,* April 26, 2013.

30 "What Is Ag-Gag Legislation?"; Animal Legal Defense Fund v. Otter, 118 F. Supp. 3d 1195 (D. Idaho 2015).

31 Rachel Tepper, "George Steinmetz, National Geographic Photographer, Arrested Taking Photos Of Kansas Feedlot," *Huffington Post,* July 11, 2013, http://www.huffingtonpost.com/2013/07/11/george-steinmetz-arrested-feedlot_n_3575593.html; "N.J. Photographer Working for National Geographic Arrested after Taking Pictures from Paraglider," *Associated Press,* July 10, 2013, http://www.nj.com/essex/index.ssf/2013/07/nj_photographer_working_for_national_geographic_arrested_for_taking_pictures_from_paraglider.html.

32 Will Potter, "Drone on the Farm: An Aerial Exposé," Kickstarter, accessed January 14, 2019, https://www.kickstarter.com/projects/1926278254/drone-on-the-farm-an-aerial-expose; Will Potter, "Fully Funded! Announcing New Stretch Goals to Expand the Investigation . . . !" Kickstarter, June 17, 2014, https://www.kickstarter.com/projects/1926278254/drone-on-the-farm-an-aerial-expose/posts/880519; Will Potter, "Extensive Update, with Photos!" Kickstarter, December 8, 2015, https://www.kickstarter.com/projects/1926278254/drone-on-the-farm-an-aerial-expose/posts/1200283; MishkaHenner, "Feedlots," MishkaHenner, accessed April 1, 2015, http://mishkahenner.com/filter/works/Feedlots; Willy Blackmore, "Here's How Drones Can Fight Animal Cruelty and Ag-Gag Laws," June 18, 2014, *Yahoo News,* http://new

s.yahoo.com/heres-drones-fight-animal-cruelty-ag-gag-laws-202747637.html; Peggy Lowe, "Deploying Drones To Get An Overview Of Factory Farms," *The Salt, NPR,* July 19, 2014, http://www.npr.org/blogs/thesalt/2014/07/19/332344201/deploying-drones-to-get-big-picture-of-factory-farms-from-above; Ariel Schwartz, "Drones Can Get Around Strict 'Ag Gag' Laws and Document Horrifying Factory Farms," *Fast Company,* July 7, 2014, http://web.archive.org/web/20161203202545/ http://www.fastcoexist.com/3032446/fund-this/drones-can-get-around-strict-ag-gag-laws-and-document-horrifying-factory-farms; Christopher Zara, "Spy Drones Over North Carolina Factory Farms Reveal 'Lagoons Of Filth,' Filmmaker Says," *International Business Times,* December 19, 2014, http://www.ibtimes.com/spy-drones-over-north-carolina-factory-farms-reveal-lagoons-filth-filmmaker-says-1763592; Christina M. Russo, "Aerial Drones Expose Vile Conditions On Factory Farms," *The Dodo,* December 22, 2014, https://www.thedodo.com/aerial-drones-expose-vile-cond-892429092.html; "Spy Drones Expose Smithfield Foods Factory Farms," Farm Factory Drones, accessed December 28, 2016, http://factoryfarmdrones.com/.

33 "What Is Ag-Gag Legislation?"; H.B. 1643, Texas State Legislature, June 2017, accessed January 14, 2019, https://capitol.texas.gov/tlodocs/85R/billtext/pdf/HB01643F.pdf#navpanes=0.

34 Michelle Slatalla, "A Brief History of Hacking," Discovery/TLC, 2003, accessed August 18, 2016, https://web.archive.org/web/20051113095604/ http://tlc.discovery.com/convergence/hackers/articles/history.html; Gabriella Coleman, "Phreaks, Hackers, and Trolls and the Politics of Transgression and Spectacle," in Michael Mandiberg, ed., *The Social Media Reader* (New York: NYU Press, 2012), 99.

35 Molly Sauter, "The Future of Civil Disobedience Online," *iO9,* June 17, 2013, http://io9.com/the-future-of-civil-disobedience-online-512193648; Molly Sauter, *The Coming Swarm: DDOS Actions, Hacktivism, and Civil Disobedience on the Internet* (London: Bloomsbury, 2014).

36 Sauter, "The Future"; Sauter, *The Coming Swarm*; Coleman, "Phreaks, Hackers, and Trolls."

37 Everton, *Dark Networks*; Howard Rheingold, *The Virtual Community: Homesteading on the Electronic Frontier* (Cambridge, MA: MIT Press, 2000); Gabriella Coleman, *Hacker, Hoaxer, Whistleblower, Spy: The Many Faces of Anonymous* (Brooklyn, New York: Verso Books, 2014), 37.

38 Coleman, *Hacker*, 2.

39 Coleman, *Hacker, Hoaxer*; Parmy Olson, *We Are Anonymous* (New York: Random House, 2013).

40 See, for example, this map showing every demonstration: "mmm map 2017 | ANONYMOUS | Million Mask March," accessed January 14, 2019, www.millionmaskmarch/map/mmm-map-2017.

41 Coleman, *Hacker, Hoaxer*; Olson, *We Are Anonymous*; David Kushner, "The Masked Avengers," September 8, 2014, *New Yorker,* http://www.newyorker.com/magazine/2014/09/08/masked-avengers; Alexandra Sims, "Million Mask March: Anti-establishment Protests Expected in Over 670 Cities across the World," *Independent,* November 5, 2015, http://www.independent.co.uk/news/world/million-mask-march-anti-establishment-protests-expected-in-over-670-cities-across-the-world-a6722286.html; Anonymous Guatemala, Twitter, November 4, 2015, https://twitter.com/An0nymousGT/status/662107871656722432.

42 Coleman, *Hacker, Hoaxer*; Olsen, *We Are Anonymous*; Janet Reitman, "The Rise and Fall of Jeremy Hammond: Enemy of the State," *Rolling Stone,* December 7, 2012, http://www.rollingstone.com/culture/news/the-rise-and-fall-of-jeremy-hammond-enemy-of-the-state-20121207.

43 Coleman, *Hacker, Hoaxer,* 62, 66, 71, 75; Olsen, *We Are Anonymous*; Eric J. Hobsbawm, *Primitive Rebels: Studies in Archaic Forms of Social Movement in the 19th and 20th Centuries* (Manchester University Press, 1971).

44 Wendy H. Wong and Peter A. Brown, "E-bandits in Global Activism: WikiLeaks, Anonymous, and the Politics of No One," *Perspectives on Politics* 11, no. 4 (2013): 1015–33.

45 Alexia Tsotsis, "LulzSec Releases Arizona Law Enforcement Data, Claims Retaliation for Immigration Law," TechCrunch, June 23, 2011, http://techcrunch.com/2011/06/23/lulzsec-releases-arizona-law-enforcement-data-in-retaliation-for-immigration-law/.

46 The revolutionary message had a hard left edge, evident in AntiSec's Robin Hood-ian theft of credit card data it used to make donations to charities. Yet AntiSec and Anonymous more broadly had always been too anarchist and anti-statist to be identifiably left-wing. Plus, its chosen charities, such as American Red Cross and CARE, were rather middle of the road. Coleman, *Hacker, Hoaxer*, 284–6; Reitman, "The Rise and Fall."

47 Richard A. Oppel, Jr., "Ohio Teenagers Guilty in Rape That Social Media Brought to Light," *New York Times*, March 18, 2013, A10; David Kushner, "Anonymous Vs. Steubenville," *Rolling Stone*, November 27, 2013 http://www.rollingstone.com/culture/news/anonymous-vs-steubenville-20131127; Hunter Stuart, "FBI Raid On DericLostutter, AKA KYAnonymous, Was In Connection With Steubenville Hack," *Huffington Post*, June 7, 2013, http://www.huffingtonpost.com/2013/06/07/deric-lostutter-raid-kyanonymous-steubenville_n_3403000.html.

48 Joseph Menn, "Cyberactivists Warned of Arrest," *Financial Times*, February 5, 2011, http://www.ft.com/cms/s/0/87dc140e-3099-11e0-9de3-00144feabdc0.html#axzz1DWB0kKHq; Nate Anderson, "Spy Games," *Wired*, February 14, 2011, http://www.wired.com/2011/02/spy/.

49 Coleman, *Hacker, Hoaxer*, 301–2; DaniilTurovsky, "Meet Anonymous International, the hackers taking on the Kremlin," *Guardian*, April 7, 2015, http://www.theguardian.com/world/2015/apr/07/anonymous-international-hackers-kremlin; "'A Man Who's Seen Society's Black Underbelly': Meduza Meets 'Anonymous International,'" *Meduza*, February 2, 2015, https://meduza.io/en/feature/2015/02/02/a-man-who-s-seen-society-s-black-underbelly. Anonymous International has engineered a number of leaks, including a photograph showing a former top official of a pro-Putin youth group (*Nashi*) sitting next to a bag stuffed with what it estimated to be 15 million rubles (about $300,000). Another leak showed what seemed like Russia's authorship of Crimea's referendum to determine whether the polity should secede and become part of Russia or remain a part of Ukraine.

50 Will Potter, "Sea World Employee Busted Infiltrating PETA," *Green Is the New Red*, July 14, 2015, http://www.greenisthenewred.com/blog/sea-world-employee-infiltrating-peta-thomas-jones/8438/; Christopher Palmeri, "SeaWorld Employee Masqueraded as Animal Activist, Peta Says," *Bloomberg*, July 14, 2015, http://www.bloomberg.com/news/articles/2015-07-14/seaworld-employee-posed-as-animal-activist-for-years-peta-says; Eric Schlosser, "Burger with a Side of Spies," *The New York Times*, May 7, 2008, A27.

Chapter 9

Conclusion

The contemporary understanding of "whistleblowing" as righteous secret-spilling dates back to the 1960s.[1] But the process has a much longer history. People we might now identify as whistleblowers have probably been spilling secrets for millennia. After all, the impetus to "blow the whistle" on perceived abuses, by publicly alerting others, is probably rooted in the common psychological need for fairness and equity. That fairness- or justice-seeking motivation is likely tied to our hard-wired propensity and capacity to detect and punish cheaters and other kinds of exploiters.[2]

However universal the whistleblowing impulse may be, closed political systems and concentrated publishing markets have, for most of history, severely limited individuals' opportunities to make impactful unauthorized disclosures. Until the late medieval period, with few exceptions, publishing was an exclusive, noncompetitive enterprise, dominated by a polity's most powerful individuals and organizations, who had little reason to disclose their own damning secrets, although they often had strategic reasons to publish secrets to harm their political or economic opponents.[3] Authoritarian repression, primitive communications technologies, and small, concentrated publishing markets gave would-be whistleblowers very few channels in which to spill secrets with the potential to hold bad actors accountable.

A key turning point came in the late 1400s, when Gutenberg's printing press decentralized publishing. The new technology initially did not do much to disrupt the still very centralized, closed market, but it enabled the eventual turn toward more open, dynamic systems with more independent, private sector actors. When societies got there, would-be whistleblowers finally had more options.

Bartolomé de Las Casas may have been the first whistleblower of the post-Gutenberg era. The Spanish colonial settler began his life in the New World as an *encomendero* on Hispaniola (modern-day Dominican Republic and Haiti), which gave him privileges and powers similar to an Old World feudal lord. His disenchantment with the encomienda system, which thrived on indigenous slavery and other abuses, led him to become a friar in the Dominican Order, where his mission became the protection of indigenous peoples from Spain's exploitative colonial system. He traveled the New and Old Worlds giving speeches and distributing books and pamphlets, starting with 1516's *Memorial de Remedios para las Indias* (Memorial Remedies for the Indians) and culminating in his most influential work, *A Short Account of the Destruction of the Indies*, written in 1542 and published in Europe in 1552. Many Europeans, as well as Spanish Americans, were shocked by de las Casas's descriptions of the cruelties that colonists inflicted upon indigenous people, made even more vivid by Theodore De Bry's disturbing illustrations (e.g., figure 9.1). De las Casas and De Bry may have indulged in exaggeration, but no one credibly disputed the broader picture of abuse at the heart of the encomienda system. Their work

FIGURE 9.1 Spanish Colonists' Abuses Illustrated in De Las Casas's Short Account. *Source*: Bartolomé de las Casas (1484–1566)/Photo © Whiteimages/Bridgeman Images.

turned Europeans against the system, which persuaded the Spanish crown to institute the New Laws of the Indies for the Good Treatment and Preservation of the Indians, which banned slavery and generally placed colonists under greater crown control.[4]

More opportunities for would-be whistleblowers arrived in the 1600s and 1700s with the emergence and proliferation of newspapers, newsletters, broadsheets (corantos), broadsides, separates (e.g., speech transcripts), and other media. The first newspaper appeared in Germany in 1605, with the snappy title *Relation aller Fürnemmen und gedenckwürdigen Historien* (Account of All Distinguished and Commemorable News).[5] English citizens saw their first newspaper in 1620 (published by the Dutch), and soon readers lapped up trivial revelations about royal scandals whenever they could. Governments there and elsewhere still worked hard to suppress independent voices with censorship and other means, but sometimes closely held secrets squeaked out. That was more likely to happen in places outside a sovereign's direct control. The English under Protestant royals in the seventeenth century, for instance, could read about Vatican officials' wrongdoings.[6]

New publishing technologies thus created new opportunities for secret-spillers, but early modern authoritarian politics still made whistleblowing very difficult. The free press had not yet arrived. Plus, the whistleblowing *idea* had not yet emerged in any of the world's political cultures. Someone with a hot secret in the United States in 2019 might immediately consider spilling it, in part because leaking and whistleblowing were familiar possibilities. Before those concepts had become commonly understood, they were not obvious communication choices, even for individuals with the whistleblowing impulse.

Several things changed in the mid- to late-1800s. Investigative journalism became a distinctive profession and calling for writers of all kinds, including many individuals with the whistleblowing impulse. New and old media forms continued to proliferate. Newspapers and other publications became common consumer goods. More and more individuals considered themselves "liberal" or found themselves under liberalism's influence. While religious laws and other kinds of traditional authority still shaped behavior, liberalism, which prizes individuals' ethical judgments and autonomy, increasingly recalibrated how people thought about their lives and personal influence within society.

The new political and cultural landscape of the 1800s created fertile soil from which whistleblowing networks could emerge. Chapter 4 recounted the case of Aleksandr Herzen's newspaper *Kolokol* ("The Bell") and its popular secret-spilling section, *"Pravda-li?"* ("Can it be true?"), which evaded the tsars' censors and regularly reported on corruption and other abuses of power. Later in the century, whistleblowers in the paradoxically titled Congo Free State exposed atrocities committed by Belgian King Leopold's colonial forces.

After American missionary William Henry Sheppard witnessed the *Force Publique's* extreme violence and exploitation of native Congolese, he and others resolved to gather evidence and publicize it as widely as possible. To do that, he collaborated with many whistleblowing facilitators and recipients, including *The New York Times*.[7]

The opportunities for whistleblowing continued to grow in the twentieth century, developing along the trajectories carved in the previous century. In the 1970s, whistleblowing became a political phenomenon with a name with heroes and villains—the Ellsbergs and Deep Throats versus the Nixons, the Silkwoods versus the Kerr-McGees. The high-profile cases, and the Hollywood films they inspired, helped to define the phenomenon in public opinion and to forge the political identity of the whistleblower. Individuals considering spilling secrets in the late twentieth century not only had numerous communications and collaborative options, but they also had the opportunity to *become* whistleblowers— widely respected modern heroes. They could *be like* Ellsberg or Silkwood or Erin Brockovich or others in the pantheon. The cultural development of the whistleblower identity and practice probably influenced many secret-spillers starting in the 1970s. While some may have craved fame and respect, many others probably found the identity's generally positive sheen as a way to validate their well-intentioned impulse to blow the whistle.

Twentieth-century history also serves up examples that remind us that whistleblowing occurs in societies before "whistleblowing." That is, the impulse and its expression predates its cultural appearance. For example, the underground contributors to the *Chronicle of Current Events* (chapter 4) built and utilized whistleblowing networks before most Soviet citizens had heard the word and imagined the identity.

Delineating the Wide World of Whistleblowing Networks

One purpose of this book was to clarify the many blurred lines in the secret-spilling universe. How do we distinguish whistleblowing from leaking, let alone other secret-spilling enterprises? Investigative journalism, for instance, "involves original work, about substantive issues, that someone wants to keep secret."[8] Truth and reconciliation commissions feature victims, witnesses, and perpetrators of war crimes and human rights violations who unearth secrets by the thousands. Gossip websites publish private sex tapes, proclaiming they do so to serve the public interest.[9] YouTube and "cop watch" apps stream police-suspect interactions they portray as police abuses. How do we separate the wheat from the chaff in this pile of spilled secrets, which is getting bigger every year?

Getting to a palatable, analytically sturdy answer took all of chapter 2. One lesson readers probably took from that chapter is that defining and conceptualizing whistleblowing is fraught with a seemingly endless stream of semantic problems. Why bother?

Karl Popper advised social scientists to "never let yourself be goaded into taking seriously problems about words and their meanings." I often agree with this Popperian skepticism of definition making. Yet when I posed the question "what is whistleblowing?" and found a hodgepodge of unsatisfactory definitions, I had to agonize over words. Without concept development, we would be stuck with our diverging subjective impressions and our dictionaries' wide-open definitions about "provid[ing] information about another's wrongdoing" (Merriam-Webster) and the like. Moreover, we would have no common understandings and standards for the variables we might try to measure for hypothesis testing—Popper's analytic priority.[10] Nor would we have any capacity to frame or help resolve public debates about tricky or especially important cases (e.g., Snowden) or to guide would-be whistleblowers contemplating disclosure.

In contrast with Popper, Hanna Pitkin suggested that "the problem is not to state the correct meaning of the word, but to specify all the varieties of its application to various contexts."[11] When researching this book, Pitkin trumped Popper, although specifying the applications of the whistleblowing concept became more of a stimulating opportunity than a problem. Going from "what is whistleblowing?" to "where and when does whistleblowing happen, and who does it?" led to a wide range of individuals, organizations, movements, and epochs, from the well-known Snowdens and Ellsbergs to the lesser-known Harry Wus and Ka Hsaw Was—hundreds of them are catalogued on the companion website[12]—as well as the whistleblowing networks not usually seen as such, including Amnesty International (AI), the *Chronicle of Current Events*, IPaidaBribe.com, and Witness.

On that Pitkinian search for varieties, it became immediately clear that most leaking and whistleblowing happens because of the work of groups. There may be a lone, heroic (or not so heroic) protagonist at the center of a case—a single individual who initiates an episode of secret-spilling. But with few exceptions, each case involves, at a minimum, that individual plus a recipient/publisher of the secret. And there are often more people and organizations involved—facilitators—who work on the receiving end or somewhere in the middle.

One reason people often miss this point about the prevalence of networks is that they tend to think about whistleblowing as a one-off occurrence: The protagonist gathers evidence of abuse, and then reveals it. Yet as we have seen, far from being ephemeral and static, whistleblowing networks are often long-lasting, with an ever-changing complex of nodes. Think of the fourteen-year run of the *Chronicle* or the constantly evolving networks supporting AI's disclosures.

In some cases for which data is plentiful, it is possible to map out all or most of a social network. The (partial) Snowden network map in chapter 1 is one example. Yet in many cases the data are not available. AI, for instance, restricts from public view a large portion of its operations and archive in order to protect its contributors. Some fear retaliation; others just might prefer privacy. In any case, anyone who wants to reconstruct a network map of, say, AI's information extraction networks in Argentina during the late 1970s military government—the networks that exposed the regime's "disappearances" and other human rights violations and had much to do with AI's 1977 Nobel Peace Prize—would need to wait until 2061. Much of AI's archive is essentially classified until the late twenty-first century. AI is not alone in this. Many secret-spilling networks go to great lengths to stay anonymous, including Anonymous, the hacker group that has sometimes gestured toward whistleblowing, as well as the *Chronicle*. Social network analysts usually use the term "dark networks" to refer to underground criminal and terrorist organizations. The *Chronicle* and other underground whistleblowing networks were unique for being dark networks that shed light.

Explaining Whistleblowing: A Framework for Multilevel Analysis

While this book is not Popperian, in the sense that it does not develop and test causal explanations for whistleblowing, it does suggest some of the key ingredients for an approach like that. Earlier I argued that a whistleblowing impulse predated the historical emergence of the named concept and that technological, political, and economic developments gradually cleared obstacles that blocked people with that impulse. The historical argument was brief and speculative, and we need more research to better substantiate it. But it suggested a path forward for systematic theory development and empirical analysis.

Explaining the amount and variation of whistleblowing requires contextual and individual-level variables and their interactions. Which contextual variables? We could start with the ones suggested earlier, including whistleblowing-enabling technologies, the presence of a whistleblower cultural identity, and the prevalence of liberal ideas and institutions. Organizational contexts also matter—specifically, variation in the incentives and opportunities that discourage or encourage whistleblowing. To what extent do they invest in "insider threat" and other leak-plugging programs? To what extent do they offer whistleblowers' protections, and if those exist formally, to what extent have organizations maintained them once someone actually makes an unauthorized disclosure? Furthermore, how do organizations differentiate between leaking and whistleblowing, and do they make the distinction clear to all members?

Organizations also vary in their levels of secrecy. The ones that are more secretive, especially those with tendencies toward excessive secrecy, create more secret-spilling opportunities (and possibly stronger motivations) simply by virtue of having more secrets. That is, individuals in organizations with a small number of closely guarded secrets have fewer opportunities to spill secrets, while those in organizations saturated with secrets have ample opportunities. Nevertheless, secret-spilling incidents probably do not increase linearly as opportunities proliferate. Just because some organizations have more secrets does not mean they will experience more leaks. Why the ratio of spills to secrets will vary across organizations depends on causes already mentioned, such as insider threat and other internal security programs, as well as others, such as an organization's history of retaliation, and the nature and degree of members' commitments to the organization.

When we incorporate other kinds of structural variables (e.g., regime types; levels and temporal patterns of human rights violations), or recognize some macro-structures as organizations (e.g., states), other kinds of contextual variables become relevant. Network-related contextual traits also vary. In addition to knowing whether individuals have connections to whistleblowing networks, which likely shape their disclosure decisions, it would be helpful to know how the structure and resilience of those networks shape individuals' incentives, opportunities, and capacities to act.

While any attempt to explain whistleblowing will require contextual variables like those just suggested, any causal story about leaking and whistleblowing ultimately hinges upon the individuals who make it happen. Researchers should examine the extent to which individual-level psychological variables matter, such as the tendency toward seeking or avoiding conflict, and the need for fairness. They should also test for individuals' history of activism, and perhaps their perceived political efficacy. We might also ask leakers and whistleblowers about their motivations, but those responses should be treated with caution. Many would likely claim that they had a moral duty to disclose hidden evidence of abuses. While they might genuinely believe that some of those individuals might also have an inflated ego and/or sense of self-importance, believing they have a historically important role to play. Others might just want the limelight. Still others might be driven by vengeance. They want to embarrass their bosses or colleagues or countries. Or they want to exact revenge upon them for real or perceived slights or transgressions. Overall, some people might have purely noble motivations that lead them to make unauthorized disclosures, while others probably have a more complex set of reasons to do so.

It might seem reasonable to restrict the whistleblower label—distinct from leaker—only to those with good intentions. Why not require purity of heart and noble motivations? The answer, as argued in chapter 2, is that verifying purity of heart and purpose is impossible. We can never be fully confident we know another's motivations, no matter what they might say. Perhaps that will change once humans develop reliable brain emulations or brain-reading implants. In the meantime, we are out of luck. Here, again, is one reason why a consequentialist approach is useful for concept development and post hoc evaluations. We can evaluate cases without presuming to know others' motivations.

Furthermore, fixating on purity of heart can also distort our case-by-case evaluations. Imagine a well-meaning person—someone with a generous heart and a desire for world peace—who fell for the Soviet regime's propaganda about how only it could usher in world peace and how the greedy capitalist United States stood in the way. Our hypothetical protagonist really, truly believed the Soviets and their witting and unwitting agents. He also happened to work at Los Alamos National Laboratory. After marinating in Soviet propaganda, it was only a matter of time before he thought to spill U.S. nuclear and military secrets—to further the cause of world peace and the brotherhood of man. From his perspective, spilling those secrets was his *duty* as a citizen of the world. In short, purity of heart is an abstraction that we cannot measure. It is also misleading, because people can be easily misguided. What matters more is the nature of the disclosed evidence, and whether its revelation brought more benefits than costs. Granted, estimating those costs and benefits is also fraught with difficulty, but framing the debate around those ideas, rather than human motivations, will likely lead to more substantive discussions.

Overall, the consequentialist approach offers a way to sidestep the motivation question when making distinctions between whistleblowing and leaking. But stripping individuals from the analysis completely would lead to impoverished causal explanations. In addition to testing for the individual-level variables proposed above, we need research about the so-called whistleblowing impulse and the cognitive, social, personality, and perhaps evolutionary psychology behind it.

To be fully satisfactory, explanations would likely need to incorporate more than two levels of analysis. For instance, perhaps there is a common misperception in the national political culture that organization X's (e.g., an intelligence agency) secrecy is excessive and harmful to democracy. An X employee who subscribes to that view will be more likely to leak some of X's necessary secrets. In this scenario we have (1) the individual and her attitudes about X and its role in society more broadly; (2) X itself, with its unique organizational configuration (e.g., actual level of secrecy, extent of insider threat programs, reputation for retaliation, etc.); and (3) the national political culture, which transmits objective and subjective/slanted knowledge about X and its history and image, along with the presence of a whistleblower identity, along with meanings attached to it. Only multilevel analysis would incorporate each of those causal influences.

In the meantime, this book offered a clearer conceptualization of whistle-blowing and a presentation of its many applications. The application-seeking, Pitkinian tromp through the world that consumes most of this book's pages brought dozens of cases into the mix, most of them not hypotheticals from the author's imagination. They contained dramatic conflicts at their core: the *Chronicle* versus the KGB; Harry Wu versus the Chinese; Peter Gabriel's WIT-NESSes versus their abusers; ordinary Indians versus their entitled bribe-takers; undercover animal welfare investigators versus meat producers; and many more. Not all of them had an unambiguous good guy or bad guy distinction. Not all approximated whistleblowing. But they all, together, illustrated how widespread secret-spilling has already become. And with the relentless pace of technological development, along with our evolving norms of privacy and transparency, the complex, secret-spilling universe will continue to expand, whether we like it or not.

Notes

[1] Ralph Nader is often credited with first using the term to describe justified secret-spilling. See, for example, Ralph Nader, "Preface," in Ralph Nader, Peter J. Petkas, and Kate Blackwell, eds., *Whistleblowing: The Report of the Conference on Professional Responsibility* (New York: Grossman Publishers, 1972). The use of "leaking" to describe secret-spilling is much older. Ben Zimmer traces the etymological history back to ancient Rome:

> The metaphor of confidential information leaking out is, in fact, an ancient one. In "The Eunuch," a comedy by the Roman playwright Terence from the second century B.C., one character says of his inability to keep a secret, "I am full of holes, I leak at every point" ('Plenusrimarum sum, hacatqueillacperfluo"). In English, blabby talkers (stereotypically women) have been called leaky since the late seventeenth century. And the phrasal verb leak out has been used for the revelation of secrets since at least 1806, when the British journalist William Cobbett, an advocate for parliamentary reform, wrote, "When any valuable information leaks out, let us note it down." An early glimpse of how leak entered American political vocabulary comes in John C. Frémont's 1887 memoirs, which recount a political event leading up to the Mexican-American War, when Secretary of State James Buchanan "discovered a leak in his department." Buchanan needed to patch a leak from below, but by the end of World War II, leaks could just as likely come from above, in the form of information revealed to reporters by high-ranking officials who didn't want to be identified. As James Reston wrote in a 1946 New York Times dispatch on postwar peace negotiations, "Governments are the only vessels that leak from the top."

Ben Zimmer, "Leaks," *The New York Times Magazine*, August 22, 2010, MM16.

[2] Examples of evolutionary explanations for humans' interest in justice include Michael Bang Petersen, Aaron Sell, John Tooby, and Leda Cosmides, "Evolutionary Psychology and Criminal Justice: A Recalibrational Theory of Punishment and Reconciliation," in Henrik Høgh-Olesen, ed., *Human Morality and Sociality: Evolutionary and Comparative Perspectives* (New York: Palgrave MacMillan, 2010), 72–131; Anthony Walsh, "Evolutionary Psychology and the Origins of Justice," *Justice Quarterly* 17, no. 4 (2000): 841–64.

[3] Exceptions could include relatively open societies, such as ancient, republican Rome, where writers and artists had relatively fewer restrictions and more opportunities for publishing.

[4] John Charles Chasteen, *Born in Blood and Fire: A Concise History of Latin America* (New York: WW Norton & Company, 2001), 59–61.

5   Kathleen A. Hansen and Nora Paul, *Future-Proofing the News: Preserving the First Draft of History* (Lanham, MD: Rowman and Littlefield, 2017), 2.

6   "Breaking News: Renaissance Journalism and the Birth of the Newspaper," Folger Library, September 2008, http://folgerpedia.folger.edu/Breaking_News:_Renaissance_Journalism_and_the_Birth_of_the_Newspaper; Randy Robertson, *Censorship and Conflict in Seventeenth-Century England: The Subtle Art of Division* (State College, PA: Penn State University Press, 2009); Robert Darnton, "Censorship, a Comparative View: France, 1789—East Germany, 1989," *Representations* 49 (1995): 40–60.

7   Adam Hochschild, *King Leopold's Ghost: A Story of Greed, Terror, and Heroism in Colonial Africa* (New York: Houghton Mifflin Harcourt, 1999); E. D. Morel, "The Third Test of Congo State Rule—Militarism, Murder, Mutilation, and the Traffic in Arms," in Anya Schiffrin, ed., *Global Muckraking: 100 Years of Investigative Journalism from Around the World* (New York: The New Press, 2014), 17–21.

8   James T. Hamilton, *Democracy's Detectives: The Economics of Investigative Journalism* (Cambridge, MA: Harvard University Press, 2016), 10.

9   Peter Thiel, "Privacy Issues Won't End with Gawker," *The New York Times*, August 15, 2016, A21.

10 Karl Popper, *Unended Quest: An Intellectual Autobiography* (LaSalle, IL: Open Court, 1976), 19; John Gerring, "What Makes a Concept Good? A Criterial Framework for Understanding Concept Formation in the Social Sciences," *Polity* 31, no. 3 (1999): 357–393; David Collier, "Putting Concepts to Work: Toward a Framework for Analyzing Conceptual Innovation in Comparative Research," Paper delivered at the American Political Science Association Annual Conference, Boston, 1998, 3–6.

11 Hanna Fenichel Pitkin, *Representation* (Berkeley: University of California Press), 8; John Gerring and Paul A. Barresi, "Putting Ordinary Language to Work: A Min-Max Strategy of Concept Formation in the Social Sciences," October 3, 2002, http://people.bu.edu/jgerring/papers/MinMax.pdf.

12 Readers are invited to add suggestions at https://sites.google.com/view/secretspillers/home.

Index

DISCARDED
Worthington Libraries